Journey of the mind
by
Pragyananda

authorHOUSE®

AuthorHouse™
1663 Liberty Drive
Bloomington, IN 47403
www.authorhouse.com
Phone: 1-800-839-8640

The front cover design was done by: Troels Oehman.

First published by AuthorHouse   12/15/2011

ISBN: 978-1-4670-0197-7 (sc)
ISBN: 978-1-4670-0198-4 (ebk)

Printed in the United States of America

Any people depicted in stock imagery provided by Thinkstock are models, and such images are being used for illustrative purposes only. Certain stock imagery © Thinkstock.

This book is printed on acid-free paper.

This book is dedicated to my little brother.
May it live to inspire him as well as to a world of his kind,
so the teaching of our beloved Sri Swamiji may nourish the
heart and soul of all who strive to live a life enriched with
a contemplative spiritual approach to life.

Introduction

I have always been amazed by this void we call the mind.
What is its substance? How do feelings and thoughts manifest in this mind? Are they a part of the mind; a quality inherent and therefore inseparable from this mind? If this mind is seated in the brain, and thus is inseparable from this body, then how is it that it can experience things far beyond this tiny 'prison', as I dare call it?
It makes sense to say that the body is housing the mind which houses consciousness.
What is it that happens within this framework of the mind in relation to the world of objects? The mind cannot be limited to just this body alone. It is so much more. The thoughts we have thought since we took our first breath are infinite in number. They are like the waves on the ocean, rising and falling. Can you count them? How can something which is subjected to both life and death contain the infinite?
How did the mind come into existence? What is its origin? How do all these notions inherent in the mind, become the mind?
We actually recognize them to be the mind, at least part of it.
I would rather say that it is something that is glued to the mind, as you will find described in the following story:

*It is like the grass being covered with unseen dew,
an invisible burden it is, I shall reveal to you.*

We may not have a concrete answer to these questions, but that does not mean we cannot do a little research into the nature of the mind.
I do not want to become too intellectual on this subject, especially when we speak of something as the very root of the intellect, the Mind, which always wants to rationalize words and sayings and categorize them.
I mainly got the inspiration to write the 'Journey of the mind' poem during my stay at the Ashram of Swami Satyananda Saraswati.
There I came across text like the 'Mohamudgar' poetry written by

Adi Shankaracharya, the 'Yoga Vasishtha' and the 'Bhagavat Gita' chapter 13 in which it talks about the body being the field; the mind its knower. Having read this chapter from the Bhagavat Gita, helped me being able to analyse and better understand the mind as a separate identity. The first and last stanza of this chapter go like this:

This body is called the field. He who knows it is called the knower of the field, by those who know of them.
Knowledge of both the field and the knower of the field is considered to be the Knowledge.
They who, by the eye of knowledge, perceive the distinction between the field and its knower and also liberation from the nature of being, unifies in the supreme.

(B.G. 13:1 & 34)

Who is this mind; what is this body in relation to the mind and how do we get to know it?
I have long thought about a way to be able to see and also separate all the many notions of the mind.

This great wide world has been providing many thinkers like Descartes—*je pense, donc je suis* (I think, therefore I am)—Plato and Socrates. Hence seers like Vishvamitra, Vasishtha, Buddha and many others you may, or may not have heard of. Socrates philosophy was enriched with tantric concepts and ideas.
It was said his philosophy was blasphemous; it opposed the religion and led the youth astray. The tantric concept has always provoked a very controlled set of rules laid down by the religions that have been governed by power and politics; because of its very free way of realizing and developing awareness that entirely aims for a higher state of consciousness in our every day. It does not speak of one God, one

7

way, but it accepts—in brief—that every human being can reach the same hight of evolution by as many means as there are species here on this earth.

But it is not only the great ones who 'once upon a time' lived on this earth who have been inspiring and guiding our life on earth. Look around and see what is hidden in fairytales, poetry, stories and songs. Throughout the story you will find that my source of inspiration lies in tellings like those of Hans Christian Andersen, Brother Grimm's, old scriptures and songs from the Vedic times. The lyrics in many Pop & Rock songs have similar messages, such as today's pop idol, Michael Jackson, who sang in 'The Man in the Mirror';

"If you wanna make the world a better place,

Take a look at yourself and make that change."

Changing our hair style, clothing, etc. won't make much of a change *in* us.

Our own actions and habits are rooted as a thought in the mind of, 'I AM so, I DO so, I THINK so' and so forth. This is where we will have to make changes.

Do thou, Arjuna, know yoga to be that which they call renunciation. No one verily becomes a yogi who has not renounced thoughts.

(B.G. 6:2)

This mind divides this world into countless categories, countries, races, religions and politics! But in the end, isn't it also that very same mind that unites everything in oneness, such as:

All rivers to the ocean lead,

so too, the King must now weigh his deed.

As for the ego, a wave rising high in search,

8

in the ocean great it again shall merge.
Be his deeds good, bad or selfish,
        his self-imposed identity too, shall vanish.

Part I

The Mind, The Field and The Knower

Let us now move on with this little journey of the mind.
This narration took place in a house not far outside of the city. The house had a small but beautiful garden with a view to a lake. A mother lived in the home with her youngest son. The boy had only just turned twelve a few days earlier and, as so many others his age, has his whole life in front of him. And so it was that his mother wanted to think of a way to give her son the best possible tools with which to walk through his life.

So listen with care to this little goodnight story, from a letter sent from afar, told by the mother to her son, called:

The Journey of the Mind

My Friend,
I shall relate to you, to my best ability,
 what's written in many fairytales and poetry.
For vast is this world of fantasy,
 of a kingdom with heroes, legends and a monastery.

In the magical mirror we shall find
 a reflection made in our own mind.
Close your eyes and follow me well,
 as I shall lead you in this tiny nut shell,
 to a land of mountains and valleys so fresh and green,
 where lakes glitters like the brightest pearls you've ever seen.
Animals and other creatures, all do they speak;
 an artist of painting, such a place would surely seek.

Within you, in the vision of your inner eye,
    follow in detail as I, to you, shall describe
    your mind, being the King of this field in this palace
    of 9 gates[1], your body, the regime of your highness.
Sitting up there on the towers highest place,
    on a throne of gold with quiver and mace.
With the exception of the roof 'and a crown' he adds,
    He sits beyond as a witness, collecting tax.

His musketeers are his dear warriors
    who act on commands given from their superiors,
    such as talking, listening, seeing and giving greetings
    to other regimes and with them has meetings.

Like this, the command of the King is carried out
    by his dearest warriors, to mention a few
        arms, legs fingers and mouth.

Next to our King is the Royal Counsellor;
    the 2'nd mind we know him as,
        always being 'against' or 'for'.

The King is never left in peace to decide;
    his council is always acting like a biting mite.
Nagging into the depth of the King, they twist,
    till agree he must, manipulated and left in a dense mist.

---

1   The 9 Gates are the nine openings in the body; eyes, nose, ears, mouth, anus and the sexual organ.

But of all he loves his musicians five,
  they put on for him the most brilliant disguise.
Entertaining him from early morning till late night,
  showing, singing, presenting and feeding him to his delight.

Their performances are such,
  to the King who's involved just as much,
  that he becomes in fact
  what they out-livingly act.

There's no limit to these, the senses five,
  Good God they are noisy and bring the King to life.
Glorifying his majesty, his strength and his might,
  avoiding the unpleasant, keeps it out of sight.
Ever, ever, and ever tries to gratify
  our King, his honour, HIM, ever to satisfy.

After a whole day of entertaining,
  of what he liked the most, our King is quietly humming[2].
Left to himself, with no one else here,
  He, roaming to and fro in memory, recalls places far and near.

In a Kingdom of his, the mind,
  you can be absolutely sure to find,
  hundreds of children all over the place,
  respectively called: Wish one to a hundred in this case.

---

2 Dreaming. When all the senses etc. are inert, the perceived objects are reflected in the mind.

A few of them mischievously keep nagging,
>to test the King if his confidence is lagging,
>by crawling all over him, pulling
>>his beard, his many limbs and ears
>and so must he deal with his own
>>desires and wants, or they bring him to tears.

But think not that all power alone is our King at hand
>with his army, councillor and a noisy band.
Behind the greatness of every a King's success
>lives in silence, a woman, to restore his mess.
She lives in the chamber of the heart,
>living entirely for others and to nourish, she works hard.
Day and night she gives as a selfless act,
>for should she stop, it'll be Hari Om Tat Sat[3].

Her beauty knows no limit,
>She is the Queen, the pulsating Spirit.
She's in fact the one who looks after the common man,
>while the King forgetting his own precious land.

Obsessed with his own selfish greed and lust he forgets
>the care for all and their well being he neglects.
But like the tower built up with mere bricks will fall,
>you, oh King, too, one day shall out cry a resentful call.

---

3   Hari Om Tat Sat is a word describing the highest reality and is used in completion of any dedicated worship or its like. So, as it here is written, it means in a bit obscure way 'finished' (the end of ones life, 'Hari Om Tat Sat!!!').

See how She, without hesitation will give.
You never let loose your frozen grip.
To take is your thing and firmly hold on.
To give is her way, that is her song.

You lament if confronted with a difficult task,
    but never will you find her pondering
        on whose advice to ask.

And so, as two different entities they live
    and it's thus left to the inmates
        to either curse, or accept and forgive.

For with a passionate mind as the King,
    the Queen alone sustains the whole
        as one and the same thing.

But Mom, interrupted the child.
please tell me more about this King.
Is it entirely his fault when acting wrong;
and is he alone to blame for this fall?
Be good to tell me thus;
how he thinks; how he works; what is he in truth?
For like a cloud which casts a shadow on land,
he too must be subjected to a higher hand,
like the sun up high; ever constant and luminous!!!
What is it that makes him act as if He is of numerous identities?

And to times, too, seems in conflict with these,
as when you described him with his hundreds of self created wishes!
Strange indeed are his ways;
ever fluctuating, never in one and the same place.
So do tell me further more of this mind, the King,
that lives here, within the mind.

My child—replied his mother—do listen with care,
 how the King being pure to become bound, I shall share.
It is like the grass being covered with unseen dew,
 an invisible burden it is, I shall reveal to you,
 how thus the senses, plus others, as a transparent layer
 affect the King and his entire behaviour.

With Kama*⁴ as his 2'nd wife,
 His band of five becomes his life.
Krodh* is his highest commander,
 the above mentioned make him sweet and tender,
 by polishing his crown and feet,
 they make him fall low and meek.

Taking their advice, how in life to walk,
 he becomes bound and deluded by their decisive talk.
Kama* ruling him in jealousy,
 Moh* his adviser, with misery.
Krodh* his commander

---

4 * 1)Kama—desire. 2)Krodh—anger. 3)Lobh—greed/selfishness and 4)Moh—
delusional thinking/idea or concept of ones own existence.

with outrageous anger
and Lobh* his selfish attendance
adds to his pride with each sentence.

Forever they him dominate
with a thousand tongues like snakes.
Giving him not a moment of peace,
their role has entirely become to deceive
the King, the ruler, the lord of them all,
making him a wicked prey, you may so call.

So too it happened to the little boy of little
poor Gerda, his neighbour friend,
in the telling The Snow Queen[5]
a witch to whom he was sent,
because of a mirror made by the Devil himself
while playing, out his hands it fell,
it splintered and perverted the sight
of what its victim beheld.

And so too it has pierced the eye through which you behold
this world, this creation, the way you see it
the way it's programmed and told
by many authorities, a friend, a saying or
as an experience that came your way,
but mainly by your parents who lived
their beliefs and fights in your everyday.

5   The Snow Queen is a tale by Hans Christian Andersen that I here refer to.

But like the paint on a house is not the wall,
   for then indeed it is sure to fall,
   He, the King, is the foundation of it all
   and should he take his right place
         he could make'em all crawl.

Knowing, Kama, Krodh, Lobh and Moh is not who I am
      lowering indeed my status as a man,
      renounce you all, for sure I can!

Look thus within, with whom your King self identifies:
As the Ugly Duckling? Let it then become a swan!
As a rigid old King whose life is bound
            by hatred and norms? Let it move on!
Like the wicked witch? As in the tale of Snow White.
Or as Rama[6] my lord, of pure and radiant light!!!

On a day, when the King was in his deep slumbers,
      a messenger of the Prince to the Queen's inner chambers
      entered and sang with wisdom pure,
      in a voice so sweet and melodic, that was to ensure,
      the King and the Queen would listen and understand.
The messenger Gentle Breeze, he thus began:

As a light ignites a flame of light in times of despair,
      when life in its whole seems scary and unfair.

---

6   Rama is the main character of the ancient told/written poetry "The Ramayana",
original written by Valmiki.

I to you have come, who lives for others,
  in you are thoughts pure and modest.

He, the eternal, the infinite whose
      existence is like the burning flame
  of whom a portion is taken and divided
      into one and all, remains the very same.

To you my Queen, continued Gentle Breeze,
  Eternity has sent me, our beloved prince,
  to wake up the King who has now grown feeble and old;
  toothless his mouth, still clinging to his stick of gold.

As if bound to the throne of yore,
  he still lingers wanting more and more.
Even with age he has reached the peak of the top,
  but his vanity hopes he never gives up.

Thus to make the king realize,
      that he is subjected to a much greater law,
  there are things in this life he never ever saw;
  words of truth never heard; feelings of
      ecstasy and bliss never felt;
  a reality so great and pure within
      our King, thus till now, he never beheld.

All rivers to the ocean lead,
  so too, the King must now weigh his deed.

As for the ego, a wave rising high in search,
　　　　in the ocean great it again shall merge.
Be his deeds good, bad or selfish,
　　　　his self imposed identity too, shall vanish.

But alas, see how the King when his palace expires
　　　　thinks it's the end, but all it requires
　　　　is a little contemplation on the waxing
　　　　　　and waning of the moon,
　　　　whose appearance and disappearance
　　　　　　is a fake, must he realize soon,
　　　　that he thus exist himself, like water
　　　　　　captured in an earthen pot on cracking,
　　　　again shall flow out freely, though a body lacking.

Time again and again these castles have been created
　　　　of sand, of clay or of flesh, yet they are faded
　　　　by the hands of time, the creation in space,
　　　　so it all thus again . . . re-creates.

He exists himself as the subtle fragrance in the wind;
　　　　once his castle is gone, he carries them all within.

And what seed in this life he has planted
　　　　shall grow in accordance as in the Vedas[7] has been chanted.

---

7   The Vedas is an old script collected in India roughly 5000 years BC. of 4 books
mainly describing the many ways of worships, how to live a dharmic life and so forth.

Like the farmer chooses with care what to sow,
     a person should think wisely in what way to grow.
According to the deeds done in his, this life, it unfolds
     as sweet, fragrant or foul, it is in the seed foretold.

If stiff and rotten, a tree shall forgo
     as food for termites it meets the end, we all know.
But the strong grow high over meadows and farms,
     purifies the air and gives shelter with outspread arms.

Stand thus up, my Queen, and see what money
     to your King, a bee who was sent for honey,
     got high and intoxicated on drinking of the flower bud,
     the sweet fragrant nectar and made it his hut.

Forgotten his purpose of coming this way,
     I've come to remind you both on this day.
Of the many things to which a King has to attend,
     he entirely forgot, in his daily life event,
     his own daughter, Jiva[8], the Princess,
     whose life is spent on her own in all pensiveness.

Alone is she, this Sleeping Beauty, staying a hundred years
     who does her daily japa[9] on her rolling tears.

---

8   Jiva means "LIFE" and is referring to the life-force that is sleeping in Mooladhare, or the Root Chakra, into which our kundalini-shakti/life energy is sleeping like the 'Sleeping Beauty' as told by the brother's Grimm's.

9   Japa is mental repetition of a mantra. Mantras are of many sorts and are found in the many different religions such as in Catholicism, Hinduism and Buddhism. One of the

Forgotten and alone she lives in this, the castle's lowest cellar
    as Sita*[10], forcefully kidnapped by
        Ravan* of evil and brutal temper.

The day to come, she eagerly awaits for,
    too much of her life spent in an enclosed cellar indoor.
With a serpents hissing she shall up rise[11]
    and with the wings of swans[12] she shall give up her disguise.

To the throne of the King first she is to reach,
    up further more, until her lord she shall meet.

The dazzled King may daze for a while
    in the spectacular union of earth and sky.
Up in the sky, our Prince so heaven blue[13]
    Jiva, with the Eternal, united in spirit true.
As she is the world's inner flame
    and He, the lord in all, ever the same.
But this, o'Queen, would be the end here of,
    for everything ceases to exist in this great love.

---

most used mantras in yoga is "SO-HAM" = I am that, which is the sound of our breath, inhalation-Sooo, exhalation-Hammm.

10 * Ref. to the Ramayana as earlier mentioned.

11 Kundalini Yoga or Tantra, explains the rising of ones prana/life energy seated in the lowest chakra, to be similar to the hissing of a snake.

12 The form/appearance of an angel.

13 Why so heaven blue? The colour blue symbolizes tranquillity. Also it is most amazing that when this black universe is lit up by the sun it turns blue in colour, just like the black skinned ones who is pitch black also appears bluish.

Thus the purpose of life has been briefly revealed to you.
    It is no secret, but a reminder is what we, too,
    need to break the habitual life repeating patterns
    of habits and actions, desires and thoughts inherent.

Self-created is our way in life; to undo them is a fight.
To break it is hard and thus to live it in a divine light.
But remember that light, within and out, is light supreme.
It is the light of thy own auspicious self, my Queen.

On this, His majesty arose from a dream thought dreamt,
    empty and alone on his throne a whole night thought spent.
Returning to His conscious state in contemplation
    on the words softly spoken, as if received in meditation,
and sang:

    Oh Gentle Breeze,
    How I've been kept blind in all these years.
    What have I gained but self pity
        and eyes sore with bitter tears?

    Oh Gentle breeze,
    I now you beseech.
    Pray teach me, an old feeble soul who fancied gold,
realizing now how I'm left with nothing but a bundle of mould.

    What is passion to an old man like me?
        Like the pond of water deprived is!

As when no honour even in the family
   Oh salvation, to you, what this world is?
Who am I? Who is my mother?
   My father? My love and kin?
Who are my, these children
   so many? How did it all begin?

Contemplating thus on his life as a falling raindrop,
  once reached the desert sand burning hot,
  like a dead born child, whose life string too quickly cut.

And again as a snowflake falling on ice cold land,
  stayed for eons as a ghost-like man,
  bound to a life of riches and an increased lifespan.

Pondering thus again, he sang:

 Like a raindrop falling from the sky

   My lord I pray
   every night and day,
 I'm like a raindrop falling in torrents of rain,
   to give up this identity,
   to merge in infinity,
 like a drop in the ocean devoid of duality.

 I fell on the tree on the ground in the river,
 to nourish the bird, the grass, the deer and the streams.

I fell in the desert on hot burning sand.
And like a snowflake so gently on ice cold land.

My lord I pray
        every night and day,
I'm like a raindrop falling in torrents of rain,
        to give up this identity,
        to merge in infinity,
like a drop in the ocean devoid of duality.

As time goes on, again I was born,
but this time I'm searching the big blue sea.
Yes as time moves on again I'm thus born,
but this time I'm in search of infinity.

Did you listen, my dear, well?
        With this, you every fairytale; its meaning can tell;
        as the swan milk from water can separate,
        thus falsehood from truth you must learn to discriminate.

It is not the Prince eternal who judges the actions done
        whether good or bad it is ignorance alone you have to shun.
Knowledge illuminates your entire being bright
        once you've overcome the notions might.

To grow up in life you must understand
       that body and flesh isn't what makes a man.
But in spirit your soul, your life, can expand
       and thus right from wrong, truth from
            lie, good from bad, wisely judge, you can.

So do thus contemplate in Gentle Breeze
       and live happily, and at ease.

Goodnight my child, sleep thou sweet and gently away,
       into the promise of another day.
To Jiva, this world is nothing but clay;
       for her, this life is a dream you may say.

With this, sleep overpowered the little boy,
       and he lived what he dreamt without regret or envy.

And his mother sang, while asleep he lay:
       To the promise of another day.

The morrow dawn again is breaking,
       like a ray of wisdom within you is awakening.

The Morning light is chasing away
       all the shadows that hide your way.

The sun has given its light to melt all fears away,
       on this, my child, a brand new day.

Part II

The Search

Consciousness is in each and everyone.
All are of That consciousness.
A portion of the Divine—is what our consciousness is,
therefore, the abode of God is in all life.
Not many live their lives in consciousness
and so, there aren't many living a life in God!!!

"Can you tell me tonight why you call the prince the eternal?" Said her son, while he did his tooth brushing the following evening. "Why is it not *he* who is the King?" "Because," replied his mother on seeing all the small bubbles of white foam, with great haste shooting out his mouth in all directions, "it is only the King who thinks himself superior enough, to spit toothpaste, out all over my carpet while talking!" And they both laughed. Having rinsed his mouth, she gently guided him into his bedroom and said to him:

"Remember the tale 'Le Petit Prince' of the author Saint-Exupéry that I read for you?" The son nodded as he recalled this fabulous telling of a little boy called 'The Little Prince'; a story his mother had told him not long ago.

"If we now imagine the Little Prince to be the soul, a portion of the supreme; his rose to be the mind; the fox the feelings; the different planets—an ironic characterisation of the many different personalities one human being acts (self identifies with) in the stages of evolution. This gives a picture of an existence pure and simple inherent in us, that have come in contact with a mind, feelings and the many notions—stages of consciousness. The rose is always envious of others, and therefore tries its level best to make the Little Prince think that there are no one like her. She, with her four thorns and beautiful red rose petals, appeals to his conscience. The fox to his feelings, because it wants the Little Prince to feel and connect with another object, and to feel 'the ways' of expectations, love and separation, parting and befriending with another being." She paused shortly before continuing further:

"If God is always looked upon as an old man, we may as well think he's going to die someday! But it is the eternal we're talking of here. That which neither is born nor dies. So why not see him as a prince? It is the prince in all tales who is the courageous one, the handsome one," she said with a smile. "Isn't it? And by the way, the human really thinks himself to be the lord of this creation. He thinks himself legal

32

and wise enough to do whatever he wants, no matter what causes great destruction and problems for millions of others, here, on this earth, that it may affect.

Anyway, Let me tell you how 'this mind' went out in search . . ."

"It starts with despondency in most cases, otherwise, why should an intellect like us even bother to think of something as unthinkable as 'a God'. An all-pervading existence! When we, the human beings, think ourselves to be so clever and capable, as to figure out the whole thing with our tiny brains and technology. Then why, tell me please, why think of something that no one can prove exists? Nor being able to get hold of it, as it is as subtle as the wind. Or, as it is your very own self, but a self that doesn't reflect in a mirror. Nor is it visible to this eye of yours that only beholds a world of objects and projections.

Well, the fact is, that just as well we cannot prove the existence of it, we also cannot prove the non-existence of it!!!

Don't feel compelled to say: 'Yes, God exists'. No. But was it man who created man? Was it man who created the sky? Or was it man who created the beauty of nature with its flowers, birds, etc. and to give it the life that it has? Ooo, it just happened like this, *boom*, the big bang, but then what!!! From where did the force come? The life energy? The Consciousness?

Man can only, and should only, help the growth of nature. Instead he destroys! The human race has been given the power to think, but that thinking should be of the supreme, the absolute, of that which is equally seated in all living beings, including the nature!

But no, see how he only thirsts for the sensual objects, to gratify his own, so called, 'needs'.

When a man like Albert Einstein, a great intellect said of God and his creation, that it is so much more than what a human is possibly able to perceive, in his small limited thinking, using only one tenth of the brain to think and analyse with, then . . . What to believe?

He simply believed in a God, whose spirit is manifested in the harmony of the universe."

The Search

The mother continued with the story:

"So The Mind, after having realized both its physical and mental limitations, began a search of 'the ways of Gentle Breeze' and came thus upon a man who sang out these lines:"

Foolish one,
memorizing all your grammar is of what use, I ask?
When old as you are now
and soon to give up your last and final life breath!
Sing his glorious name of the Omnipresent one.
Sing his name, O foolish one, the name of the Omniscient one.

Dear friend. From where have you come
and thus with clinched fists?
To what place must you leave
when your hands finally let loose, out stretched?
The name of Ram is an ocean of bliss,
leave me with nothing but Ram on my lips.

"His singing came to a hold when he realized he wasn't entirely alone in this deserted place in which he lived. Our traveller—the Mind—was maybe just a bit too curious to know, to whom he might have been singing and so had come quite close.

He looked at the newcomer who had reached this creepy and unpleasant place, lying behind an old deserted church, where no one else dared to come, because of its ghost-like looking ruin. The traveller was dressed in nice, no, in a *very* nice city suit, which seemed a bit odd in such a place.

To his new visitor the Sadhu spoke:"

A Real Blessing

It is a real blessing to go hungry a day, for him who has everything in terms of money and wealth; just as it is for the poor to be blessed with at least one meal a day.

And so it is a real blessing to share your joy, and to share it with those who have no joy. To give them a hand, help them make a stand, for their own joyous selves.

And for him, that lazy fellow, what a blessing it is for him to get some hard work. Think of him who always works hard, who never gets a rest, you'd think he might like a little rest too!

And just like the dirty little child roaming the streets gets a bath, maybe, once a week, so do let your little overprotected child, who always is kept so clean and fine in dress, let him splash in the mud to the pleasure of his soul.

But what is the use—he shouted out loudly, as for the whole world to hear—to set the bound man free when he, himself, denies his freedom?[14]

What's the use of wisdom to he, who like a goat is bound to a pole of rites and norms—either created by a religion or a society—and does nothing but circle round and round the pole till utterly tied up and can go no further?

And What, as well, is the use of telling the fish of the great ocean, when its home is in the water anyway?

"Having finished the last line, the Sage looked at the seeker with his small bushy eyebrows raised up high on his forehead saying:"

And so I say, A real blessing it is for him, who lives his life in darkness, to see the coming of the light.
As it is to him, who lives in the light unchangeable, to experience the darkness, so to have a greater understanding!

"Our travelling friend, who'd gone in search to find answers to life, asked the sage to identify himself."

The Sadhu sang out:

---

14 As described in 'The Cave' by Plato.

Know me thus

Wanting to be good; I am not I am not.
Wanting to be free; I do not I do not.
Driven to be bad; I am not I am not.
Living in madness; I do not I do not.
Like the deep blue sea, I am,
into which restless rivers of desires flow from all directions.
I am perfect, whole and at ease.
Untouched like the sky with the roaming wind, birds and clouds,
I am in Thee, I am in Thee.

Running after a world so empty; I do not I do not.
Rejecting its objects; I do not I do not.
Wishing or demanding; I do not I do not.
Forgetting or remembering; I do not I do not.
Steady like the sun seated in infinite space,
shining equally on all; the witness I am.
In all ages I exist as time eternal,
as beginning-less and so without a origin or an end.
In Thee I am, In Thee I am.

Family and relative; I am not I am not.
Desire and longing; I am not I am not.
Passion and dispassion; I am not I am not.
Many or none; I am not I am not.
Forever and ever I am;
like the mighty blowing wind so subtle it can't be grasped.

God is truth, this world a lie.
Jiva, the individual soul, and God verily are one and the same.
I am in Thee, I am in Thee.

Free or bound; I am not I am not.
A human of any race or sect; I am not I am not.
Enlightened or ignorant; I am not I am not.
Birth and death; I am not I am not.
In religious matters I am Love,
not a judge, so ask me not, cause;
Sins and virtues, I divide them not.
Let alone Love be the one and all.
Thus I love. I am love.

"He fell silent and remained thus.

When the evening approached, our traveller sat upon a high hilltop of the area in which he was and looked at the evening sun lowering in the horizon. A silence came over him at the sight of the great nature experienced at dawn. When all life's thoughts seemed too calm and he silently sang out, into the sky, in front and above:"

Devotion

Late in the evening, I see the sun go down, into to the sea.
And it plays its game with all the colours in the sky,
slowly we flow into the night.
Into a peace, what else can it be but paradise?

Child kiss the sky, child kiss the sky,
We are gonna fly, you and I,
in this starlight night.
Another world awakens in our sight.
Who am I?

Who am I?
The same question confronts me all the time.
I'm surrounded by this, this light.

What do I feel?
What do I seek?
What am I?

"Our traveller stayed a day or two more, but the sadhu did not steer from his meditation and so he went on.

After a few days of constant walking he came to a little village with lots of active people. All moving about in a seemingly relaxed atmosphere, walking to and fro doing all sorts of things. At a field nearby the village, he came upon a man cutting down a wilderness high and dense with a machine, and he asked:"

The Worker

His Boat.
"Excuse me, what are you doing?"
The working man looked at the newcomer with a silent look in his
eyes. He thought what he should reply, as you do when you are
doing the most obvious of things; in this case cutting wild grown

grass and bushes. To the traveller he said:

"It's my Naiya—my boat," he translated.

"Yes, my boat," he said confirmative.

"Why?" He said before the newcomer even got a chance to ask.

"Because it helps me crossing this samsara—this world existence," he again translated himself on seeing the question mark on the visitors face.

"Yep. It helps me reach the other side quite safely. 'Cause in here are many snakes and scorpions hiding, finding prey for their living. And should I too become a prey here of?" He laughingly asked.

"In here," he said and pointed at the tall grass in front of him, "lives many creatures enjoying themselves like the frogs. And in here lives those chasing prey, like the poisonous snakes. And I have come to stir them a bit, for resting here can be a danger for my friends and family, guests and visitors like you and others living in this area. But I shall tell you why it has to be like this."

And he shared with the new visitor a concept of a life seen and lived in his, the workers mind.

The Grass.

"Grass shrinks and looks grey and dead when dried in the hot season of May. Yet it grows high and strong when there's a mixture of sun and rain that comes in the few months when it's heavy laden with clouds above.

From looking dead and lifeless, grass is transformed into a sight for the eye to behold, so splendid and green when grown anew. Till this, a huge uncontrollable mess in which many dangerous

creatures hide, take shelter and kill whatever comes their way.
O yes, truly it's a paradise for frogs, that live their lives herein to
become huge, but for what reason? To be able to fill the stomach of a
snake? I ask!"

"Strange this creation is. Man is no different than the frog, nor is
he any different to the snake. And all this is caused due to this high
growing grass that, at first looked so nice, soft, and green. It
becomes a hiding place for robbers and thieves and yes, for these
great *Bhogies*—the sensual enjoyers—living just to eat, have sex
and be merry. BUT, with the danger of being eaten too. HA!" He
laughed out, a loud but short laugh.

The Garden.
"The grass too is like us humans. Our minds are like a garden. If
you don't maintain it well, it'll grow wild. The mind needs to be
maintained in the same way you look after a garden. You have to
look after it all the time! If not well looked after the weeds, the
grasses and all, grows wild. The beautiful flowers that grow like the
noble thoughts in you, will drown in all the messy thoughts of
everyday worrying."

"Fears too find a way in here, like the creeps. And the trees, they
also just grow wild, casting huge shadows of doubts for those
beneath them. And you freeze in your own doubts of this illusory
overcast shadows in the mind.
But you can remove these doubts, like you cut the unnecessary
branches of the trees to let in streams of light.
Remove the weeds and let the flowers beauty come forth and thus

the noble thoughts in you, grow visible in the light of your ever-shining self."

The Purpose.
"The purpose of life is to live a life perfectly in balance with nature. Not to disturb nature for your own purpose, sustenance, greed or sensuality. Not to exploit nature, but to *live* with nature. Swami Sivananda had said:
Any community that lives with nature follows a divine path. Nature is not created by divinity, but it is a part of divinity. There is silence and simplicity in the lives of those who live with nature."

The Circle of Life.
"A life comes as a buried seed in the soil.
Life is hidden somewhere in the unknown, as it secretly swells up a mother's stomach, as if to say:
—Hi, here I come again. And the happiness seen on its parent's faces is even more thrilling to see than, of course, just seeing the beautiful work of nature in the form of a new bright looking lawn. But in a way, I'm telling you, it is the same. Why? Because if you do not know how to take care of your child, it'll grow up just like the wild grass and entertain evil and poisonous thoughts like the snakes residing there. And live to enjoy, to gather and to grow big, in all ways, the way a frog too lives here."

And he exclaimed:

"But old and lifeless it thus quickly shall grow,
        when unattended and left to its own.
So the sweet innocent child thus out lives,
        his youth to old age and in vain his life up gives.

For what's the purpose of living a
        life for own selfish greed,
    when a whole world out there is in terrible need.

His life again shall wither away, like the
        grass in May dried and lifeless as it seems,
    only to return anew into this world
        and to grow up again by all means.

Again and again we take birth in the
        womb of mother nature,
    again and again must we give up
        our this, chosen creature.

So why not live to maintain this earth, as you see,
        it is to be taken care of, just like you and me."

"O Lord supreme," he said with his eyes gently closed. Streams of sunlight from the lowering sun behind the traveller glowed golden on his face.
"Thou art the only one to save us from this cycle of birth and death. Thou art the indweller of all hearts; causing ignorance to darken

our sight; thou art the one who makes the knowledge of your existence blossom in our hearts. Thou verily art the scripts, the author of all scriptures and the knower of it all. Do please, my lord, have mercy on us foolish and selfish beings, by shining thy bright effulgent warmth of your love on us, in which we feel safe and at ease."

He fell silent.

Kept the silence a few moments.

Then, again he looked up to intake the scene as it stood before him. But it was as if he saw it in a different way, which I'm sure he did. "And so I say to you, it is with my boat that I am to cross this fearful existence of hidden cruelties, that ruthlessly has to be cut asunder; I must keep moving. Ever active and alert we surely have to be in this world. And while in it, to keep bad habits far away. Ever alert! They may come back your way when you least expect it, so be thou always ready to shun them."

The Cow of Plenty.

"But see!" He said with a sudden big smile shining on his face. "See how this grass can nourish and give life, to our cows who in return give us milk in plenty. Cow dung to make gas of and keep the fire of the house alive. See how the milk can be made into cream, cheese, butter . . . ah," he exclaimed, "you know. I try my level best to work like nature works."

Growth.

"A tree gives fruit in plenty. Often more than can be consumed. But never does it hold on to its own given fruits. It need not

44

worry for itself and so I believe too, that I'm looked after, as long as I don't accumulate."

"And, with hard work, your children shall grow up healthy, as long as you keep them in the right spirit. That's the most important work of parents. Children are the future of this world. They are to learn and understand the indifference of the absolute in them. Each life, and the supreme spirit, are *one* and the *same*. They are no different. Although, mind you, bind them not to your belief and thinking. Let them be themselves; children of innocence nature. Do show them, if you are able to, that life is much more than this," he said, referring to his hands that he held outstretch before him.

"Flesh and bones." He looked up again and said:

"I'll give you something to think about:

The Absolute is inherent in everything. It is the oblation, and, it is the offering. The Absolute is the oblation poured into the fire of the Absolute. The Absolute verily shall be reached by him who always sees the Absolute in one and all.

(B.G. 4:24)

Or;

That is full, This is full. From full, the full is taken. The full has come.

If you take out the full from the full, the full alone remains."

(Ishavashya-upanishad)

"Our traveller stayed here in this lovely little village of theirs, for a much longer period as he really thrived being amongst people of many different casts, religions and races. Taken by the constructive pleasure of being constantly active and working with the soil of the earth."

The world is a home to all who are members of the human family. Creation is organic and no one is alone and separate. If people recognize the worth of others, protect animals and see all life as sacred, then the world will be a beautiful heaven of peace and tranquillity.

(Sw. Sivananda Saraswati)

"And so," the mother continued:
"Having stayed a few years in this society, he finally took leave of the worker, to continue his search of the Prince; the all-pervading spirit that he was introduced to by . . . By who?
He thus thought:
A voice in my own inner being; was it just a dream? But yet, if a dream, it must have come from somewhere! And he thought and thought, but got nowhere in his thinking. He sat thus on a stone in a deserted place; silently grumbling to himself with slow moving lips, that almost whispered the unspoken words of his thinking, out into the silence, of the silent witness, of a silent existence that now, here, seemed to fill him.
Where had he gone? He felt somehow at home, or at least at ease. Up he looked, but did not know the place.
Never had he been to such a deserted place. No one could be seen for miles around. Not much sign of life in the nature around him here either. Had he come to the desert?
Never had he been so far away from the noise of the city life.
—Did I really quit my job and sell my apartment, he thought to himself?
Never had he been so much on his own. He had mixed feelings of being lost and empty. Yes, even his own thoughts, his own demanding wife Kama—desires—the senses and all the many wishes, the hundreds of

children that ever were all over him. Even they seemed to have been left behind in the tumult and chaos of the city."

"He had got some direction from the worker as to where to find their still living master. He who taught them the way of living this joyous and simple life. But how to find it? He had been walking and walking for days now. His legs felt tired and sore from constant walking. Alone he was . . . Alone he sat . . . Though, not entirely alone . . . Unaware of a presence within him awakening. A gentle breeze was blowing, as if whispering in his ear, into a now 'ripened' mind. Come to help and guide this open, humbled, and silenced space of the thoughts 'creator'. Yes, the mind!!!"

To take is to bind—To give is divine

So again, down you fell, mourning and complaining.
Being a fatalist, so sad at heart you lament "Oh poor me!!!"

Down like one on the battlefield caught in the grip of despondency,
You take to your head, drowned in selfish misery.

The day before you claimed truth as the light
            absolute and pure. We ought to walk this way,
        in our every day life, so what happened to
            you now? What is it your mind wants to say?

"It's worth it not," Because you're lost and down.
Taken to fatigue, you're like a lifeless corpse on ground.

Feeling pity on you? Oh no, I surely do not.
But do thou rise once again,
            stand up. We can still do a lot.

Stand up and bring back the innocent smile of a child.
Go back murmuring, it brings you no good
            it's of no avail. Hey, be mild.

What you have so gravely mistaken for
            being the truth, is a lie.
What is the use to keep saying: "But they
            said so. They told me so." And see now, you cry.

The clouds cover a starlight night
            as well as hiding a clear blue sky,
      but change its origin, it cannot
            like the tranquillity behind this disguise.

So do rise. Up shall you rise my child,
      or stay down, blocked and blind,
      thinking your only escape is to take flight,
      and thus claiming death to be thy only right.

You know for sure the truth; yourself within.
Seeking others help, is not a sin.

Many on your way have given a view or a hint;
      waste it not, think of their ways of living it.

Thus to make a stand in life, for you to live
    in truth, in bliss, as an immortal soul
        of the auspicious, try it, learn to give.

      -To serve will make you see;
          To take is to bind.
      -To give you'll be;
          Forever Divine.

His mother found him in a deep sound sleep as she looked up from the letters she had been reading. She held them close to her heart and sat there in silence, looking at the peaceful face of her sleeping child. She noticed he had entered a deep state of sleep. Into that dreamless stage we enter, where even thoughts release their grip within this human scull; the most refreshing stage of a human sleep. Samadhi—the culmination of meditation—is said to be like deep sleep, but with full knowledge of the Self. She thought of those who could withdraw the senses, as a turtle withdraws its limbs, and remain steady in this meditative state.

In that peace all pains are destroyed; for the intellect of the tranquil-minded person soon becomes steady. (B.G. 2:65)

Part III

Union

Attachment is a psychic gravitation.
Attachment to dreams and objects has a psychic pull.
Bondage is the outcome of attachments.
Release it; develop detachment; be content;
content with what is; content with what comes.
Let this psychic gravitation of yours release.
Devoid of attachments equals a peaceful mind.

Art of life

You are the architect of your life.
In front of you;
a blank piece of paper
awaiting your hands to make a blue print.
You write, you draw,
you paint this life of yours with the colours of your choice.

You smear it, you mould or decorate it the way you choose.
It is, after all, your life;
it is your painting, so do it the way you think right.

Undo it if necessary, but do not stop.
Scratch it, erase it, throw it away if you have to, but do not give up.
Do make an attempt to make it again the way you've imagined it.

Do try again and again if necessary,
as there are wishes and dreams and beliefs within your being,
awaiting to manifest on this thin sparkling white paper.
Desires, ideas and thoughts, created within this universe of yours,
wanting to attain a shape and a form.

Whether it takes the form
of a self-imposed determination of hard work,
or you let it be shaped by the will and influence of others,
it remains in the end, an unwritten book.
It remains as water that seemingly has gained a form

(by the grace of a container) though liquid, shapeless of nature
and therefore has no form;
thus you can describe the unchangeable soul of nature.

Contentment, contentment, contentment,
how I seek thy eternal shore.
Lead me ever to thy divine door.
In those who really strive for you my lord
dost Thee manifest thy gracious form.

This is the art of life; expressing an existence,
carving a sculpture in the image of your soul.

But, having thus witnessed the many writings and scribbles
of colourful and colourless thought-patterns;
an unlimited and free imagination that ever tried to decorate
its purity . . . it remains intact, untouched and pure.

My goodbye

I'm walking down below the sky
I look up in the big blue; only a few clouds.
The sun shines its light on me, so I can grow.
Slowly I spread my wings and in the wind I flow.

Like a bird I cross the sky.
Through the wind I fly, I fly.
I pass great fields and valleys.
To heaven I fly and the earth I leave from now on.

Now I'm an angel, I can fly as a bird.
I have done my work on earth.
And now I go on to something new,
I am free I can do what ever I want.
Now I'm an angel. I live in the life of love.

Beauty is everywhere; a great big warmth of love is here.
Divinity we're blessed with here, there is nothing else here.

I have said my goodbye to the world.
I might not see the earth again, in physical form.
I've lived my time there,
and cried my sea of tears.

The following day.
His mother continued telling the story from where she had reached
the night before:

"A while after having scrambled these texts down on a tiny piece of wrinkled paper, along with scattered sketches of drawings, he went on in the direction given by the worker.

He walked towards a new territory that lay in a simple and well maintained area. As the seeker found his way a bit further down the bare landscape to a place with fields, houses and trees so fresh and green, he thought of the worker. The worker had often described this place, and now he was there himself. As he entered the premises he was invited inside to a satsang—a discussion on truth—that was being held by the saint who lived there.

Seeing the newcomer entering the hall, the saint nodded approvingly and guided him to a seat nearby.

The newcomer, our travelling seeker, was stunned on seeing the saint's bright looking being.

Then it struck him. At first, he recalled, the essence of the saint was more of a feeling, an internal sensation which words could not describe. Then as a voice heard within his own mind space. And now, in a living three dimensional form so verily visible to his own two eyes. He forgot everything happening around him, and these few seconds felt like an eternity in the moments of this revelation.

He regained his present state of awareness, as the surroundings were caught in a silent pause that filled the entire hall they were sitting in.

God in Nature

"God is One" the saint said, "and only One. It is not a mathematical 1 that gives 2 on putting them together. But it's an Infinite One, where 1 + 1 + 1 + 1 plus plus plus . . . Makes one.

This world of the supreme is self-luminous, complete and whole.

Though it is divided into all of us; it remains intact like the flame of the candle, which ignites a light of its own to another. It enjoys through our senses though It is devoid of senses. Subtle like the wind, It exists both nearer to you than your own breath and thoughts, and also very far. It is the digestive fire in all, the soma—nectar—of all life, the creator, provider and so too the destroyer.

It is dear to none, yet it does not reject anyone. All is THAT. But the human has been given the ability to think and so, that being who thinks of God, reconnects to his or her own Self in *That*, the supreme."

The mind
"What the mind thinks of, is what it becomes!

A flower seen within your conscious mind is the form that your thoughts take in that very moment. You become that flower within your inner vision.

God IS the mind. Remember, He is the Mother of all and also the seed-giving Father. He is the friend, the enemy, the lover, the master, the lord and the disciple. God is in us, but then why do we not see it? We, with our minds, are not in God but ever with our thoughts dwelling in the realms of passion and attachment. All you sitting here," he pointed at us, "are all Ravans[15]." His stomach was jumping up and down in tune with his gentle laughter.

"In fact," he said again, "You are all Demons." That is what he meant.

His presence was enormous. Little was his size in body, but huge his energy that seemed to envelop the whole hall into his being. His voice was equally heard in all corners. Everyone in there was captivated by that single voice, that spoke ever so gently, and had an uplifting laughter that slipped out of his being every now and again.

---

15 Ravan is, as earlier mentioned, the demon king who kidnapped Sita in the tale "The Ramayan."

Destination

"God lives in this body as the witness, just as a passenger is seated in a wagon. The mind is the chariot driver and the senses are his horses, the driving force. The reigns are in the hands of the chariot driver and are in his control. But the untrained charioteer (mind) either holds the reigns too loose and gets dragged around by his horses (the senses), or holds on too tight and therefore gets no where.

You have a destination. We all have one. To get there you'll have to learn how to drive this chariot and learn how to train these wild horses. Learn how to Become their master, so your passenger can reach its destination.

If I have to go somewhere, say Berlin, there are many ways for me to get there. I can take a bus, an airplane, a train or I can walk." He laughed his gentle laughter again before continuing.

"To have the witness become what it is, the origin, the beginning, the path, the goal, is what every human has to do sooner or later. But there are many obstacles on your way to get there."

In that moment he calmly leaned forward, with such an expression that everyone knew, that what he was about to say, was of utmost importance.

"And for this you need a guru." He broke the short moment of silence with a sudden move back in his seat and said in a raised voice: "If you are so convinced that you don't need a guru, because he's already there within you, then show me!" He added, his whole body moving with gentle laughter. "Then show me!" He reached out warmly as if welcoming any of us to reveal it.

"I served my guru for twelve years. From washing his clothes, preparing food and constructing buildings. And I managed all the activities of the ashram at the same time. I learned everything in my guru's ashram. Yes, I was taught grammar and mathematics in school, but school didn't teach me how to live life; how to manage and deal with life. That I learned only in my guru's ashram. An image of your guru or God is not going to correct you when you go off track. It's not going to stop, nor direct you, when you do wrong actions. Who is there to guide you physically and to stand as an example, of how to deal with the mind, and manage the difficulties in life? The guru is one who can set the guidelines to follow. The guru can bring out the hidden treasures from your very own self. But a Guru isn't easy to find."

Attachment

"Man has to understand the ways of desires seated in this body. For, to be honest, it is not at all the fault of the other sex or object, that you should feel a longing; a desire to become partners, or to develop an attachment towards him/her.

Is it attachment to the toxic stuff you're having? Or is it to the soul? Is it the hair, skin, sweat, eyes and bones, all these toxic outlets of the body that you are having such passion for?

A girl's beautiful hair—and don't mind me say this—is nothing but toxins. A way the body gets rid of its own waste products, such as sweat, dead cells in form of nails, hair, urine and your own cistern! So think twice before you fall prey for lust's unreasonable ways. What a waste of energy it is to run after others waste products!

Look thou upon all with equal feelings. In the Gita it says:

Be equal to foe and friend, honour and dishonour, praise and its opposite."

"My guru-dev always loved to sing. He once sang:

Eyes is a not fetter, seeing is not a fetter, beauty is not a fetter.
But the exited desire is a fetter, knows this point well.
Ears is not a fetter, hearing is not a fetter, music is not a fetter.
But the exited desire is a fetter, knows this point well.

60

Tongues is not a fetter, taste is not a fetter, coffee is not a fetter. But the exited desire is a fetter, knows this point well."

Desires

"Desire is an enemy of peace. Desire causes restlessness of mind. It isn't this world of objects that can make you truly happy. Desires are not bad, don't take me wrong. They can lift you to the highest realm of your existence, just as they can lower you to the lowest. Desires are the drive force; It is the one and single minded desire that have to be directed towards your goal. Living this life with a desire that makes you strong is the driving force of life. But, but, but . . . Desires can be a fetter, a trap of ignorance if you direct them toward this world of objects only. We are not talking of needs! Your needs are basically a different matter. It's not many of you who knows how to simplify your needs, for that you need to spend at least some time behind boundaries, or best . . . in an Ashram environment."

Feelings

"When hating someone, you think of nothing but of him with whom you feel enmity. When in love, that too is all a feeling that has enveloped your entire being. When a feeling is directed to a worldly object, we call it 'Falling' in love, right!" He asked with a smile on his face. "You *fall* in love, and that leads to attachment. But when love is directed towards something beyond, as St. Francis of Assisi did with Christ, or as Meera Bai did with Lord Krishna, it is called divine love and brings about union; that is when you *rise* in love."

The third eye

Someone in the hall asked:
"Swamiji, what is the meaning of the three stripes drawn on shivas forehead; what do they symbolize?"

He answered:

"The three stripes represent the three stages of consciousness.

1. The two eyes of the body are like one eye. They see this world and its objects and that's all.

2. The second eye is the eye through which you see the mind. It is called the inner eye. It sees the thoughts visualized within the mind space.

3. The third eye is the eye that sees the subtlety of energy. It sees the spiritual world. In the Gita it says about the level of perception of the third eye, that even though it has no sun, nor a moon, nor fire to illuminate this world. It is always luminous. Arjuna was given the 3'rd eye—Divya-dhrishti it is called—to see Lord Krishna in his Self-luminous state, as it is described in the Bhagavat Gita chapter 11. This luminous world is not a concept. It is the reality. Our microcosm is the home of the macrocosm. The cosmos exists within us. Even on this do the scientist agree to. Science do not believe in God, but wholeheartedly deny the existence of it, that too they can't do!"

Meditation

Our seeker gathered up his courage to ask a question. He was a little unsure of himself in this gathering of foreigners. His fear of not asking exactly what he wanted to know made him stumble through his words.

"Would you please tell me about Meditation. I've come to a dead end; not knowing what it is or how to move on!"

The master looked straight at him with eyes shining of tapasya (austerity) and said:

"Meditation is not a thing you just sit and do, as you may think. Meditation is an *on-going* process, including being aware when active. Like when people here do karma yoga. We call it 'Seva'. When you're consciously aware at all times, Meditation becomes a flow of awareness in both action and inaction.

Meditation alone can lead you to blinding darkness; action done
without awareness is just as blinding, it leads the soul to attachment to
the body and its senses.
He who knows both knowledge and ignorance together crosses death
and obtains immortality. So it is stated in the Ishavasya-upanishad."
And further it goes:

*Your soul is motionless, but it is swifter than the mind. Senses can
never overtake it, it runs ahead of them.*

(Ishavasya 4'th stanza)

Karmas
"It is in the soul of each individual that the karmas has been placed, or
the desire to do. It is the ego; it is the "I" notion.
If you try to sit on this "I" you are sure to go mad and confusion is all you
end up with. It can only lead you to the mental hospital.
The mind is like a monkey, jumping here and there. Therefore learn how
to be at peace even while your body is active.
Also you'll find in the Gita chapter 12 verse 12, it says that better than
practice is knowledge. Better than knowledge is meditation.
But better than meditation is the renunciation of the fruit of action,
because peace of mind immediately follows renunciation."

Keeping the mind occupied
"Man has to deal with just *one* thing, and that is the mind.
Be ever vigilant and ignore this mind. Don't suppress it, let it speak
as it speaks. You have to somehow trick it and keep yourself busy.
Remember that work done with awareness is a form of worship. Lighting
a stick of incense before an idol, or something similar, is what we think
worship is. But cleaning your room, washing your clothes and brushing
your teeth are all forms of worships too. Adi Shankarachariya
mentions this in the text Sri Saundarya Lahari. He says that my

63

walking is my circumambulation to Thee; my talking is my mantra uttered to Thee; my sleeping is my prostration to Thee; my eating and drinking is my oblation to Thee and so forth. In this way meditation becomes worship in all your doings whether asleep, eating, active or quiet and at ease."

His mother continued:
"In this place, our traveller had found a nourishing lifestyle in which to grow and expand. Swamiji never criticized anything or anyone. Never did he try to impose any belief or religion on anyone.
What he said was:
You have all been given a destiny, whether it is to become a great artist, a cook, a sailor or whatever. The seed to become who you are, or those qualities you're born with, unfolds itself through hard work. This monkey mind has to be kept busy at all time."

"This is partly what made one feel able to grow and expand in this place. The place had many different personalities, but they all learned from the ways of seeing, communicating and understanding through their differences.
There wasn't a religion taught there like Buddhism or Christianity. It was what they called The Sanatan Dharma[16]—the ancient righteous way of living."

"One day, as the seeker sat on his own, he thought:"

---

16 Righteous way of living.
(Some falsely translate Dharma as religion, but Dharma is not a religion.)

The Supreme

Who am I to try to force the Divine to show me its existence?
I should have to succeed at becoming THAT;
only then have I attained the purpose of life!

But;
The ways of God, I understand them not.
As King of the earth, Lord of the entire creation,
you reside in space unchanged.
Given is the form of all life herein;
that which contains a portion of thy never-ending self.
Your Queen is energy shaped to uniformity,
manifested in thy conscious space to form life.
Alone her thoughts, they dwell on you my Lord,
as the lover of the beloved would be when merged in Thee.
But alone and lonely, as if imprisoned in a cage she is,
'cause the 'I' notion has come into existence.
Asking and begging the mind, this stubborn selfish enjoyer of void,
to thus think of you, is of little use.
Free me here of, is only something you can do, O Shiva-Shakti[17].

---

17 'Shiva, the steady and unbroken flow of consciousness, is endowed with the power to
create when united with Shakti; otherwise he is unable even to stir.' That is the first line of
the Sri Saundarya Lahari. Sri Krishna says: 'Neither agency nor actions does the Lord
create for the world, nor union with the fruits of actions. But it is nature/Shakti that acts.'
(B.G. 5:14). In the Ramacharitamanasa by Tulsidas Shiva says to Parvati (another name
for Shakti): 'No one is ignorant nor enlightened, all are as Lord Hari/the Divine wills
it.' (Balakand doha 124). And when asked by Parvati whether there is a predetermined
focus in life, or if the human race is free to have their own goal and focus, Shiva answers in
the Pashupata yoga sutra: 'The goal of every manifest life form is predetermined just as
nature is predetermined. The life-span, heart beat, breath etc is all predetermined.'

"Shiva-Shakti?" The child interrupted and his mother explained. "Shiva means The Auspicious One. It is consciousness supreme. Shakti is energy, that which all matter is a product of. Matter is made up of tiny molecules or atoms that . . ."

"Yes I know," replied the child anxiously. "We were taught in school that atoms are something like 99% empty."

His mother answered:

"You could say so. I would say that they are pure energy of which a small percent has become matter. Do you see this stone you have on the table over there?" The child nodded.

"It is made up of atoms?" Her child gave a heartily laughter and said: "Are you saying my stone is empty?"

"Void," she said. "Energy has been very much compressed in the atmosphere into a grain of sand, and then slowly into a stone, then a rock, then a mountain." She paused.

"Life is a product of energy. Energy is inherent in all life, be it something as hard as a stone or as subtle and fine as air. Energy has a life force and consciousness too. Consciousness without energy is like a dead body.

Life lived without consciousness is a blinding darkness. It is like scattered movements without direction.

A battery has both plus and minus right! Consciousness and energy are the same. Consciousness= + and energy=—. That is why he praises Divinity, or the supreme reality, as Shiva and Shakti."

She continued the story:

In the Bhagavat Gita Sri Krishna further says: 'The Lord dwells in the hearts of all beings, o Arjuna, causing all beings, by his elusive powers/Maya (again another word for Shakti) to revolve as if mounted on a machine.' (B.G. 18:61)

The way to release the source of life
        is long and dangerous and might
    take days, 8[18] nights, 8 years or lives
        once you've started your freedom fight!

Hard as stone; you are still a mass of energy,
        awaiting the day, again to be set free.
If courage doesn't fail your faith so tender,
        long is indeed the road your walking legs have to render.

From the highest star at bindu[19] the nectar slowly does fall.
Above it is the crown, the immortal, the supreme, the lord.

From here, you went out on your own
        a lonesome walk for some.
For neither of your relatives or friends
        to existence, along with you, have come.

And so, alone you too must find the way back again.
In void, all empty, the centre of mind space from the
        world refrain.
Awaiting the light to ascend, or the phantoms of
        forms and shapes will drag you to a lower place.

---

18 The number 8 refers to the 8 main chakras/psychic centres, located from the bottom
of the spine to the top of the head and each individual acts and thinks in accordance to his
state of evolution. Nature is of eight qualities. The supreme is One. The soul is shoonya
or 0. 1-0-8, the auspicious number used on a garland.

19 Bindu is the second highest point of the 8 energy centres, placed a bit back on the
top of the head, where some keeps a little tut of hair.

Here, a poisonous stream of gasses in the throat,
　　　its purity is transformed into a haze.

The down falling life as nectar, still further down,
　　　where spirit in matter unites, leaks.
In the heart, it finds union, but doubts in
　　　its great love and so still further on seeks.

A creature of flesh and bone is what we became, eventually;
　　　a being of limitations, wrapped up in a spellbound reality.

Taken to the notion of 'I'-ness and 'Mine'-ness thus
　　　falls even further down to burn in the digestive fire.
In the heat of the all devouring flames
　　　the nectar burns; spares none from the higher.

But think not this to be the end
　　　of your long walked journey,
　　'cause life taken to inertia gets drowned in
　　　the waters with little memory.

Sea monsters and dark self imaginary cripples
　　　devouring its bright shining soul so ruthlessly,
　　making you a being of theirs; of lust
　　　and greed, is just a fraction of its cruelty.

A day spent in its grip,
        this sump of illusion, feels like an eternity.
Life after life, you herein live,
        but move not a fraction in this dark sea.

Many are lost to a life's true pleasures of
        real bliss. Truth, they call it, this illusion.
This place is at the bottom of your spine
        in which your mind has sunk in confusion.

Down further more. You can hardly fall lower,
        but get buried in the soil, but herein resides a great power.
It's a purity that remains intact
        and untouched in its muddy water;
        She is Jiva. She is just like the lotus flower.

Thus you shall rise upwards
        to the utterance of the eternal sound;
        mind you, it is the intensity that counts
        the labour and not the amount.

Attachment to body, dreams, wealth
        and family is the pull of gravity;
        hence a detached mind is peaceful and free
        able to perceive the great reality.

Move thus upwards from the roots in the mud,
        and bring the nectar back up to its flower bud.

Thus by rewinding the process by going back up,
     back to find union in heart, cooling
          the nectar and blow it up the top.

Opening wide the lotus, again to blossom at the crown chakra.
Expansion of consciousness, this is Tantra.

These messengers of the lord become rooted in Thee.
They're like the upside down growing tree.

With branches down, they
          here in this world with ease can be,
     as nourished from above in truth,
          they know their true identity.

Few are those, who have escaped this mad appearance,
     but with hard and constant efforts made you too shall dance.

Having cut asunder, with the axe of
          detachment, the roots that creep in,
     roots of lingering feelings and
          attachment to them, and so move up again.

Up through a self-created appearance
          they again do merge,
     by constant practice and with inquiry
          into their nature shall search.

Piercing each chakra with a constant
            one pointed awareness,
        awakening the life-force inherent within
            to reunite in oneness.

Reversing the process of life, to once
            again become merged with bhakti[20].
In That, an unforgettable revelation of consciousness supreme,
            inherent in all life, as Shiva-Shakti.

With streams of nectar gushing from Thy feet, irrigating the five
elements again from the region of illumination (the crown chakra), Thou
returnest to Thy home via the six chakras21. Converting Thyself into
the individual self, or jivatman, Thou sleepest in the deep pit of Thy
own home (in the root chakra), like a serpent of three and a half coils.

            (The Sri Saundarya Lahari
            by Adi Shankaracharya verse 10)

The abode of Devi/Shakti in the brain is called Kundalini yoga in
tantra. The entire circuit of Devi starts from a point, and goes down
the spinal column. Where the spinal column ends, at the tailbone, behind
the uterus, it meets with the gland behind the womb in the cervix. That
gland is mooladhara. From ancient times this structure has been called
an inverted tree. Many traditions has spoken about it. The Bible has
references to it. How will a tree performing headstand pose look like?

            (Swami Satyananda Saraswati)

---

20 Bhakti=Devotion.

21 Although it here in this verse only mentions 6 chakras, with the crown chakra being the
7'th, we presume that it here excludes the bindu chakra which is at the top of the back of
the head, and sees it as being a part of the crown chakra.

They (the wise) speaks of the indestructible peepul tree, having its roots above and branches below, whose leaves are the metres or hymns; he who knows this is the knower of the most profound knowledge.

(B.G. 15:1)

Afterward

A few days had gone after completing the story, when one day at dinner the son asked his mother:

"Is that story you told me . . . shall we call it 'The Journey of the Mind', a true story; or did you just make it up yourself?"

He looked partly at her and partly at his own plate of food waiting for an answer. She said:

"Hmmmm, in a way, yes." He looked back up saying:

"What's that supposed to mean, is it true or not," he demanded to know! She hesitated, but finally said:

"It was to share with you how your brother, upon having an encounter with his subconscious mind, found within himself a change, that he could not describe in words, and therefore suddenly left home. He set out on a journey, which was more internal than external, in search of the meaning of his existence. Also he wanted to gather knowledge to help accelerate the experience of that hidden self-luminous being existing within each and everyone; like the flames covered by smoke are held secret. A search for contentment and tranquillity."

Part IV

Stepping up the ladder

*A thought linked with an emotion
becomes an extremely forceful current.
Destiny is shaped due to such a combination
as we act on it; as we self-identify with it.*

River-stream

I am a river.
I'm floating down the landscape
giving life to the nature around me.

My purpose is neither to give nor to take
that is something I simply do
on my long walked journey.

I have a beginning and an end.
My source of existence is deep within.
The great sea awaits my final whim.

I may be able to delay.
People may build dams
to prevent my further journey.
I may try to twist and curve my path,
but I cannot help but to reach the great sea
where I'll have to give up my identity.

I mix with other rivers.
A resting place is offered.
A lake of comfort is given.

We shape the nature.
We give birth to new river streams,
but further on we'll have to go.

Rivers we are.
We each have our way
navigating through the landscape of mother earth.

We are all rivers of various places
bestowed with a time span on earth.
Each of us has a purpose to fulfil.

We meet, we join, we part, expand and separates
as we move towards the same and final destination;
as we all are to meet as one in the all-mighty ocean.

Whether you call it the Atlantic, Pacific or Indian ocean;
believe in one or many lives and Gods or none;
it is thus where we all once and for all shall *merge*.

Dispersed into various directions we are no more;
as rivers of name and identity slips into the deep blue sea
to gather as a whole, devoid of duality.

Our minds desire wealth, children, name and fame, but the desire of the spirit is different from that of the mind. The spirit desires to remove the darkness; become established in luminosity and unite with the supreme spirit.

(Swami Niranjanananda Saraswati)

The Christ consciousness, that Jesus obtained, revealed that the human mind *can* evolve to a great extent. Jesus lived and practiced his teachings, as his one and only aim was to '*become established in luminosity and unite with the supreme spirit*'. He called God his father and stated "my farther and I are *one*". He broke the concept of duality in the western part of the world. The prophet of Arabia, Muhammad, who appeared roughly 600 years later, received a divine revelation of "Allah"—the God—and said that there is only that *one* God. Saint Francesco of Assisi followed both concepts. He lived the master and servant relationship—Thou Art That, I am Thine—and the opposite, as he expressed in his song 'Brother sun Sister moon': "I am Gods creature of Him I am part!"

Just as salt has many names, as each language has its own word for it, the Source of this entire creation has also been called by many different names. The purpose of describing and naming the infinite is to help the mind expand into greater realms. The Source has therefore been named and explained by different means, to enable the human mind to somehow "grasp the ungraspable".

Non-dualism is a well known concept in Hinduism. It is believed that he who has unified in the supreme consciousness (also named as Shiva as well as Christ or Krishna consciousness) has become identical with the Omnipresent spirit.

Adi Shankaracharya called it "Brahman", or "The Absolute" as it is all-pervasive. He also spread the wisdom of the human beings true identity: "Ayam Atma Brahman"—My true nature is the supreme. Buddhism also has its roots in this philosophy and carries a similar message.

The meaning of Yoga is union, or to *unite*.
The purpose has again and again been to help people gather under the same roof and to unite the many races living in different societies. The purpose of Yoga is this:

1. To bring union amongst human and nature.
2. To evolve from an animal state of gross awareness, so that the basic instincts are no longer driving us.
3. To develop brotherhood and equal mindedness.
4. To be able to work together as a uniform nation and to raise from bondage to liberation through constant effort.

There are three main factors that have been dealt with here. One is Karma Yoga, the Yoga of action—as described in length through the poem "The Worker". This Yoga is to help us raise from our lower nature of gross awareness. This is the foremost Yoga that is widely accepted amongst all others. In Buddhism they have the legendary story of Milarepa (the young Tibetan Yogi) who entered the supreme state of consciousness through hard selfless work.
The other two paths are respectively Bhakti Yoga, the Yoga of devotion as dealt with in the poem "The Supreme", and Jnana Yoga, the Yoga of knowledge as in the first poem "Journey of the mind".

One path is not superior to another. They are different expressions just as the human is of different natures. Jnana Yoga is for the rational. Bhakti Yoga is for the emotional and Karma Yoga is for the active—and is therefore ideal for all, since we are all of active nature.

The human race is divided because of the mind associating with its lower nature, or as Sigmund Freud described it 'being driven by the subconscious mind'. 'The Shadow'—a narration by the Danish author H. C. Andersen—illustrates this concept well; showing how a *well* composed person gets deluded and suppressed by his own "shadow" side (subconscious mind). The mind which divides the entire world into numberless names and forms also unites the whole as one creation. One existence. One living organism.

But the mind is exposed to the changes of mental patterns. From being calm and composed, something causes it to develop a schizophrenic side. So what exactly is causing our minds to change so rapidly from having common sense and clarity, to cloudiness, doubts and confusion? In the 2'nd chapter of the Gita it says that it is the object we behold in our minds that we develop an attachment to. Attachment to an object, a thought or a dream gives rise to a desire to posses or obtain it. This is not the actual problem, it is only normal that we have dreams and ideas of what we want or desire to become. The problem arises when we hanker after material acquisitions and our only endeavour is to satisfy our desires. When we thus realize that we cannot fulfil all cravings of an anticipated mind, anger and frustration are the sure outcome. From anger and frustration, delusion arises. Due to anger we lose the power of discrimination. Swept away by the impulse of passion and emotion we act irrationally. The mind and the senses are naturally endowed with the two currents of attraction and repulsion. Swami Sivananda recounts the whole mind scenery like this:

Thinking is real karma. Thought moulds your character. Thought materialises and becomes an action. You can deliberately shape your character by cultivating sublime thoughts. You sow an action and reap a habit. You sow a habit and reap a character. You sow a character and reap your destiny. Hence, destiny is your own making. You can undo it by entertaining noble thoughts and doing virtuous actions and changing your mode of thinking.

(Swami Sivananda Saraswati)

So if you really want to make this world a better place to live in, take a good look at yourself and make that change!!!

Every individual is responsible for his/her own self and we ought all to realize this.
No one can change another person. This is the conclusion you sooner or later will have to accept. Every person is responsible for the changing of their own good or bad traits.
I am the one who can improve myself. A psychologist cannot do it for me. The police cannot do it for me. The sages of all time have said this.

(Swami Satyananda Saraswati)

It is left to ones own will and self-esteem to want to advance. Whatever is within you, sorrow, alcoholism, scepticism or any other bad habit, it is not possible for some one else to remove it from your life. Accept your own good qualities and eliminate the undesirable qualities through your own conviction.

To get rid of these negative traits you must learn how to be indifferent to them. Stop being so obsessed with them. The more obsessive you are, the stronger they will hold you in their clutches. All these habits, concepts, beliefs, analysis, etc. are just expressions of the mind. Attachment to worldly objects has a psychic pull. Release it, be content and develop detachment.

And so it is the responsibility of each living creature to move from an inert and selfish state of mind, to rise above this self imaginary illusion of wrong perception, gross thinking and negativity. You have been gifted this life. Why waste it?

May we thus live our lives in the spirit of divinity.
Guided and led through life we walk and walk but get nowhere, until the grace of the supreme self in us looks our way. A single glance of this presence is enough to change our life-patterns completely. Our Sri Swamiji used to say that as a matter of fact, we are all worshipping Shakti.
This entire creation is Her manifestation and we could try to approach Her as a child does to its mother; that is something our minds can comprehend. I also remember him saying:
"Perhaps She doesn't speak English. Perhaps She doesn't speak German, Celtic or Sanskrit, but She speaks the language of the heart."

O Consort of Shiva! Thou art mind; Thou art ether; Thou art air;
Thou art fire, water and earth too. When Thou hast transformed
Thyself into the form of the universe in this way, there is nothing
beyond that is not included in Thee. This form of consciousness and
bliss that Thou assumest rules in the form of Shiva's consort.

(Verse 35)

The indescribable Aruna Shakti, the grace of Shiva, shines
compassionately for the protection of the universe.

(verse 93)

(From the Sri Saundarya Lahari by Adi Shankaracharya)

A New Era

Thus
. . . I sit here in the corner of my window,
viewing the busy street stretching far down below,
reflecting on the life I've lived over these last 12 years.

I feel as empty and vacant as the hall behind me
from which much has been cleared out over the last decade.
I am, as if looking from the edge of my eye vision,
seeing the objects outside just as clear as on the inside.

Alone
. . . I sit and watch the walk of life.
Thousands and thousands of people moving about;
like ants in a huge nest moves in streams;
as a torrent river flowing across the path;
below my dwelling place.
Each one of them; a product of lust's unreasonable ways.

I have told my story here in brief;
how I, another such product of flesh and bones,
have experienced an entire regime of
attachments, thoughts, desires and other notions.

Having left the seclusion of a secure life,
I walked into the dead silence of the unknown desert;
to renounce these notions inherited from birth;
to work with nature in the spirit of dharma.

I acquired
. . . a skill, to learn and understand a broader concept.
A concept of a life lived as an individual being,
finding inspiration to move up the ladder placed in front of me;
a ladder on hand to climb since birth
which I did not have the courage,
nor the understanding, to climb.

Till now
. . . back to where it all once began.
Left with a cleared vacated space within,
while the world outside remains unchanged,
ever the same; although,
this feels like the end of an entire era;
sitting at the threshold of a new chapter.

Now:
Am I to re-furniture this hall?
Am I to start anew, creating a new life?
Am I to follow a flow, a destiny already lying in front of me?
All this I ask myself, but
. . . I do not know.

I turn to the songs being sung within this (mind) space;
I dwell in that, letting go of the world around me.
I slip into a presence of this now, that,

all in all, ever to haunt this human soul
with an infinite state of being
that has infinite forms and expressions;
infinite ways to be reached,
as infinity is, and always will remain, infinite.

Namo Narayan

(I greet the Divine in you)

Pragya

Acknowledgement:

From the button of my heart, my first and foremost heartfelt gratitude goes to our Sri Swamiji, Swami Satyananda, whose presence is like the steady sun in space, shining equally on everyone. My Guru Swami Niranjananandaji and Swami Satyasanganandaji who are the living examples of his knowledge and power.

To all the people living in and around Rikhia, all of you have taught me a lot, here, in this one life.

To Patrick M. Houser (author of 'Fathers to be') thank you for the support you have contributed with in writing this book.

To Gitte Snefstrup for inspiring me accomplishing my task and for your support in writing this book.

To Troels Oehman for the front and back cover illustration and Julie Bitcsh for her help and support.

To my entire family, loved ones and friends with whom I have been able to learn and understand the many sides of life through their ways of living.

BACKSTAGE
PASS

BACKSTAGE PASS

CATERING TO
MUSIC'S BIGGEST
STARS

John D. Crisafulli
Sean Fisher
Teresa Villa

Cumberland House

Nashville, Tennessee

Published by Cumberland House Publishing, Inc., 431 Harding Industrial Drive, Nashville, Tennessee 37211-3160.

Photo Credits
© Dan Gluskoter Photography (303/235-0065): pp. 5, 16, 29, 39, 67, 104, 128, 143, 152, 167, 180, 190, 227, 296; © Mitch Haddad Photography (818/841-4585): pp. 19, 30, 74, 91, 96, 134, 158, 207, 221; p. 120, photo by Dana Fineman, © Starstruck Entertainment; p. 265, photo by Russ Harrington; p. 266, photo by Russ Harrington, © 1998 Warner Bros. Records

Cover and text design by Gore Studio, Inc.
Typesetting by Mary Sanford.

Library of Congress Cataloging-in-Publication Data
Crisafulli, John D., 1970–
    Backstage pass : catering to music's biggest stars / John D. Crisafulli, Sean Fisher, Teresa Villa.
      p. cm.
    Includes index.
    ISBN 1-58182-001-1 (pbk. : alk. paper)
    1. Caterers and catering—United States. 2. Cookery. 3. Musicians—United States.
I. Fisher, Sean, 1960–   . II. Villa, Teresa, 1965– . III. Title.
TX911.2.C74   1998
642'.4—dc21   98-27719
                                          CIP

Printed in the United States of America
1 2 3 4 5 6 7 8 — 02 01 00 99 98

ACKNOWLEDGMENTS

Special thanks to the following individuals whose time, efforts, and support have gone a long way toward making this book happen:

Our family and close friends for their encouragement and interest in this project. Leah and Ashley Fisher for their creative inspiration; Jennifer Crisafulli and Ron Villa for their love and patience during our long hours and late nights backstage; Sherrie Dixon, our friend and agent; all the Behind The Scenes catering staff; Allison McGregor and the staff at Bill Silva Presents; Moss Jacobs and the crew at Goldenvoice; David Swift and the staff at Avalon Entertainment.

Finally, a thank you to all the musicians who continue to tour the country entertaining their fans and sharing their talents and lives with all of us.

Contents

~~~

··· CONTENTS ···

··· CONTENTS ···

JACKSON BROWNE

JB

8/30

CATERER

COSMIC
the
B-52'S
TOUR
CREW

INTRODUCTION

~~~

Backstage. It's the place everyone wants to be. It's where the stars hang out and fans wish they could. If only they could see their favorite stars up close: touch them, know their secrets, take a picture with them, eat with them—how great that would be!

The excitement and energy felt backstage at a concert can engulf one's senses. It is a slow, smoldering anticipation that builds throughout the day of a show. Upon the crew's arrival, the pace is slow, yet deliberate. The seasoned crew members all have specific jobs to complete before curtain. By midday, the setup pace quickens and the light and sound equipment is put into place. By early afternoon, the band members' instruments are unpacked from road cases and positioned on stage. Lighting and sound equipment is powered up and the sound check begins. You begin to feel the short outtakes of the concert, to take place in mere hours, pulsate through your body. Crowds start to form at the backstage door, as fans hope to catch a glimpse of their favorite musician. The doors to the venue open an hour before curtain time, and the seats of the concert hall quickly fill. The backstage area begins to buzz with the chatter of band guests, promoter VIPs, radio contest winners, and the production staff filling last minute ticket orders.

The resonant noise from the crowd now fills the venue. The performers emerge from their respective dressing rooms after donning their stage attire and makeup. The crew makes final adjustments to the sound and lighting just as the music and lights come up with the announcement of the main attraction. The musicians take a deep breath and a final stretch, the music kicks, and the stars run up the steps to the stage. Band members retrieve their respective instruments and begin the show with a recognizable song. The crowd goes wild as the emanating sounds reverberate throughout the backstage area. Your heart skips a beat as the music pulsates throughout the venue . . . remembering that you were a part of the hard work throughout the day that made these music stars look so good.

Our company, Behind the Scenes, is a full service catering company that has been serving the music industry for more than twelve years. During that time, we've worked with artists from all over the world, representing all styles of music. The goal of Behind the Scenes is to meet the needs of the performers, their crew, their management, and their guests backstage.

The first thing people ask us is What's it like backstage? What did the star request? What are they really like? After so many years of fulfilling food and beverage needs and miscellaneous desires and appetites backstage, we have gained a great deal of insight into their lifestyles. This perspective is often quite different from the media image of the performers. It is this unique perspective that fans of these performers long for. *Backstage Pass* will take you behind the curtain and expose the answers to these questions and more. Find out what the stars must have in their dressing rooms. Get a peek into the excitement backstage before, during, and after a concert.

A lot has to happen before the fans pour into a venue. Artists touring on the road travel with a regular road crew whose job it is to ensure that the staging, lighting, sound, pyrotechnics, and instruments are all just right before the band takes the stage. A local crew is often used to unload trucks and assist in setting up the show. Typically, a state-

of-the-art arena-style concert takes sixty to seventy crew members to unload, assemble, and create. There are extreme cases, however, such as Janet Jackson, with one hundred traveling crew members and an additional thirty to thirty-five local crew members.

To produce a full feature concert production, it takes an entire day of setup, tuning, playing, and breakdown. The prerigging typically begins at 6:00 A.M., load-in commences by 8:00 A.M., and the remainder of the morning is devoted to unpacking equipment, cable, lights, and instruments. The afternoon is spent assembling all the pieces to produce a light and sound extravaganza. Setting the power, sound, and lighting cables, and "flying" the lighting and speaker trusses from the rafters of the venue can

typically take eight to ten hours. Stadium concert shows, however, take approximately five days to setup. The breakdown and load-out is much faster, three to four hours for an average concert, twelve to fourteen hours for a stadium concert.

The road caterer's day usually begins very early, with a hot breakfast for the road crew, sometimes as early as 4:00 A.M. As the day progresses, lunch is served, and dressing room requirements are put into place by late afternoon. After the sound check, our main event, dinner, is served. However, our job is far from over. Those big, beautiful tour buses the bands and crew travel on must be stocked with drinks, snacks, and hot food. Often bands request after show meals in their dressing room, since many do not eat before taking the stage. At about 1:30 A.M., the trucks and buses roll out of the venue packed, refreshed, and headed to the next gig.

Dinner time is when we have an opportunity to meet the performers and provide for them an atmosphere in which they can relax away from the frenzy of the show. As you'll see, menus vary widely, just like the styles of the musi-

cians themselves. The one constant is that all the artists require superb quality food—and plenty of it! Most of today's artists are eating healthier than in years past. Over the years, as tastes have evolved, so has the manner in which menus are planned and prepared. The '90s have spawned the emergence of the health-conscious star (and crew). The grind of working long hours combined with the excesses of the past have caught up with many in the music industry. We are cooking a lot lighter, and adding spices, textures, and flavor combinations that can't help but make them sit up and take notice. We are also finding an increased demand for low fat and vegetarian alternatives. There's something for everyone here.

Along with our wonderful cuisine, we have collected many stories over the years. For example, Billy Idol, the rebel rocker, donned a lavender jump suit during the encore on his "Whiplash Smile" tour. Little did the fans know that Billy found the garb rather constricting. So upon returning to his dressing room, he stripped down to nature, hoisted a large flower arrangement into his arms and worked the crowd standing outside his dressing room. He gave a new definition to the term streaking—and with all the hooting and hollering you'd have thought he was still on stage!

Did you know that Ozzy Osbourne is very much a family man, down to earth and extremely gracious? Or that Robert Plant and Jimmy Page know how to do laundry? Did you know that Sheryl Crow takes her dog on tour with her?

All these facts and information have made for fascinating conversation over the years. John Crisafulli, co-owner of Behind the Scenes, has been sharing these stories with friends and associates for years. The stories date back to the mid-1980s, the pop culture era when Miami Vice was the hot television show and groups like A-ha topped the charts. In fact, it was during an A-ha concert that the idea for this book was born.

John was asked to check the band's dressing room, to see if the beverages needed more ice. A-ha was performing in a very old downtown venue, the Cali-

fornia Theater, which was built back in the early 1900s and has since been condemned. The backstage area was hardly glamorous at this venue, nestled in the dark and musty subbasement of the building. The hallway was lit with crude, temporary lighting and the dressing rooms were no more than converted storage closets. The heavy lead-painted doors opened into the hallway, allowing no room for traffic. Typically, we knock on the dressing room door before entering. However, the band bus had not yet arrived, so John assumed the dressing room was empty. Well, not quite. As he opened the heavy door, he discovered the lead singer lip locked in a compromising position with his girlfriend. Completely embarrassed, John placed the bucket of ice on the rickety counter and left the room apologizing for the interruption. The next day, it made for a great story when he was asked about his workday.

A year or so later, at a Berlin concert, John was asked to deliver a fruit tray to lead singer Terri Nunn's dressing room.

This particular dressing room was nothing more than black drapes sectioning off a corner of the backstage mezzanine level. Upon reaching the draped area, John was instructed by the tour manager to go on in and place the tray on the refreshment table. Upon entering, he was confronted by the singer and told very abruptly to fetch her suede boots from across the cubicle. More than willing to help, John quickly set the tray down in an attempt to fulfill Ms. Nunn's request, only to be further accosted by the artist for not moving quickly enough. Needless to say, Ms. Nunn was not in ideal spirits that evening. John later received an apology from the tour manager for the berating he received earlier in the evening.

The more concerts John, co-owner Teresa Villa, and chef Sean Fisher work, the more stories they collect from their experiences. Some are humorous, like the Harry Connick Jr. interruption, and some are a bit more interesting, like Frank Sinatra's cherry Lifesavers. In years past, the backstage area was a party of sorts with a constant parade of guests, women, contest winners,

and fans. Liquor and drugs, often a staple in previous years, are now the exception. The concert industry is much more business-oriented in the 1990s. Our knowledge and insight of this backstage world is what we have decided to share with this book. You will also learn what each musician requests in their dressing room. Learn which musicians are vegetarians, which follow strict diets, and who indulges in sweets and chocolates.

So come into our backstage world. Feel the enthusiasm and excitement of being literally *behind the scenes.* Learn more about your favorite musicians and what they enjoy eating. Learn how to duplicate their dining choices in your own home. This is your *Backstage Pass* . . . please join us!

Teresa, John, and Sean

ABOUT THE AUTHORS

Behind the Scenes, Inc. is owned by the brother and sister team of Teresa Villa and John Crisafulli. The company specializes in backstage catering for concerts, major sporting events, national broadcast compounds, movie and commercial sets, and special events throughout California and the nation. Their clientele has included The Eagles, Janet Jackson, Pearl Jam, Frank Sinatra, Bette Midler, Aerosmith, ESPN, NBC, CNN, and the NFL to name but a few.

While they were in college, Teresa and John both worked with the company's former owner, which gave them a taste of what was to come. Their degrees helped prepare them for the business of doing business, but nothing could truly get them ready for the long days and last-minute changes that come when the artist arrives! Teresa has worked backstage for more than thirteen years, and John for almost twelve years. During that time, they've met and catered for countless artists, many of whom are still shining stars, as well as those who have since left the spotlight. Fame can be a fleeting thing!

Teresa worked her way through college by holding down numerous jobs, one of which included backstage catering. After completing her degree in journalism, she secured a positions with a public relations and advertising agency. Teresa's tenure with the agency proved invaluable in teaching her the fine points of promotions, marketing, product introduction, crisis management, advertising, and media placement. During that time, she kept her hand in catering (on a very part-time basis), never knowing it would be a business opportunity in the making.

John began his college career at Boston University and eventually graduated from San Diego State University with a degree in finance. While in high school and college, John worked backstage polishing his culinary skills, something he takes great pride in as a hobby. During his years at SDSU, he took a position with University Relations and Development, as special assistant to the vice president. In that position, he worked with countless community leaders and major donors, taking responsibility for fundraising, special event planning, and donor relations. Since leaving the university in 1994, John continues to involve himself with SDSU events as time allows.

Sean Fisher is the Executive Consulting Chef for Behind the Scenes, Inc. He has nineteen years of restaurant and culinary arts experience. Having served with some of Southern California's premier chefs, Sean has drawn on his own creativity and individual study to put together innovative menus with taste. Over the years, he has overseen the opening and management of several restaurants in the San Diego area. Sean has had a hand in everything from construction and menu planning to sales, personnel, and purchasing. Over time, he has mastered several different types of cuisine, including Italian, Mediterranean, and Southwestern. During the more than fourteen years he has worked backstage, Sean has cooked for just about every artist who has gone on the road. Sean is also one of the west coast's premier international wine brokers. His expertise in recommending appropriate wines to compliment the various dishes is recognized by not only his all-star clients but by the food and wine industry as a whole.

In January 1993, John and Teresa took over Behind the Scenes from a long-time friend who wanted to move on and continue her travels. Since then, Behind the Scenes has grown at an astounding rate. Company sales have increased more than 35 percent annually under John and Teresa's management. Since building its reputation and becoming the exclusive concert catering company in San Diego, Behind the Scenes has expanded and ventured into the areas of production, media, and corporate catering. The company's growth can be traced to uncompromising attention to detail and quality, not only in the food served, but in personnel and service as well. Never ones to look back, John, Teresa, and Sean continue the adventure into a future that looks rosier all the time.

Behind the Scenes coordinated and served the worldwide media during the 1995 America's Cup campaign that took place off the coast of picturesque San Diego. The International Broadcast Center was home to ESPN, NHK, One World of Sports (New Zealand), TV Espana (Spain), and many more. Behind the Scenes provided meals for the chase boats, helicopter crews, camera people, commentators, producers, directors, and editors. Due to

In 1997, Behind the Scenes began a new adventure, catering to the athletes and crew of the ESPN Winter X Games held in Southern California, as well as the ESPN Summer X Games. This exciting and thrilling competition took the crew of Behind the Scenes into the deserts and mountains of Baja, Mexico, to feed the athletes and crew of the ESPN Xventure Race, a team-based endurance race. The Behind the Scenes crew set up camp for the participants in river washes, cliffside, and on the Baja shoreline as the athletes rock climbed, mountain biked, hitched horseback, ran, walked, swam, and kayaked throughout the back country of Baja until reaching the U.S. shoreline by kayak. The race ended on the shores of Southern California where the Summer X Games were underway.

In 1998, the company finds itself moving backstage once again. Hosting such talented musicians as Elton John, Jimmy Buffett, the Spice Girls, and Chicago, Behind the Scenes caters to the stars at the new Coors Amphitheatre in San Diego. This outdoor arena is state of the art. Built specifically to host touring musicians and rock concerts, it contains the latest sound and video technology. The venue hosts the biggest names in the

unusual weather conditions which prolonged competition, Behind the Scenes served meals almost daily for four months, without once repeating a menu!

In August 1996, the company took on the challenge of feeding the thousands of broadcasters who converged on San Diego for the Republican National Convention. This included more than 5,000 meals a day, around the clock, for two weeks to the production crews and staffs of NBC, CNN, ABC, FOX, MSNBC and others. Behind the Scenes could also be spotted on the set of the Hollywood Pictures summer blockbuster "The Rock," starring Sean Connery and Nicolas Cage. Behind the Scenes fed the crew, scuba divers, and camera people as they filmed scenes of Navy Seals storming Alcatraz.

industry, and a tentative plan is in the works to offer VIP box seat holders an opportunity to order the same meal served to the artist backstage.

You can also find Behind the Scenes on location with companies such as Lands' End, Orvis, and Chevrolet as they shoot their catalogs and commercials, as well as with top fashion industry shoots, with models from Ralph Lauren and Calvin Klein.

John, Teresa, and Sean invite you to share in their experiences and food talents. Enjoy new and exciting menus served to the stars. Create your own star-studded events with the many recipes and stories in this book. Learn more about your favorite artists, gaining a greater perspective into their personal lives. Join them as they take you . . . Backstage.

BACKSTAGE
PASS

CHAPTER 1

VAN HALEN

Gourmet dinners, a connoisseur's wine list, enough munchies and drinks on the crew buses to feed an army, and lots of chocolate milk!

Big Ass Shrimp Scampi

Your Basic Shrimp Stock

Van Halen's Bourbon Whiskey
   Peppercorn Filet

Demi-Glace

French Roux

The sun rose bright and fiery into the brilliant azure San Diego sky on that early April morning in 1995. It was 7:30 A.M. sharp, and breakfast was ready! The trucks and crew buses rolled in with a fury, arriving at the San Diego Sports Arena about an hour later than scheduled. The all-male road crew piled slowly off the buses, still half asleep, and staggered down the loading ramp toward the catering area, located deep in the tunnels of the arena. They made their way to the coffee and breakfast waiting to give them a jump start on the long day ahead.

The morning spread was a breakfast lover's paradise, although the crew's first priority was strong, steaming black coffee, and lots of it. When the caffeine finally forced their groggy eyes open, crew members discovered a treasure trove of pastries, waffles, eggs cooked to order, fresh juices, hot and cold cereals, energy bars, and fresh fruit waiting for them. Oh, and let's not forget one gallon of low fat chocolate milk.

After the crew had finished breakfast, still not fully recovered from the previous night's performance, they sauntered down the long cement tunnel to begin unloading the seven tractor trailer trucks packed full of equipment. Van Halen is one of the few bands left on tour that really typify a rock 'n' roll arena show. Do you like lights? They have two trucks full. Is loud music your game? Two more trucks are packed with speakers and amplifiers. And if television screens and high-tech video effects are your thing, don't worry, you won't be disappointed. Van Halen puts on a multi-media performance that leaves the audience begging for more. It's a veritable circus for the senses!

As morning gave way to the noon hour, lunch was served. Good thing, too. The crews were famished! Philadelphia steak sandwiches, homemade garden burgers for the vegetarians, and a delicious variety of salads were served. No prepackaged food allowed here. The crew works and plays long, hard hours. They and the band demand the freshest foods and attentive service. Oh, and don't forget two more gallons of low fat chocolate milk and a can of honey roasted peanuts. Lunch is served over a three- to four-hour period, allowing the crew and the band, upon arrival, to eat at their convenience.

As the buffet tables were cleared and reset for dinner, a crew began to prepare the dressing rooms for the artists' arrival. All the trucks had been off-loaded, road cases unpacked, light and sound equipment assembled and hoisted to the rafters of the arena, and the stage assembled. Everything was ready to dazzle the 14,000 screaming fans who would soon arrive.

Eddie Van Halen was on the brink of forty during this tour. He had traded in his long hair, rock 'n' roll look of the '80s for a clean cut, boyish hairstyle. This seventeen-year seasoned rocker also now donned a goatee to polish his truly '90s style. The short haircut was originally the result of a golf bet with Buffalo Bills quarterback Jim Kelley. Eddie lost the bet and shaved his head. Discovering he liked the new image, he decided to keep his hair short.

Van Halen has toured for many years, often stopping in San Diego. The 1995 stop was during the "Balance" tour. This new album, *Balance,* had found the band with a more controlled sound and a new look. Eddie Van Halen has sworn off alcohol and cleaned up his act and thus garnered even more respect from his fans and music critics as a result.

The artists' dressing rooms had to be setup, and beverages iced down by 3:30 P.M. The dressing room requirements list for Van Halen looks like it was made by someone who was really hungry! Artists and road managers don't use the word "picky," they prefer "specific." And Van Halen was definitely specific.

The artists arrived at 3:45 P.M. to take part in the sound check. The band members hopped out of a Mercedes and a Lincoln Town Car. All were very friendly and talkative to the production staff and crew, who had been working throughout the day to prepare for the show. Upon the band's arrival, the backstage atmosphere was somewhat light and casual. As time passed and show time approached, the atmosphere became increasingly structured and serious.

It was 4:45 P.M. and all one could hear was an English accent, "Check 1,2 . . . Cheeeek 1 . . . Check 1, 2 . . . Yo, Yo, check 1, 2, 2, 2 . . ." (We don't know why, but for some reason, every band in the world seems to have a Brit running the sound check.) The band emerged from their dressing rooms in cut-off shorts and tattered T-shirts to take the stage for sound check. Eddie Van Halen, Sammy Hagar, and the band checked instruments, played parts of songs, tested microphones for distortion and proper sound levels, and instructed their sound and lighting engineers to adjust the appropriate controls or lights to their liking. After about forty-five minutes, they retired to their dressing rooms.

Dinner was served at 5:00 P.M. The band opted to snack on the buffet set up in their hospitality room while the rest of the production staff and crew filled their plates. The band was saving their appetites for the feast that would follow the concert.

Collective Soul, a band whose sound is synonymous with the new wave of '90s rock, opened the show for Van Halen at 8:00 P.M. Their first album, *Hints, Allegations, and Things Left Unsaid,* was a huge success and spawned a loyal following and support for their second album, *Collective Soul.* The band is best known for their top ten hit "December" and later "The World I Know." Van Halen took the stage around 9:00 P.M. and played past 11:00 P.M.

The band finally retired from the stage at 11:30 P.M. and showered in preparation for their after show meal.

After the concert, the dressing room furniture was moved out and the room was transformed into an intimate dining room. The table was set with linen, fine china, and crystal stemware. We referred to the scene as the "King's Round Table," because it reminded us of being summoned to prepare a meal of royal proportions in the middle of the night, then serving it upon command around the "Master's Table." It was actually quite entertaining and enjoyable.

By the time the band had cleaned up and changed, orders were taken and the meals were ready to be served. Eddie Van Halen ordered the Bourbon Whiskey Filet, medium rare and prepared without the bourbon whiskey in the sauce. The others ordered the Big Ass Shrimp Scampi, including Sammy Hagar, who personally chose the wine selections: a 1990 Domaine La Flaive Batard Montrachet ($85) and a 1984 Chateau LaFite Rothchild ($185). He is definitely a man who knows his wines. All this at midnight in the sports arena! Excessive? Yes, absolutely!! But as a tour manager explained, "They are millionaires. They can have anything they want!" And they certainly did.

Van Halen Dressing Room Requirements:

HOSPITALITY ROOM REQUIREMENTS:

When not specified, quantities in the band hospitality room should be sufficient for six people with large appetites.

Cold Drinks:
- 1 case Coke
- 1 case Pepsi
- 1½ cases 7Up
- 1½ case diet soft drinks (Diet Pepsi, Diet Coke, etc.)
- 2 Bottles of Plain Seltzer (no salt)
- 1 case natural non-alcoholic fruit cooler drinks (Cranberry Kiwi-Lime Naturally Carbonated)
- 1 quart low-fat milk
- 1 quart fresh squeezed orange juice
- 1 six-pack small disposable juice boxes—pink grapefruit
- 1 six-pack small disposable juice boxes—apple
- 1 six-pack small disposable juice boxes—cranberry
- 1 six-pack small disposable juice boxes—white grape
- 30 liters Evian water
- 2 gallons distilled water
- 1 case Sharps non-alcoholic beer (must be in cans)
- ½ case regular local beer (must be in cans)
- ½ case premium beer (Grolsch, Pilsner, Urquell, Corona)
- 1 pint Jack Daniel's (Black Label)
- 1 pint Absolut Vodka or substitute with Finlandia or Stolichnaya
- 1 bottle Bacardi Anejo Rum
- 2 bottles white wine (Please consult with production manager)
- 1 bottle red wine (Please consult with production manager)
- 1 bottle tequila—the best you've got! (upon request)
- Small bottle of Grand Marnier, Cointreau
- Ingredients for Bloody Mary's
- 6 whole limes and margarita salt and 4 shot glasses

Food:
- assorted fresh-cut cold meats including turkey, ham, salami, and roast beef
- coleslaw
- potato salad
- macaroni salad (note: dry, not much mayonnaise, served in separate bowls)
- 3 large loaves fresh-baked bread (i.e. rye, whole wheat, sourdough, pumpernickel)
- cutting board, 2 knives
- ketchup, mustard, mayonnaise, salted butter, salt and pepper
- 1 tray cheese and vegetables: jack, muenster, cheddar, and brie (all cheeses in blocks); carrots, celery, tomatoes, scallions, broccoli, cauliflower
- two dips (i.e. sour cream and onion, avocado)
- assorted crackers (minimum 3 types, i.e., Saltines, Ritz, Finn Krisp, Stoned Wheat)
- cold mixed pasta salad (no oil or vinegar — just organic pasta and vegetables)
- fresh fruit platter including: apples, oranges, grapes, pears, bananas, kiwi fruit, melons (all fruit kept whole except melon)
- fresh whole organic vegetables for juicer including carrots, celery, garlic cloves (chill and serve on ice)

Hot Drinks:
- hot coffee (fresh-brewed, not instant)
- hot water (for tea)
- 12 Lipton tea bags
- 6 fresh whole lemons
- cream and sugar
- Equal and honey

Munchies:
- 1 pound tortilla chips with salsa and gua-camole
- 1 pound Ruffles potato chips
- 1 pound twist pretzels
- 1 pound mixed salted nuts
- 1 pound unsalted peanuts
- 2 dips for chips
- 12 Reese's Peanut Butter Cups (full-size, individually wrapped)
- 4 assorted Dannon yogurts
- 1 can honey roasted peanuts

Supplies:
- 150 16 oz. plastic cups
- 50 10 oz. plastic cups
- 18 dinner plates (china only)
- 12 bowls (china only)
- 18 each: forks, knives, spoons (metal not plastic)
- serving utensils for all food items
- 3 corkscrews
- 5 bottle openers
- 6 wineglasses
- tablecloths for all catering tables
- 300 paper napkins
- 2 rolls Bounty paper towels
- 2 large bars Ivory soap
- 2 ashtrays (metal or plastic)
- 5 full-size Bic lighters
- ice
- 1 large roll aluminum foil
- 1 large roll plastic wrap
- 1 carton Winston Ultra Lights
- 1 carton Winston Regulars (upon request)
- Tabasco Sauce (a must)

DINNER

Dinner will be served in the band hospitality room buffet style. At the close of the artist's performance, a freshly prepared meal for eight persons should be served including:

- 4 meat dishes
- 4 vegetarian dishes
- fresh salad with 2 dressings
- two cooked vegetables
- potatoes, pastas or rice
- breads and butter
- dessert (something special)
- any appropriate condiments

MIXER BOARD DRINKS

The following drinks, on ice, in three separate bus trays, are to be brought to the sound mixer, the light mixer, and the production office:

- 6 Sundance Cranberry Coolers
- 1 gallon spring water
- 6 Cokes or Pepsis
- 1 quart orange juice
- plastic cups

BUS FOOD

To be available at 10:00 P.M. for three buses (one to be selected):

- 40 assorted man-sized sandwiches, condiments on side, freshly made (not soggy)
- 13 assorted pizzas:
  4 plain
  3 pepperoni
  3 mushroom
  3 house specialty

- 40 assorted hot sandwiches (meatball, sausage, eggplant, tuna melt)
- chicken wings or assorted finger foods, (160 pieces)

BUS DRINKS
The following drinks (in cases or cartons) are to be given to production manager at 7:00 P.M.:

- 6 cases of beer (3 domestic/3 import)
- 2 cases assorted soft drinks

- 12 assorted bottles of fruit juice: (cranberry, orange, grapefruit, apple)

These drinks are for three buses; please have 50 pounds of ice ready per bus at 10:00 P.M. (150 pounds total).

The Menu

Big Ass Shrimp Scampi

Your Basic Shrimp Stock

Van Halen's Bourbon Whiskey Filet

Demi Glace

French Roux

BIG ASS SHRIMP SCAMPI

4   pounds raw shrimp (U10, "Big Ass Shrimp")

¼   cup olive oil

10 cloves fresh garlic, chopped

4   cloves shallots, chopped

    pinch salt

    pinch ground white pepper

1   cup Your Basic Shrimp Stock (recipe follows)

2   tablespoons shredded fresh basil

1   tablespoon dry whole leaf oregano

½   cup (1 stick) butter, cubed

1   tablespoon chopped fresh parsley

1. Peel and devein the shrimp. Reserve the shells for Your Basic Shrimp Stock.

2. In a large sauté pan combine the olive oil, garlic, shallots, salt, and pepper. Sauté over medium heat until the garlic and shallots appear translucent.

3. Add the cleaned shrimp and increase the heat to medium-high. Sauté the shrimp, continually turning, until almost firm.

4. Remove the shrimp and set aside.

5. Add the shrimp stock, fresh basil, and oregano to the remaining contents of the pan. Reduce the heat and simmer approximately 3 minutes until liquid begins to thicken.

6. Add the partially cooked shrimp and butter. Sauté until the sauce thickens. DO NOT overcook the sauce or shrimp, because the sauce may break and the shrimp will toughen.

7. Remove the pan from the heat.

8. Place the shrimp on a platter, and top with the remaining sauce. Garnish with fresh chopped parsley.

Serve with 1990 Domaine La Flaive Batard Montrachet ($75)—Sammy Hagar's personal selection.

SERVES 8

YOUR BASIC SHRIMP STOCK
BASICALLY THE BEST!

2   tablespoons olive oil

    shells from 4 pounds shrimp

½   cup white wine

1   cup water

½   stalk celery, chunked

½   fresh carrot, peeled and chopped

½   ripe tomato

¼ white onion, chopped

1 whole bay leaf

---

1. In a saucepan, heat the olive oil and sauté the shrimp shells over medium-high heat until the shells reach a bright pink color.

2. Splash with wine and water. Add the celery, carrot, tomato, onion, and bay leaf. Bring to a boil.

3. Reduce the heat and simmer for 35 to 40 minutes.

4. Remove from the heat and allow to cool. Strain through a fine mesh strainer, and discard the strainer contents. Then you have a beautiful shrimp stock!

VAN HALEN'S BOURBON WHISKEY PEPPERCORN FILET

¼ cup olive oil

6 cloves shallots, finely chopped

4 cloves fresh garlic, finely chopped

1½ cups bourbon whiskey*

½ cup red wine (preferably a Cabernet)*

2 cups beef consommé

1 cup roux mixture (recipe follows)

1½ ounces green peppercorns in brine

4 pounds filet mignon, cut to 8-ounce portions, medallion shaped

1 teaspoon salt

1 tablespoon cracked black pepper

1 pint heavy cream

1 sprig fresh rosemary (garnish)

---

1. In a saucepan, heat the olive oil. Add the shallots and garlic, and sauté over medium-high heat until a light golden color.

2. Add the bourbon whiskey and flambé (see Glossary of Recipe Terms) until the flame dissipates. Add the red wine and consommé, and bring to a boil. Reduce the heat and simmer for 15 minutes.

3. Thicken by slowly adding the roux mixture to the sauce approximately 1 tablespoon at a time. Beat into the sauce with a whisk. Add the peppercorns. Set the sauce aside.

4. Dust the cleaned filets with salt and cracked pepper. Grill to each band member's liking. Remove from the grill.

5. Bring the sauce back to temperature over medium heat, continually stirring. Add the heavy cream slowly, being cautious not to overheat to prevent the sauce from breaking. Continue stirring until the sauce thickens.

6. Pat the filets on a clean dry towel to remove excess liquid. Place the filets on a serving platter, top with peppercorn sauce, and garnish with a sprig of fresh rosemary.

Eddie Van Halen prefers his sauce without the bourbon whiskey and red wine.

SERVES 8

DEMI-GLACE

3   tablespoons olive oil

5   pounds beef bones

1   leek, chopped

1   medium white onion, chopped

2   medium carrots, chopped

4   quarts spring water

½   cup brandy

1   cup diced Roma tomatoes

1   6-ounce can tomato paste

¼   cup chopped fresh parsley

3   fresh garlic cloves, peeled

½   cup beef base (dry)

1   tablespoon whole black peppercorns

5   whole bay leaves

2   tablespoons whole dry thyme

Optional: Add 2 cups red wine at step 4 to make a Beaujolais sauce.

1. Preheat the oven to 325°.

2. Lightly oil a large roasting pan with olive oil. Place the beef bones in the prepared pan. Roast the bones in the oven for approximately 30 to 45 minutes, rotating every 15 minutes, until browned.

3. Add the leek, onion, and carrots. Add 1 quart of spring water, cover with foil or lid, and roast an additional 30 minutes.

4. Remove from the oven, and transfer the contents of the pan to a large stock pot. Add 3 quarts of spring water, brandy, tomatoes, tomato paste, parsley, garlic cloves, beef base, black peppercorns, bay leaves, and thyme.

5. Bring to a rockin' boil, reduce the heat, and simmer for approximately 2 hours. Cool mixture.

Note: If you are running short on time, look for powdered demi-glace at a gourmet store or substitute a brown gravy concentrate such as Bisto.

FRENCH ROUX

1   cup (2 sticks) butter

1   cup all-purpose flour

In a saucepan melt the butter. Blend in the flour and cook over low heat until the mixture reaches a pasty texture. Be careful not to brown or burn.

indigo girls

AUG 00 1997

local crew

RECYCLED PAPER

BECK
tour 97

Working
Personnel

FEB 19 1997

CHAPTER 2

BONNIE RAITT

Bonnie Raitt is an artist with loads of talent and a whole lot of class to boot. She isn't afraid to indulge in spicy foods, but requires low fat dining. Anyone for a Weight Watchers Popsicle?

World's Greatest Caesar

Sourdough Croutons

Bonnie Raitt's Quick Red Beans
and Rice

Killer Tortilla Soup

Sundried Tomato & Roasted Garlic Pasta

Bonnie Raitt is an artist with not only loads of talent, but a whole lot of class to boot. Her appearance at the Hollywood Bowl in Los Angeles was somewhat of a contradiction. Headliners at this landmark Hollywood venue tend to be more pretentious and demanding than Bonnie, who turned out to be as charming and lovely as can be.

Everyone who is somebody and everybody who thinks they are somebody tend to appear at these Hollywood Bowl concerts. Limousines, Ferraris, Porsches, and Range Rovers abound in the VIP parking area adjacent to the stage.

The hospitality area was located under a stream of tents, directly behind the large half-dome stage backdrop. The tents were carpeted and filled with plants to create a relaxing and peaceful outdoor atmosphere for the performers and crew. All meals were prepared on site in our remote kitchen facility, housed in an adjacent prep tent. Throughout the day there was a bever-

age station for Bonnie's crew and production staff to help themselves. For the health conscious staff, band, and crew, there were plenty of fruit juices, fresh fruit, and healthy snacks available.

Our crew arrived at the venue at 4:00 A.M. to set the tents, unload our equipment, and prepare the hospitality area for the extensive breakfast buffet. The traditional hot breakfast was served at 7:30 A.M., upon the arrival of the road crew and production staff. As the trucks began to be off-loaded near the hospitality area, Bonnie's production staff finished perusing *USA Today,* the *Los Angeles Times,* and the *New York Times.* These are the three most requested newspapers by bands on tour. The newspapers help the band and crew stay informed on their journey across the nation. While on tour, it is very easy to become isolated from the world around you.

The pace quickly picked up as more tractor trailer trucks were backed in.

Equipment began to pour off the trucks at a hurried pace. This steady action of the crew continued until 10:30 A.M. when the bell sounded. All work ceased, immediately, and the local crew wandered into the hospitality tent for a coffee break! The Hollywood Bowl is a union-controlled house; therefore, the local crew were provided scheduled break times, beverages, and meals at specific time intervals, all according to their contract. If their work continued even five minutes past the designated schedule, it could cost the band or promoter extra dollars due to meal penalties and overtime. In an attempt to minimize these costs, crew work schedules are tightly adhered to.

After the break, the local crew returned to their jobs for two and a half hours, and again the bell sounded. Lunchtime! A hot lunch was served over a two-hour period. The road crew ate at their leisure while the local crew lined up and ate immediately.

As the afternoon drew to a close, Bonnie and the band arrived at the venue. After a quick survey of the stage and dressing rooms they quickly made their way to the hospitality area for refreshments. Bonnie joined us in the kitchen, wearing jeans, an embroidered sweatshirt, and casual shoes. She appeared very comfortable and low key. No big hair, heavy makeup, or big sunglasses for this renowned blues musician. Curious as to the evening's dinner selection, she chatted with the chef and tasted the tortilla soup simmering on the stove.

We reminded her of the orange Weight Watchers Popsicles we had stashed away for her per her request. She was thrilled and promised to hurry back after sound check for dinner. She genuinely couldn't wait.

Bonnie and the band returned to the tent after a short while and readied themselves for dinner. They started with a bowl of our low fat Killer Tortilla Soup then they slowly moved through the meal one course at a time. Bonnie chose the Sundried Tomato and Roasted Garlic Pasta as her entree. She loved it!

The band members, including Bonnie, all had specific meal preferences, mostly based upon health concerns. Some requested no oil while others preferred whole wheat pasta. Bonnie was thrilled with her meal, and she announced that fact to all seated in the hospitality tent. "Compliments to the chef for a fabulous meal. Has everyone tried the soup? It is fabulous!" she exclaimed. She followed her compliments with a round of applause for the chef. Gracious and rare are two very appropriate adjectives for this musician. It is not often that a renowned artist takes the time to recognize the efforts of those around him or her.

Time for dessert . . . Weight Watchers orange Popsicles were brought to Bonnie's table, where she was dining with the band, atop a silver tray. Bonnie laughed at the decadent treatment and personally passed the tray around to others in the tent interested in her choice of dessert for the evening. "Looking forward to our meal in San Diego later this week," said Bonnie as she left.

Bonnie Raitt's concert at the Hollywood Bowl attracted several legends from the music industry, including Jackson Browne and Elton John. Bonnie's father, Broadway star John Raitt, joined the festivities and made a surprise appearance to sing a duet on stage with his daughter.

Jackson Browne, whom we had catered for two weeks earlier in San Diego, was a guest of the band's at the concert. About midway through the performance, Browne's assistant came rushing into the hospitality area looking for a bottle of Evian water. "For whom?" we asked. "Jackson Browne; he must have a one-liter bottle of Evian," he responded. Unfortunately, all the one-liter size bottles were in Bonnie's dressing room. His request then became a bit more urgent—

as if it were a Jackson Browne concert—so we made our way to Bonnie's room and "borrowed" a bottle of Evian water for Jackson Browne.

Elton John dashed into the venue in a white, police-escorted limousine, and he left just prior to the end of the show. Other Hollywood "be's" and "wanna be's" mingled in the VIP area adjacent to the stage. Most were not necessarily waiting to speak with Bonnie Raitt, but were more interested in being recognized as part of the "scene."

The concert was a huge success in Hollywood, as well as in San Diego four days later. The band, crew and most importantly Bonnie were thrilled with the service and food they were provided. Yet another satisfied customer!

—*mm*—

Bonnie Raitt Dressing Room Requirements:

- 1 gallon spring water (room temperature)
- 2 quarts Perrier
- 1 quart unfiltered apple juice
- 1 quart Rice Dream (original lite flavor)
- assorted summer fruits
- whole grain crackers
- baked tortilla chips (lightly salted)

Special Requests:
- Weight Watchers orange Popsicles

The Menu

World's Greatest Caesar

Sourdough Croutons

Bonnie Raitt's Quick Red Beans
and Rice

Killer Tortilla Soup

Sundried Tomato and Roasted
Garlic Pasta

1. In a blender combine all dressing ingredients except the olive oil. Blend at medium high for approximately 45 seconds. Continue to blend, slowly adding the olive oil, until the dressing emulsifies.

2. In a large mixing bowl combine the lettuce, croutons, and 1 cup of Parmesan. Toss the salad, gradually adding the dressing, until well coated. (You will most likely have leftover dressing.)

3. Place the tossed salad on serving plates or in a large serving bowl, garnish with the remaining Parmesan cheese, and serve.

SERVES 8 +

WORLD'S GREATEST CAESAR

Dressing

3	egg yolks
2	tablespoons whole grain Dijon mustard
¼	cup anchovy fillets
1½	tablespoons chopped fresh garlic
¼	cup lemon juice
½	cup red wine vinegar
1½	tablespoons coarse black pepper
¼	cup Worcestershire sauce
½	teaspoon paprika
	Dash Tabasco sauce
¾	cup olive oil

Salad

3	heads romaine lettuce, outside leaves removed, cleaned and coarsely chopped.
3	cups sourdough croutons (recipe follows)
1½	cups fresh Parmesan, shredded

SOURDOUGH CROUTONS

1	cup olive oil
2	tablespoons fresh garlic, finely chopped
½	cup (1 stick) butter
1	tablespoon whole dry thyme
1	teaspoon salt
1	teaspoon black pepper, ground
1	large sourdough baguette, cubed (3/4")
1	teaspoon paprika

1. In a small sauté pan heat the olive oil over medium heat. Add the garlic and sauté approximately 4 minutes. Add the butter, thyme, salt, and pepper.

2. Sauté for approximately 5 minutes, do not burn!

3. Preheat the oven to 375°. Place the bread cubes in a large mixing bowl, and slowly

toss with the butter and oil mixture until well coated. Place the seasoned bread cubes on a baking sheet. Sprinkle with paprika.

4. Bake 10 to 15 minutes or until golden brown. Be sure to stir/rotate the croutons halfway through baking time, to assure even cooking.

BONNIE RAITT'S QUICK RED BEANS & RICE

¼	cup olive oil
¼	cup white onion, chopped
3	cloves fresh garlic, peeled and chopped
8	cups chicken or vegetable stock
3	cups uncooked converted white rice
1	tablespoon dry whole leaf oregano
1	tablespoon whole dry thyme
1	teaspoon coarse black pepper
½	teaspoon cayenne pepper
¼	cup Worcestershire sauce
1	tablespoon Tabasco sauce
2	56-ounce cans red beans

1. In a medium saucepan, heat the olive oil. Add the onion and garlic, and sauté over medium heat until onions appear golden.

2. Add the chicken or vegetable stock and bring to a boil over high heat.

3. Add the rice, oregano, thyme, peppers, Worcestershire sauce, and Tabasco. Cover and simmer approximately 10 minutes. Stir in the red beans, cover, and continue to simmer an additional 5 to 10 minutes until the rice and beans are tender and the dish appears saucy. . . . Pile it on!

SERVES 8 +

21

KILLER TORTILLA SOUP

1	cup canola oil
¼	cup peeled and chopped fresh garlic
½	cup chopped white onions
10	cups vegetable or chicken stock (Bonnie Raitt prefers this soup vegetarian)
2	cups fresh chunky salsa
1	tablespoon mexican oregano
1	tablespoon cumin
1	cup chopped red, green, and yellow bell peppers
1	tablespoon chili powder
1	10-ounce can whole kernel corn
¼	cup chopped fresh cilantro
1	cup French Roux (see index)
12	corn tortillas, sliced into strips

1. In a large stock pot heat the oil over medium heat. Add the garlic and onions and sauté until the onions are tender and golden.

2. Add the stock, salsa, oregano, cumin, peppers, and chili powder and bring to a rockin' boil. Reduce the heat, and add the corn and cilantro. Thicken with the French Roux.

3. In a separate sauté pan heat the oil to medium-high. Fry the tortilla strips until crispy. Remove from the oil and cool on a paper towel to remove the excess grease.

4. Serve the soup in colorful bowls garnished with tortilla strips and sprigs of cilantro. Optional: Add a dash of sour cream to the top of the soup prior to garnishing.

SERVES 8+

SUNDRIED TOMATO & ROASTED GARLIC PASTA

2	cups sundried tomatoes, julienned, poached for about 5 minutes
2	cups extra-virgin olive oil
1	cup peeled and chopped fresh garlic
1	cup diced white onion
1	teaspoon salt
1	teaspoon black pepper
¼	cup shredded fresh basil
¼	cup chopped fresh parsley
1	tablespoon chopped fresh oregano
1	tablespoon chopped fresh rosemary
5	bay leaves
2	pounds fusilli pasta (regular or whole wheat), cooked al dente

Garnish:
   fresh grated Parmesan
   chopped Italian parsley

1. In a large sauté pan or saucepan heat the olive oil over medium-high heat and sauté the garlic and onions for 5 to 8 minutes until golden brown, stirring constantly.

2. Reduce the heat to low, add the sundried tomatoes, and simmer for 10 minutes.

3. Stir in the salt, pepper, basil, oregano, bay leaves, rosemary, and fresh parsley. Remove the pan from the heat, and let stand at room temperature for about 1 hour to allow the flavors to marry.

4. Bring back to temperature over low heat prior to serving. Toss the cooked pasta in the sauce. Serve garnished with fresh grated Parmesan and a sprig of Italian parsley!

SERVES 8+

Bonnie Raitt's band went crazy over this dish at the Hollywood Bowl in Los Angeles!

CHAPTER 3

ELTON JOHN/BILLY JOEL

Billy Joel hasn't lost his sense of humor after being on the road all these years. And Elton John will never lose his sense of style.

Achiote Chicken

Killer Tropical Melon Salsa

Mediterranean
  Chicken/Seafood

Roasted Red Pepper Pineap-
  ple Salsa

BTS Green Bean Bundles

Billy Joel has been on tour many years and has seen his share of "road food." In spite of this, he keeps his sense of humor and keeps the crowd cheering. We have catered for this musician several times throughout the years. Prior to one of Billy's earlier concerts in Long Beach, California, John was walking backstage carrying a tub of dirty water. Billy Joel walked by silently, without a word spoken, just a devilish grin on his face. Thoughts started racing through John's mind: Was that really him? Would he be at the venue so early in the afternoon? Couldn't be him! How full of himself can he be, not even to say hi? Maybe it wasn't him. Just look and see. So John stopped after about twenty paces and turned to look. It *was* Billy Joel, and Billy had stopped to see if John would look. Billy started to laugh as John turned beet red, and said, "I knew you would look." John shuffled off in embarrassment, only to be further teased when he entered the dressing room later to re-ice the drinks and had the whole story told in front of Christie Brinkley (then Billy Joel's wife) and the band members who were present.

Throughout the "Bridge" tour, the "Stormfront" tour, "The River of Dreams" tour, or his most recent U.S. stadium tour, in 1995 with Elton John, Billy Joel has continued to pack the crowds into his concerts. As evident in the above story, he possesses a wry sense of humor. The 60,000-plus fans at San Diego's Jack Murphy Stadium loved him. There was only one problem: Everyone was betting on the fact that it "never" rains in San Diego. Well, it did. The skies darkened and let loose one of the strongest and wettest storms in San Diego history the day of the show. The dining tent had buckets everywhere collecting the water leaking through the tent. The 30 mph wind blew down smaller canopy covers in the parking lot. Our staff gave in to Mother Nature and continued working, soaked to the bone.

In general, the backstage area at a stadium show resembles a monstrous tent city. This concert was no different. There was a hospitality catering tent to serve all the band and crew meals. There was the hospitality/VIP tent, provided for special guests of the band, the promoter and the production staff. This tent resembled a cozy 2,000-square-foot living and dining room. The night of the Joel/John concert, this tent was filled with a full array of food and beverages for the special guests. Nothing terribly fancy though; believe it or not, even Billy Joel and Elton John have a budget.

Artist dressing rooms were set up in large, temperature-controlled, forty-five-foot office trailers. Couches, oriental rugs, lamps, tables, and plants were brought in to spruce up the tight accom-modations. Extra efforts were made to keep Billy Joel's and Elton John's dressing rooms, wardrobe, guests, and management completely sepa-rate, so as not to offend or provide prefer-ential treatment to either artist, and to respect each performer's privacy. These accommodations are sparse compared to years back when venue management would fill dressing rooms with four-foot flower baskets, personal bartenders, and life-size murals of the artist. Prominent entertainment attorneys would also send flowers and gifts to the dressing rooms

with cordial notes. Those days are now gone. While the dressing rooms are very comfortable, they pale in comparison to those of the 1980s.

Sound check was about to begin when two members of the touring crew ran into the tent and started emptying our full gallons of milk. Although it was odd, we said nothing. They must have had a good reason, we thought. Finally, the stage manager entered the tent and informed us that the gallon jugs, when cut properly, make great water scoops. On stage (stadium field level), the crew was using our milk jugs to keep the rain from col-lecting on the tarp roof atop the perform-ers and their instruments during the sound check.

By showtime, the rain subsided and we were able to grill outdoors. That night we tempted everyone's tastebuds with our Tropical Melon Salsa. The salsa was such a hit that Billy Joel's band members all requested extra be brought to their dressing room after their set. We decided to lighten up the night by decorating the tables with bright colors and Caribbean decor. Not to be outdone, Elton John appeared that evening in a bright blue vinyl suit. He was surrounded by his own staff, but still managed to break free to talk with guests backstage. He's a legend on stage and off.

We were able to witness Elton John in rare form again during his two shows at the Hollywood Bowl in Los Angeles, just months later. The concerts were part of his solo "Visa Gold" concert tour. Once again, the Hollywood elite came out in droves. Planet Hollywood converted the top of the VIP parking structure (adjacent to the stage) into a dazzling party serving sushi and martinis, the hip '90s drink. The likes of Ru Paul, Dennis Hopper, and Jean Claude Van Damme could be seen in the crowd. Unfortunately for Planet Hollywood, they ran out of food and drinks after about forty-five minutes. This was their first backstage party, and they didn't realize that in Hollywood everyone brings extra guests to show off. The idea is the more guests you bring to the party—and are able to get in—the more "connected" you are.

The crowd slowly grew restless. The concert wasn't scheduled to begin for about an hour. They slowly attempted to drift down into our band and crew hospitality area. We were still serving dinner. As we fought off the backstage party crashers, we were completing the preparation of a separate Elton John meet and greet room for his personal guests. We had to have a carpet cleaning company come to shampoo the carpets in the room just two hours before the room was needed. Also, all the original furniture was removed and new stuff brought in—it just wasn't to the taste of Elton's expected guests. After all this preparation, the room ended up being used only by a small group of people, while the real VIPs were taken to the dressing rooms, which we had staffed with a personal server/bartender for the evening.

—⁓⁓—

Billy Joel/Elton John Dressing Room Requirements:

BILLY JOEL DRESSING ROOM REQUIREMENTS:

Food:
- 1 gallon orange juice
- 12 liters Poland Spring water
- 1 quart cranberry juice
- 1 six-pack Coke
- 1 six-pack Diet Coke
- 1 six-pack ginger ale
- 1 six-pack Budweiser (in bottles)
- 1 six-pack Miller Lite (in bottles)
- 1 bottle Dewar's White Label
- 1 bottle Stolichnaya vodka
- hot tea service (including Red Zinger, Lipton, peppermint and chamomile)
- fruit tray
- vegetable tray
- fresh popcorn

Accoutrements:
- sofa
- easy chair
- coffee table
- lamps
- carpeting
- full length mirror

ELTON JOHN DRESSING ROOM REQUIREMENTS:

Food:
- 12 small bottles of Perrier
- 18 small bottles of spring water
- 24 Diet Coke
- 12 Diet 7Up/Diet Sprite
- 1 quart fresh-squeezed orange juice
- 1 quart whole milk
- 1 jar pure honey
- 1 bottle apple cider vinegar
- tea service (including herbal, English breakfast tea)
- coffee service
- whole fruit basket

Accoutrements:
- couch
- easy chairs
- table lamps
- coffee tables
- large green plants
- large arrangement of colored flowers (no chrysanthemums, lilies, carnations or daisies)

Special Requests for Stage:
- Lots of water!
- Snapple Iced Tea
- assorted Gatorade
- Isotonic
- orange juice
- cranberry juice
- Perrier

Keep replenished!!!!!

The Menu

Achiote Chicken

Killer Tropical Melon Salsa

Mediterranean Style Herb Marinade
for Grilled Chicken/Seafood

Behind the Scenes Roasted Red
Pepper Pineapple Salsa

ACHIOTE CHICKEN

1   tablespoon chopped fresh garlic

1   small red/Bermuda onion, cleaned and
stripped

¾   cup achiote concentrate (spiced annato
seed paste/powder)

1   bunch fresh cilantro, cleaned, no stems

2   tablespoons chicken base concentrate

2   tablespoons dry whole oregano

1   12-ounce can orange juice concentrate

½   cup lime juice

1   teaspoon coarse black pepper

⅛   teaspoon ground cayenne pepper

8   6-ounce boneless/skinless chicken breasts

    Killer Tropical Melon Salsa (recipe follows)

1. In a blender, combine all of the ingredients except the chicken. Blend on medium high for 1½ minutes until the liquid appears thick and emulsified.

2. Place the chicken in a 6-quart bowl. Pour the blended marinade over the chicken, and stir the breasts around to assure they are well coated. Refrigerate for 6 to 8 hours.

3. Preheat the grill to medium-high heat. Place marinated chicken on the grill for approximately 4 to 5 minutes on each side, simply to mark the chicken and seal in the flavor. Be sure not to overcook on the grill! Before the chicken is fully cooked, place the grill-marked breasts on a baking sheet and finish in a 350° oven for approximately 8 to 10 minutes.

4. Remove from the oven, garnish with Killer Tropical Melon Salsa and a sprig of cilantro.

SERVES 8

KILLER TROPICAL MELON SALSA

1 ripe cantaloupe, finely chopped

¾ ripe honeydew melon, finely chopped

1 cup finely chopped mango spears

3 kiwi fruit, peeled and cubed

1 medium white onion, finely chopped

1 bunch fresh cilantro, cleaned and chopped (no stems)

¼ cup seasoned rice wine vinegar

¼ cup red wine vinegar

¼ cup lemon juice

2 tablespoons lime juice

2 tablespoons white wine Worcestershire sauce

1 teaspoon salt

½ teaspoon white pepper

1 tablespoon chopped dry basil

¼ cup sugar

2 tablespoons olive oil

2 dashes Tabasco sauce

1. In a medium bowl, combine all of the ingredients and toss well. Cover and refrigerate for 1 hour.

2. Remove from the refrigerator and drain the excess liquid. Add sugar to taste, toss, and serve. Serve over grilled chicken or fish, or as a side dish atop long grain white rice. Simply cook rice in chicken or vegetable stock to give it flavor, and top with salsa.

MEDITERRANEAN STYLE HERB MARINADE FOR GRILLED CHICKEN/SEAFOOD

Marinade for 8

⅓ cup lemon juice

¼ cup white wine (alternative: rice wine vinegar, seasoned)

¼ cup sugar

3 stalks fresh rosemary, stripped from stem

2 tablespoons chopped dry basil

1 tablespoon chopped dry thyme

1½ teaspoon salt

1½ teaspoon coarse grind black pepper

1 cup Virgin olive oil

Roasted Red Pepper Pineapple Salsa (recipe follows)

Citrus Vinaigrette (see index)

1. In a blender, combine the lemon juice, white wine or rice wine vinegar, sugar, basil, thyme, salt, and pepper. Blend at medium speed.

2. Keep the blender running at medium speed and slowly add the olive oil to the mixture through the top of the blender. Continue to blend for 20 to 30 seconds to emulsify.

3. Pour the mixture into a shallow dish and marinate seafood or chicken as follows.

IMPORTANT: Seafood should be marinated no longer than 1 hour prior to grilling. Chicken should marinate in a refrigerator no longer than 24 hours prior to grilling. Both seafood and chicken will become oversaturated and will fall apart on the grill.

4. Preheat the grill to medium-high temperature (this will sear the seafood or chicken, sealing in the natural juices). Grill the chicken or seafood for approximately 2 to 4 minutes on each side (just long enough to cover with grill marks and seal in the natural juices). Be careful not to burn or allow the grill to flame up. (Use a spray bottle filled with spring water to extinguish flames, if necessary).

5. Place the chicken or seafood on a coated sheet pan. Finish in a 375° oven for approximately 10 to 15 more minutes. It is ideal to finish your grilled items in the oven to prevent charring on the grill and to assure proper and safe cooking of the entrée.

6. Serve the entrée topped with Roasted Red Pepper Pineapple Salsa or drizzle with Citrus Vinaigrette, and garnish with fresh fruit.

BEHIND THE SCENES ROASTED RED PEPPER PINEAPPLE SALSA
(A HOUSE SPECIALTY)

3	16-ounce cans pineapple chunks
16	ounces roasted red peppers, diced
1	medium white onion, chopped
1	bunch fresh cilantro, rinsed and chopped
¼	cup lemon juice
¼	cup lime juice
¼	cup sugar (or more to cut vinegar)
2	tablespoons dry chopped basil
1	tablespoon granulated garlic
2	teaspoons salt
2	teaspoons lemon pepper

1. In a large bowl, combine the ingredients in the order listed.

2. Taste and adjust the sugar if necessary. Refrigerate the salsa for at least 1 hour prior to serving. Drain excess liquid before serving.

3. Serve the salsa atop grilled chicken or grilled seafood, or on a bed of white rice for vegetarians. Makes an excellent side dish for outdoor barbecues.

BTS Green Bean Bundles

SERVES 8

2   pounds fresh green beans, washed, cleaned, ends removed

1   bunch extra long chives

⅓   cup walnut oil

1   tablespoon lemon pepper

1   teaspoon seasoned salt

3   tablespoons fresh grated parmesan cheese

1. In a medium sauce pot heat 2 quarts of water to a medium boil. Drop in the green beans and blanche for approximately 30 seconds. Quickly remove from the heat, drain, and rinse with cool water.

2. Select 5 or 6 beans of varying lengths. Select a long blade of chives. Dip the chive in walnut oil to prevent breaking. Wrap the bundle of beans with the chive several times, eventually tying a simple knot at the center of the bundle. Set aside. Although this may seem like a frustrating task, as you will have chives break on you, keep in mind that appearance of your meal accounts for 50% of the taste!

3. Just prior to serving the meal, in medium sauté pan heat approximately ½ inch of water to medium-high temperature. Place the bean bundles in the water and cover. Steam for approximately 35 to 45 seconds or until tender.

4. Drain the water from the pan. Drizzle with the remaining walnut oil. Sprinkle the bundles with lemon pepper, seasoned salt, and Parmesan cheese. And away you go to dazzle your dinner guests!

CHAPTER 4

~~~

AEROSMITH

Wheatgrass, wheatgrass, and more wheatgrass! Wayne's World 2 excerpts were being filmed during this concert stop until 4:00 A.M. However, those wheatgrass shakes and low fat meals kept them going like Energizer bunnies.

Tortellini Gone Wild

Grilled Vegetable Sandwich

Garlic Herb Aioli

Green Linguini

Aerosmith emerged onto the rock and roll scene in the mid 1970s. Lead singer Steven Tyler led band members Tom Hamilton, Joey Kramer, Joe Perry, and Brad Whitford on a quick ride to the top, collecting numerous gold and platinum albums along the way. The band has maintained a feverish pace of producing and releasing albums accompanied by long tours. The hard work paid off, and the band has been successfully touring, making music, and selling albums for more than 25 years.

It was the extensive tour schedules that drove Tyler and Perry into the excesses of alcohol and drugs. With their rehabilitation the band emerged with a new outlook. Success continued to follow the group with hits as "Angel," "Dude Lady," and "Ragdoll," from their 1987 release *Permanent Vacation*. The album *Pump* was released in 1989, followed by *Get a Grip* in 1993.

Aerosmith's new health-conscious attitude is apparent just by looking at the support staff the band now surrounds itself with. The crew and the production staff all seem to subscribe to the new fresh attitude Aerosmith has adopted. The rage backstage was healthy. Wheatgrass, wheatgrass and more wheatgrass! Band members realized that if they were going to maintain their grueling tour schedule, they needed to take care of themselves. That they did with low fat prepared meals and dressing room edibles.

Their San Diego performance carried quite an encore. The "US" tour was coming to an end and the band and crew were looking forward to some quality time off. First, however, there were some anxious fans to perform for. Aerosmith fans never leave a concert disappointed, and that show was no exception.

The crew started load-in by 6:00 A.M. and worked feverishly to empty six trucks of sound and lighting equipment, as well as stage props. The sports arena was converted into an unforgettable light and sound show. The movie production equipment rolled in after the stage trucks were emptied. Scenes from the movie *Wayne's World 2* were to be filmed during and after the concert.

Tyler and the band were very friendly and talkative to all those backstage, from lighting technicians to caterers. The band also spent a considerable amount of time talking with special guests invited backstage after the concert. However, due to the movie scenes that were to be filmed, socializing was kept to a minimum. Paramount had cameras on hydraulic booms, hanging from the lighting trusses, and perched in the corners of the arena. Many in the crowd didn't realize they had stepped onto a Hollywood set, since extensive lighting is par for the course at an Aerosmith concert.

Aerosmith took the stage at around 9:00 P.M. The crowd couldn't get enough of the rock 'n' roll sounds emanating from the stage. Fans were a bit perplexed about the cameras at first, since no video screen accompanied the stage backdrop. Most assumed they were going to be stars in an MTV rock video. Imagine their surprise upon discovering that they were to appear in a feature film. The band continued playing until close to 11:30 P.M. Even though Tyler knew they were going to shoot the close-up shots after the performance, he didn't dare cut the concert short. He wanted to give the band's devoted fans a 100% percent performance.

After the exhausting show, Tyler stepped to the microphone and asked the crowd to stay a bit longer so they could shoot a few more scenes. The enthusiastic crowd was quite receptive to the invitation. After a short break, Aerosmith returned to the stage. The music cranked up and Tyler belted out the song "Dude Looks Like a Lady," from the *Wayne's World 2* soundtrack. The band played and played and played. It was 2:00 A.M. and the dude was still looking like a lady. At 3:00 A.M. you would expect the dude to be tired, but no, still looking like a lady. It was close to 4:00 A.M. when they called it a "wrap." Tyler, absolutely exhausted, walked into our kitchen area, adjacent to the

dressing rooms. He looked as tired as we did, but with a bit more stage makeup. He settled on some Cheetos and cookies, foregoing health food just this once for childhood comfort food. He kindly thanked us for our help, made his way to the dressing rooms, and we were finally able to call it a night.

Aerosmith Dressing Room Requirements:

HOSPITALITY ROOM REQUIREMENTS:
- brown rice—no oil, no butter
- 6 fresh ears corn on the cob—cooked 4 minutes only
- 2 roasted breasts of turkey—no oil, no butter
- 1 baked roaster chicken—leave on bone
- 1 tray of assorted vegetables with dip
- 2 cans white albacore, dolphin safe tuna in spring water
- assorted vegetables for juicing
- 1 flat of wheatgrass
- 15 pounds of organic carrots
- 4 pounds of organic beets
- fresh ginger
- 1 tray of assorted fruits including green seedless grapes, melons, mangoes, watermelon, pineapple, apples, and bananas
- dried fruit—no sugar coating
- assorted fresh fruit for juicing including 3 pineapples, 5 Golden Delicious apples, 3 Granny Smith apples, 4 mangoes, 4 papayas, 4 bananas, 1 bunch seedless green grapes, 2 pints of strawberries, 1 whole watermelon
- 1 bag Medjool dates
- 7 baked potatoes—no butter
- 1 loaf of good whole wheat bread (NO Wonder Bread)
- 6 bags Hain rice cakes (apple cinnamon, honey nut, caramel)
- 3 packs of low sodium, no fat rice crackers (sesame, nori, plain)
- 12 hard boiled eggs—do not peel
- 6 containers nonfat yogurt (including three plain)
- 1 pound undressed spaghetti noodles—no oil, no butter

- 1 jar Jif crunchy peanut butter
- 1 jar smooth health store peanut butter
- 2 jars All Fruit, fruit juice sweetened jellies
- 1 bottle of virgin olive oil
- 1 bottle of Newman's own natural light italian dressing
- 1 bottle of Grey Poupon mustard
- 1 bottle of balsamic vinegar
- 1 bottle of Kikomann soy sauce—light
- 1 box of Equal sugar substitute
- salt and pepper

Drinks:
- 12 bottles Sundance sour cherry soda
- 12 bottles Snapple iced tea—lemon flavor
- 8 bottles Diet Snapple iced tea
- 1 six-pack Diet Coke
- 1 six-pack Caffeine Free Diet Coke
- 1 case 6-ounce bottles Perrier—assorted flavors
- 2 gallons spring water
- 1 case Evian (1.5-liter bottles)
- 1 quart fresh-squeezed orange juice
- 1 case Miracle Water (fortified with electrolytes)
- 1 quart grapefruit juice
- 1 pound gourmet decaffeinated coffee
- 1 pound gourmet regular coffee—kona
- tea service—zingers and ginseng
- 4 large Pellegrino
- 1 pint skim milk
- 1 quart Ocean Spray cranberry juice
- 1 quart Ocean Spray cranapple juice
- 1 quart Welch's grape juice
- 1 quart unfiltered organic apple juice
- large packs of Wrigley's Extra, Wintergreen, Spearmint, Double Bubble
- No alcoholic beverages allowed

AFTERSHOW DRESSING ROOM REQUIREMENTS:

- 10 hot meals to be served buffet-style including:
  3 steamed vegetables (including spinach)—no butter or oil
  7 baked potatoes with sour cream, butter and chives on the side
  healthy salad—no cheese—dressing on side
  extra fruit including watermelon
  nonfat cookies and muffins—no wheat flour

JACKYL (THE OPENING ACT) DRESSING ROOM REQUIREMENTS:

(Well, this looks pretty normal until you look at the "Other Requirements")

Food:
- 1 fresh fruit bowl
- 2 jars Planters Peanuts (honey roasted and salted)
- 2 packs Carefree spearmint gum
- 1 bag Chips Ahoy chocolate chip cookies
- 1 bag Werthers Original candy

- 2 boxes Nabisco Snackwell's (raisin/chocolate)
- 2 boxes Nabisco Fat Free Newtons (fig, apple, strawberry)
- 1 bag dip-style chips with French onion dip
- 1 bag tortilla chips with salsa
- 1 jar real mayonnaise
- 1 jar spicy brown mustard
- 2 loaves bread (whole wheat and white)
- 2 large deli trays with all white meat (preferably whole prepared chicken and turkey—smoked or baked)
- 1 condiment tray with lettuce, tomato, and onion
- side pasta and potato salads
- 8 cans StarKist white tuna in spring water
- 1 half gallon whole milk
- 1 half gallon chocolate milk (Hershey or Nestlé)
- 1 half gallon orange juice
- 4 cases Evian water (liters)

- 24 assorted soda
- 12 assorted diet soda
- 24 assorted Very Fine juices
- 6 quarts of Gatorade

Other Requirements:
- 1 three-foot wooden bar stool (to be destroyed by artist)
- 1 shaved gerbil (rodent)*
- 12 fine point Sharpie pens
- 1 carton Marlboro medium cigarettes
- 3 Bic lighters

*No, we did not provide the gerbil! We draw the line when it comes to requests for small animals.

The Menu

Green Linguini (with Pesto)

Tortellini Gone Wild (with Wild Mushrooms)

Grilled Vegetable Sandwich

Garlic Herb Aioli

GREEN LINGUINI (WITH PESTO)

1   pound fresh basil, cleaned, stems removed

1   cup pine nuts

1½ tablespoons chopped fresh garlic

1   cup Parmesan cheese, grated

1½ cup olive oil

1   teaspoon salt

½   teaspoon black pepper

1   tablespoon lemon juice

2   pounds linguini, cooked al dente and kept hot

Garnish:

     fresh basil, shredded

     pine nuts

     Parmesan cheese

1. In a blender combine half of the basil, half of the pine nuts, half of the garlic, half of the Parmesan, and half of the olive oil. Blend at medium speed for 1½ to 2 minutes. You might need to stop the blender and stir the basil leaves into the mixture with a spoon.

2. Add the salt, pepper, lemon juice, remaining olive oil, and remaining basil. Continue to blend for an additional 1 minute, until smooth. Continue to blend as you slowly add the remaining pine nuts and Parmesan until the sauce thickens.

3. In a large skillet over low heat combine the piping hot pasta and pesto. Toss vigorously, remove from the heat, and serve. Garnish with basil, pine nuts, and Parmesan.

Although this dish is not low in fat, the band gobbled it up.

SERVES 8

Tortellini Gone Wild (with Wild Mushrooms)

2   tablespoons olive oil
2   tablespoons diced shallots
1   tablespoon finely chopped fresh garlic
2   cups sliced button mushrooms
2   cups mixed wild mushrooms (Porcini,
Morel, Oyster, Portobello, etc.), fresh or recon-
stituted dried, julienned
½   cup brandy
4   cups heavy whipping cream (Can substi-
tute lowfat or nonfat milk and thicken with a
French Roux and a touch of cream to retain
the dish's body.)
1   teaspoon salt
½   teaspoon black pepper
1   cup shredded Parmesan cheese
3   pounds fresh tortellini (cheese- or meat-
filled)
2   tablespoons chopped Italian parsley

1. In a large saucepan heat the olive oil over
   medium heat and sauté the shallots and
   garlic for approximately 4 to 5 minutes.
   Add the mushrooms, and continue to
   sauté for 5 minutes. Add the brandy and
   flambé. Sauté for an additional 5 minutes.

2. Increase the heat to medium-high, add the
   heavy cream, and bring to a rockin' boil.
   Add the salt and pepper. Reduce the heat
   to medium and simmer for an additional
   10 to 15 minutes, stirring constantly, until
   the sauce begins to thicken into a smooth
   creamy texture.

3. Add ½ cup of Parmesan and the hot
   tortellini. Toss and serve. Garnish with the
   remaining Parmesan and sprinkle with
   Italian parsley.

SERVES 8

Grilled Vegetable Sandwich

8   whole grain sandwich rolls, toasted or
grilled
     Garlic Herb Aioli (recipe follows)
     Grilled Assorted Vegetables (see index)
8   leaves red leaf or green leaf lettuce
16   slices Roma tomatoes
8   ounces goat cheese (chevre)
1   cup sunflower or alfalfa sprouts
1   teaspoon salt
1   teaspoon black pepper

1. Griddle/toast sandwich roll, spread Garlic
   Herb Aioli onto bread. Layer the sandwich
   with the grilled vegetables.

2. Top with lettuce, tomato, crumbled goat
   cheese, and sprouts. Season with salt and
   pepper. Graze away!

SERVES 8

Garlic Herb Aioli

2   egg yolks
1   tablespoon chopped roasted garlic
¼   teaspoon dry mustard

½   teaspoon salt

½   teaspoon white pepper

1   cup olive oil

1   tablespoon apple cider vinegar

½   teaspoon dry oregano

½   teaspoon dry basil

1. In a blender, add the egg yolks and blend to stir. Add the garlic, mustard, salt, and pepper. Blend on medium.

2. Slowly add the olive oil. Continue to blend and add the vinegar, oregano, and basil. Blend until you reach a mayonnaise consistency. Refrigerate until chilled, and serve.

CHAPTER 5

~~~~~

METALLICA

From opening for Guns n' Roses to flying their own private plane to the stage for a concert in a "dust bowl," Metallica had to have their pears and tissues.

Seared Ahi Sandwich
Roasted Red Pepper Mayo
Santa Fe Chicken Sandwich
Black Bean Spread
Pineapple Tomatillo Salsa
Rock 'n' Roll Gazpacho

Metallica established itself in the 1980s as one of the most influential heavy metal bands of the era. The release of their 1983 album *Kill 'Em All* launched the band into the heavy metal underground. Metallica consists of James Hetfield, Kirk Hammett, Lars Ulrich, and Jason Newsted (who replaced Cliff Burton after a 1986 tour bus crash in Sweden, which resulted in the band member's death). It was their 1991 self-titled release, *Metallica,* that found the band crossing over into the mainstream, touring with popular groups such as Guns n' Roses. That album went to number one after selling over seven million copies in the United States alone.

During one stop on their 1994 tour, entitled "Who Gives a Shit," the band arrived in their own vintage military cargo plane. The venue was Brown Field, adjacent to the United States/Mexico Border. The concert stage was erected alongside an alternate runway in a dirt field. Twenty-five thousand fans packed the makeshift venue. It was 93° in the shade—if you could find shade. Santa Ana winds blew throughout the day, constantly stirring up the dust and dirt.

Metallica arrived just as one of the opening acts finished its set. The crowd's attention was focused skyward as the plane made a wide approach to the airfield. Fans began to scream and yell as the plane tipped its wings back and forth to gesture to the crowd upon final approach. The plane landed and taxied alongside the stage. The band exited the plane and rushed off to their dressing room to prepare for the show.

Metallica survived the 1980s, quite an accomplishment considering many bands in the heavy metal world fell to the wayside after three or four years in the spotlight. This survival and success is attributable to not only their devoted fans, but to the band's management. They may not have been easy to work with, but they were professional in the sense that they knew what they wanted and needed, and they knew when and how they wanted and needed it.

For this particular concert, a promoter booked the show with certain promises to the band's management. This airfield venue was completely fabricated from the ground up, with the band flying in for its dramatic entrance as the highlight of the event. Details such as the two-hour traffic jam on the only road into the area and portable office trailers used for dressing rooms weren't brought to light. The fans standing in dirt and weeds for several hours in the hot sun, waiting for the show, and planes continuing to land at the functioning airport added to the tension. The accompanying dust, dirt, and heat left everyone a bit on edge. Lunch served to calm the discord backstage between the promoter and band management. They argued all day long about percentages of gross tickets and concessions, backstage conditions, and other issues. The only thing they didn't argue over was the delicious meals we served backstage, under less than ideal cooking conditions.

Prior to Metallica's grand entrance, a last-minute dressing room need nearly ended the concert before it began. Once we had unloaded the supplies and equipment, traffic on the lone road in and out prevented any quick trips back to civilization. So when the band demanded four more pears and a box of Kleenex, we asked how serious this "need" was. We were told the band would not play without them. *HELP!!*

Metallica had already asked for—and received—dressing room requirements that filled twenty-four feet of table space. The band had provided us with a detailed three-page dressing room rider, as well as a blueprint of how the items were to be placed on the tables. Also attached were specific instructions on the type of linens to be used and other miscellaneous details. With all this in mind they needed four more pears and a box of Kleenex?! We were told that, yes, without these extra items they couldn't perform. So our staff went into action. We are hired to provide hospitality services for the band, that is exactly what we did.

We called a friend at a local pizza place and desperately asked for help. We didn't tell anyone the items were coming from his home. Forty-five minutes later, we received the four pears and a box of Kleenex—not tissues but *Kleenex brand tissues*—and the band went on as scheduled. We have to admit as soon as we saw the pizza delivery truck pull up, the Mighty Mouse theme went running through our heads: "Here I come to save the day!"

Metallica's Kleenex and pears arrived just as the band did. They were thrilled with the dressing room spread and took the stage on time. With the band and crew content, we packed up some essential items and sent out our "Road Team" with the catering truck to Los Angeles that evening. Harry Connick Jr. was performing at the Hollywood Bowl the next night. That meant breakfast and load-in starting at 6:30 A.M. We got a few hours sleep.

mm

Metallica Dressing Room Requirements:

This band is so precise about their dressing room that they have created a blueprint of the layout of the food and beverage table. Everything must be just so.

Food:
- fresh fruit bowl to include: 4 apples, 4 pears, 4 oranges, 12 bananas, 3 plums, 2 kiwi, 2 lemons, grapes, 1 honeydew, 1 whole bulb garlic, 1 avocado, 1 cucumber—all uncut
- 1 bowl fruit salad
- cheese and crackers
- 1 deli platter—including 4 grilled boneless chicken breasts
- tray of fresh vegetables and dip—heavy on the carrots
- 1 bowl of hummus with pita bread
- 1 platter of lettuce, sliced tomatoes, and sliced onion
- 1 bowl tuna
- 1 bowl tossed green salad
- 1 bowl pasta salad—no olives
- 1 bread basket including whole wheat, rye, sourdough, french, croissants, bagels, hot dog buns and assorted rolls
- 6 containers of yogurt including coffee, vanilla, strawberry, blueberry, wild berry
- 2 pints of Häagen-Dazs coffee ice cream
- 1 can mixed nuts
- 1 package hot dogs
- 1 package of vegetarian tofu hot dogs
- 1 bag pretzels
- 1 bag potato chips
- 1 bag Fritos dip size
- 1 box Premium saltines
- 1 bag pistachio nuts—not red
- 1 bowl assorted candy bars
- 1 bowl assorted hard candy
- 1 box assorted granola bars
- 1 jar strawberry preserves
- 1 jar Skippy peanut butter
- 6 assorted individual cereals
- 2 sticks sweet butter
- 1 container low-cal margarine
- 1 jar Grey Poupon mustard
- 1 jar Hellman's mayonnaise
- 1 bottle ketchup
- 1 bottle bleu cheese dressing
- 1 bottle Italian dressing
- 1 container of sour cream
- 1 package of Philadelphia cream cheese
- 3 raw eggs
- 1 bottle Hershey's chocolate syrup

Drinks:
- 6 cans Dr. Pepper
- 6 cans Diet Pepsi
- 6 cans Sprite
- 6 cans Mountain Dew
- 6 cans Canada Dry Ginger Ale
- 12 cans Coke
- 6 bottles natural soda in assorted flavors
- 2 large bottles Perrier
- 15 liters Evian water
- 1 quart unsweetened iced tea
- 1 quart V-8 juice
- 1 quart grapefruit juice
- 1 quart apple juice
- 8 bottles lemonade Gatorade
- 4 quarts orange Gatorade
- 2 quarts fresh-squeezed orange juice
- 1 quart Ocean Spray cranberry juice (not Knudson's)
- 1 gallon 2% lowfat milk
- 1 quart cranapple or crangrape

- coffee and tea service
- 2 cases Heineken beer
- 2 cases Pacifico beer
- 1 case Miller Lite beer

Hot Food Before the Show:
- vegetarian pasta dish
- meat dish

- potatoes
- vegetable
- homemade vegetarian soup

The Menu

Seared Ahi Sandwich

Roasted Red Pepper Mayo

Santa Fe Chicken Sandwich

Black Bean Spread

Pineapple Tomato Salsa

Rock 'n' Roll Gazpacho

SEARED AHI SANDWICH

¼ cup dry white wine

¼ cup lemon juice

1 tablespoon coarse black pepper

1 teaspoon chopped fresh rosemary

1 teaspoon dry whole oregano

2 tablespoons finely chopped fresh garlic

½ teaspoon salt

2 bay leaves

1 teaspoon fresh Italian parsley

2 tablespoons diced red/Bermuda onion

½ cup olive oil

8 fresh 6-ounce Ahi Steaks

8 round sandwich rolls

8 leaves butterhead lettuce

8 slices beefsteak tomatoes

8 thin slices red/Bermuda onion

Roasted Red Pepper Mayo (recipe follows)

1. In a medium mixing bowl whisk together the white wine, lemon juice, black pepper, rosemary, oregano, garlic, salt, bay leaves, parsley, and diced onion. Whisk in the olive oil. Place the ahi steaks in a marinating dish and coat with marinade. Cover and refrigerate for 30 to 40 minutes.

2. Preheat the grill to high. Remove the ahi from the refrigerator and place the steaks on the hot grill. Sear for 4 to 5 minutes per side, depending upon thickness. Remove from the grill and set aside.

3. On the top half of each bun layer the lettuce, tomato, and onion. Place the seared ahi steak on the bottom half, and smother with Roasted Red Pepper Mayo. Cap off and dig in!

SERVES 8

ROASTED RED PEPPER MAYO

½ cup roasted red bell pepper

2 egg yolks

¼ teaspoon dry mustard

pinch cayenne pepper

pinch white pepper

1 tablespoon apple cider vinegar

1 teaspoon roasted garlic

1 cup olive oil

pinch salt

1. In a blender purée the roasted red peppers. Set aside in a separate dish. Rinse and dry the blender.

2. In the clean blender mix the egg yolks at low speed to stir. Add the mustard,

cayenne and white peppers, vinegar, garlic, and salt, and blend on medium high. Slowly add the olive oil until it reaches a mayo-like consistency. Scrape into a small bowl, fold in the roasted red pepper purée, and spread.

Note: If the mayo starts to separate, don't panic; simply add another egg yolk!

Santa Fe Chicken Sandwich

8   Torta sandwich rolls or soft sourdough rolls, grilled or toasted
    Black Bean Spread (recipe follows)
8   leaves green leaf lettuce, washed
8   Achiote Chicken breasts (see index)
    Pineapple Tomatillo Salsa (recipe follows)

1. Coat the inner surfaces of the rolls with Black Bean Spread. Top with a leaf of lettuce followed by an Achiote Chicken breast.
2. Scoop a few heaping spoonfuls of salsa atop the chicken. Cap with bread and serve.

SERVES 8

Black Bean Spread

1½ cups black beans (homemade or canned), drained
1   teaspoon chopped jalapeño chilies

½   teaspoon chopped fresh garlic
½   teaspoon finely diced onion
2   tablespoons red wine vinegar
1   tablespoon cilantro
1   teaspoon mexican oregano
½   teaspoon salt
½   teaspoon pepper

1. In a blender or food processor combine all of the ingredients and purée on medium for 1½ minutes or until smooth.
2. Transfer to a serving dish. If the spread is not needed right away, place in a container with a cover and chill.

Pineapple Tomatillo Salsa

1½ cups pineapple chunks, drained
1   cup fresh tomatillos, peeled, poached and cubed
1   bunch fresh cilantro, cleaned and chopped (no stems)
1   serrano chile, cleaned and finely chopped
¼   cup diced red/Bermuda onion
¼   cup chopped green onion
2   tablespoons sugar
¼   cup lime juice

1. In a medium bowl toss all of the ingredients together. Cover and refrigerate for 45 minutes to 1 hour.
2. Drain the liquid, toss, and serve.

ROCK 'N' ROLL GAZPACHO

1	tablespoon olive oil
1	cup diced white onions
2	tablespoons finely chopped fresh garlic
8	cups tomato juice
1	16-ounce can crushed tomatoes in purée
1½	cups diced zucchini squash
½	cup diced yellow squash
½	cup lemon juice
½	cup lime juice
¼	teaspoon cayenne pepper
1	teaspoon Tabasco sauce
2	tablespoons white wine Worcestershire sauce
1	teaspoon dry whole oregano
1	tablespoon shredded fresh basil
1	tablespoon chopped Italian parsley
1	teaspoon salt
½	teaspoon black pepper

Garnish:

fresh chopped parsley

diced cucumber

1. In a large stock pot heat the olive oil and sauté the onions and garlic over medium heat for 3 to 4 minutes. Add the tomato juice and crushed tomatoes, heat an additional 7 to 10 minutes, stirring constantly. Remove from the heat and let cool.

2. Add the zucchini, yellow squash, lemon and lime juice, cayenne pepper, Tabasco, Worcestershire sauce, oregano, basil, parsley, salt, and pepper. Stir well. Cover and refrigerate for 1 hour.

3. Remove from the refrigerator, stir, and serve garnished with fresh chopped parsley and diced cucumber, if you prefer.

John Cougar MELLENCAMP

CATERER FEB 87 ?

WORKING PASS

The Lonesome Jubilee

cure

24.6.92 wish tour '92

ACCESS ALL AREAS

CATERING

squeeze

babylon and on

2/20
world
tour
87/88

C

CREW

CHAPTER 6

~~~~~~

THE EAGLES

Hell truly did freeze over, bringing the Eagles back to the stage to perform for a sold-out stadium crowd of over sixty thousand fans. Band members maintained separate dressing rooms, yet came together for our luscious pasta bar.

Spinach Salad with HOT Pancetta
  Dressing

Penne with Smoked Salmon

White Bean and Sage Salad

Hell truly did freeze over when the Eagles got back together. The sellout stadium crowd of over 60,000 fans yelled as loud as they could when the group stepped on stage. The years were reflected in their faces, but the music remained unchanged and they sounded great! Each had gone on to enjoy separate careers after the band's breakup.

The band, with Don Henley (vocals, drums, percussion, and keyboards), Glenn Frey (vocals, guitar, slide guitar, and keyboards), Don Felder (vocals, guitar, slide guitar, steel guitar, mandolin, and keyboards), Joe Walsh (vocals, guitar, slide guitar, and keyboards), and Timothy Schmit (vocals and base guitar), parted ways during the 1980s. The band members' separate musical careers produced surprising success. Each member's ability to sing and play multiple instruments aided their transition to solo careers.

However, 1994 brought a rash of reunion stadium tours. Pink Floyd led the pack, selling out every concert date upon release of the tickets. The Eagles, who had promised their band wouldn't reunite, started to rethink that prospect with the reality of 60,000+ fans offering to pay good money for a chance to see them play together one last time. So the Eagles put their differences aside and became the "Boys of Summer." They sold out stadiums coast to coast playing such hits as "Hotel California" and "Desperado." The band hadn't played together in more than ten years.

The backstage atmosphere wasn't as united as their stage presence. Behind the Scenes set up private dressing rooms for each band member, including a private gym for Glenn Frey. Every band member had his own needs that had to be met. The Eagles spent more time socializing with friends and family members traveling with them than with each other. They were much more concerned on this tour about their comfort and convenience than about budget issues, so money was almost no object. The stadium parking lot was converted into a carpeted oasis of plants, tents, food, and beverages. The traveling production staff even joked about setting up a private airstrip in the stadium parking lot, so the band wouldn't be inconvenienced by the fifteen-minute limousine ride from the airport.

The crowd, unaware of any backstage isolation, thoroughly enjoyed the onstage reunion of the band. All fans saw was the massive stage and lighting display that took five days to erect. (Surprisingly enough, the design of the stage was simply borrowed from a previous outdoor tour by another artist. The crew hung a simple mountain backdrop from the rear of the stage, flew some video screens to the side of the stage and flipped the switch. It was very much pulled off by the seat of their pants.) The Eagles practiced the show only in studio, from what we were told. All this last minute preparation, or lack thereof, certainly was never evident—the concert was a resounding success!) The Eagles took the stage and with a few strums on the guitar, kicked off the show with "Hotel California." Just over two hours later the concert came to an emotional end with their classic song, "Take It Easy."

The show was in progress when a couple of gentlemen from the Eagles' management team joined us in our portable kitchen, which had been set up in the stadium parking lot. San Diego was the first stop on a twelve-city tour. We talked about what was ahead and expectations the band and management had for the overall tour. The amount of money spent to make this tour "comfortable" for all participating was astounding. Nonetheless, the Eagles had matured and become more casual and sophisticated; they found our company a perfect fit. A hearty thank you was offered by the management and production crew for our delicious work.

The Eagles Dressing Room Requirements:

GLENN FREY DRESSING ROOM REQUIREMENTS:
- coffee service
- tea service including Celestial Seasonings Sunburst C and Lipton Orange Pekoe
- 1 squeeze container of honey
- 1 quart nonfat milk
- 12 cans Coke
- 12 cans Diet Coke
- 12 16-ounce bottles Evian
- 1 bag Eagle brand thin potato chips
- 1 bag Eagle brand mesquite BBQ thin potato chips
- small bowl of mixed nuts
- 1/2 pound brown sugar
- vegetable tray
- small fruit platter
- cheese and cracker tray
- 1 bag Halls mentholyptus regular and honey lemon cough drops

DON FELDER DRESSING ROOM REQUIREMENTS:
- 12 16-ounce bottles Evian
- 6 cans Coke
- 6 cans Diet Coke
- fresh organic fruit
- tray of vegetables with fat free or lowfat dip
- 1 bag of rice cakes — sodium free or low sodium

DON HENLEY DRESSING ROOM REQUIREMENTS:
- 6 cans Coke
- 6 cans Diet Coke
- 12 16-ounce bottles Evian
- tea service including Celestial Seasonings Chamomile and Sunburst C
- Tabasco sauce
- crushed red pepper

- salt shaker with salt
- fresh organic fruit
- vegetable tray
- 1 bag sodium free plain rice cakes

JOE WALSH DRESSING ROOM REQUIREMENTS:
- coffee service
- tea service including Lipton Orange Pekoe and Throat Coat
- 6 black ceramic mugs
- 1 squeeze container honey
- 1 pint mocha mix
- 8 bottles assorted Ocean Spray cranberry juices
- 6 liters lemon lime Gatorade
- 1 bottle fresh carrot juice
- 12 16-ounce bottles Evian
- vegetable tray
- fruit tray
- 1 half pound pistachio nuts—No red
- 1 half pound roasted, in the shell, unsalted peanuts
- 1 pint Listerine
- 2 ashtrays
- 6 cans Coke
- 6 cans Diet Coke

TIMOTHY SCHMIT DRESSING ROOM REQUIREMENTS:
- 12 16-ounce bottles Evian
- 6 10-ounce bottles Perrier
- fresh organic fruit
- 4 fat free fresh baked bran muffins

Special Requests: All coffee cups, both ceramic and paper, had to be black.

The Menu

Spinach Salad with a HOT
Panchetta Dressing

Penne with Smoked Salmon

White Bean and Sage Salad

SPINACH SALAD WITH A HOT PANCHETTA DRESSING

2	tablespoons olive oil
½	cup chopped Panchetta
1	cup diced red/Bermuda onion
¼	cup Pernod (may substitute brandy)
2	tablespoons Worcestershire sauce
½	cup balsamic vinegar
½	cup red wine vinegar
2	tablespoons whole grain mustard
	pinch salt (adjust to taste)
	pinch coarse black pepper (adjust to taste)
½	cup firmly packed light brown sugar
2	pounds spinach tops, cleaned
1	cup feta cheese
½	cup toasted pine nuts (8 to 10 minutes in a 400° oven)

1. In a medium pan heat the olive oil over medium heat and sauté the panchetta until almost crisped. Add the red onion and continue to sauté until the onion appears translucent.

2. Add the Pernod and flambé.

3. Once the flame subsides, add the Worcestershire sauce, vinegars, mustard, salt, pepper, and brown sugar. Simmer for approximately 10 minutes at low heat. The sauce will begin to slowly thicken and achieve a syrupy consistency.

4. Place the spinach on serving plates and cover with plastic wrap. Microwave on high for 30 to 40 seconds to warm and wilt the spinach slightly. Remove from the microwave and remove the plastic wrap immediately.

5. Ladle the sauce over the spinach and finish with crumbled feta (or dry goat cheese) and toasted pine nuts.

SERVES 8

PENNE WITH SMOKED SALMON

½   cup olive oil

1   tablespoon finely chopped garlic

2   tablespoons finely chopped shallots

½   cup dry white wine

2   cup shrimp stock (see index)

½   cup large capers

2   pounds smoked salmon, sliced thin

1   teaspoon salt

½   teaspoon coarse black pepper

2   tablespoons lemon juice

2   pounds penne pasta, cooked al dente and kept hot

1   tablespoon coarsely chopped Fresh Dill (no stems)

2   tablespoons butter

2   ounces black caviar (optional)

1. In a large sauté pan heat the olive oil over medium heat and sauté the garlic and shallots for approximately 5 minutes or until the shallots appear soft.

2. Increase the heat to medium-high and add the wine and shrimp stock. Stir and simmer for 10 to 15 minutes. Reduce the heat to medium-low. Add the capers, smoked salmon pieces, salt, pepper, and lemon juice. Stir well.

3. Increase the heat to medium. Add the piping hot pasta, dill, and butter, and toss vigorously to coat the pasta. Garnish with a dollop of black caviar and a sprig of fresh dill, and save.

SERVES 8

WHITE BEAN AND SAGE SALAD

8   cups white beans (cooked or canned)

1½   cups diced red/Bermuda onion

1   tablespoon minced fresh garlic

2   tablespoons chopped fresh sage

1   cup olive oil

1   teaspoon salt

1   teaspoon cracked black pepper

2   tablespoons dry white wine

1   tablespoon lemon juice

1. In a large mixing bowl combine all of the ingredients and toss well. Cover and refrigerate for at least 1 hour.

2. Remove from refrigerator, toss and serve. Makes a great summer salad aside a hearty sandwich served with ice cold lemonade!

CHAPTER 7

JANET JACKSON

This caravan included fifteen tractor-trailer trucks; nine custom coach buses; and a mind-blowing stage, light, and sound system. Also, don't forget Janet's personal recliner and stereo wall for her dressing room.

Black Bean and Rice Soup

Spring Salad with Citrus
  Vinaigrette

JJ's Chicken Fajitas

Janet Jackson's career began to blossom in 1986 with the release of her smash hit *Control,* which sold more than eight million copies. Next came *Rhythm Nation* in 1989, again selling more than eight million copies. It was this album that made Janet Jackson the first artist in music history to have seven top five singles from one album (four of which hit #1), on the Billboard charts. The following year, Janet set out on her first concert tour. That tour was seen by more than two million fans.

This is a performer who has truly made her place in the music industry. Janet's career has progressed tremendously, so that her most recent concert tour consisted of fifteen tractor-trailers and nine customized buses. Janet has toured the globe, selling out arenas on almost every continent. These successful tours started with the "Rhythm Nation" tour. The stage on that tour consisted of an industrial elevator, twisted steel and aluminum, and lots of lights. She and her troupe of limber dancers dazzled the crowd with their sheer energy. The artist performed nonstop for more than two hours. This energy and enthusiasm was carried over to her "janet" tour, years later. Janet had lost the pudgy cheeks and emerged with a new '90s style. Her fans couldn't get enough. The stage on this tour transformed itself into numerous settings. Huge video screens popped up on all sides of the stage and fell from the rafters as the Diva strutted her stuff. The stage twisted and turned throughout

the show creating dance platforms for her fifteen or so male and female dancers.

All this stage excitement didn't continue backstage, however. Janet's dressing room was very solemn. It was draped in black and furnished with a black leather massage recliner and a state-of-the-art video and sound system. The room was heated, humidified, and dimly lit. The humidity and heat keep the singer's vocal cords moist and loose.

Outside the dressing rooms, the well-toned dancers began to stretch and prepare for the show at about 4:00 P.M. They broke for dinner around 5:00 P.M. You might think these chiseled dancers would be careful how much they eat three hours before a performance. Not a chance. They loaded up on carbohydrates and vegetables. There are no waistline worries for this troupe—they burn it all off while on stage.

Janet had a special fat-free meal prepared and delivered to her dressing room prior to the show. The dinner consisted of a thin tortilla filled with an array of julienned garden vegetables with a light southwest seasoning. The only delay in her meal service was the security guard posted at the door checking everything that went in and out. We even asked if he wanted to taste her meal, although he didn't appreciate our attempt at humor.

Janet Jackson remained in her dressing room throughout the late afternoon and evening. There was no mingling with other band members or dancers, with the exception of the banter that occurred during the makeup session.

The curtain rose and the crowd enjoyed every beat of the fabulous show. The stage twisted and moved with the dancers. Janet was on the catwalk, on top of the video screens, and stage center, swinging and jiving to the beat of her music. The performance left both Janet and the crowd literally breathless.

After the show, some Jackson family members had arrived, including Jermaine Jackson. Janet seemed to let her guard down a bit once the show was over. She became much more per-

sonable with her family and backstage guests. The atmosphere on the whole was a bit more lighthearted, however, the crew was hard at work repacking the fifteen tractor trailers of equipment and staging. The singer took time to talk with her brother and other special guests. Then it was off to her limousine for the trip home.

Janet Jackson Dressing Room Requirements:

- 1 vegetable tray
- 1 fruit basket
- 1 fresh fruit tray
- 1 bowl of raisins
- 2 pounds carrots, some beets and parsley for juicer
- 6 1.5-liter bottles NAYA water (No exceptions)
- 1 quart fresh-squeezed grapefruit juice

- flowers including one vase with 12 white roses and 6 red roses, one vase with 12 yellow roses and 6 red roses and one coffee table arrangement

Entire room must be draped in black—including all table linens.

Special Requests: "NAYA Water is the only acceptable water for the artist and her entourage. There can be no substitutions! So, find six cases somewhere. . . ."

- 1 quart fresh-squeezed orange juice
- 1 quart cranberry juice
- 3 bottles Snapple (Kiwi Strawberry or Melon Berry)
- 3 bottles Clearly Canadian—Loganberry
- 3 bottles Clearly Canadian—assorted
- 6 cans Kerns—peach, apricot and papaya
- tea service including Bigelow decaffeinated orange & sweet spice tea
- fine china, linen and silverware

The Menu

Black Bean and Rice Soup
Spring Salad with Citrus Vinaigrette
JJ's Chicken Fajitas

BLACK BEAN AND RICE SOUP

2   tablespoons chili powder (mild)
1   teaspoon ground cumin
12   cups chicken stock
1   cup diced red/bermuda onion
2   tablespoons finely chopped fresh garlic
3   cups black beans, uncooked, presoaked
overnight
¼   cup Worcestershire sauce
1   teaspoon Tabasco sauce
2   teaspoons salt
1   tablespoon coarse black pepper
1   tablespoon beef base
1   cup cleaned and diced green bell pepper
1   cup cleaned and diced red bell pepper
1¼   cups long grain rice
1   bunch fresh cilantro, cleaned and chopped
(no stems)
     sour cream

1. In a large stock pot combine the chili
    powder and cumin. Toast over medium
    heat, stirring constantly, approximately 3
    to 4 minutes. This brings out the full fla-
    vor of the seasonings. Increase the heat to
    medium-high.

2. Add the chicken stock, onions, garlic, pre-
    soaked black beans, Worcestershire sauce,
    Tabasco sauce, salt, black pepper, and
    beef base. Bring to a boil. Reduce the heat
    to medium low and simmer for approxi-
    mately 30 minutes, stirring occasionally.

3. Stir in the bell peppers and simmer an
    additional 30 minutes, stirring occasion-
    ally. Add the rice and simmer an addi-
    tional 20 to 25 minutes, stirring
    occasionally. Stir in the fresh cilantro.
    Serve with a dollop of sour cream, if
    desired.

SERVES 8+

Spring Salad with Citrus Vinaigrette

2   pounds spring mix lettuce
     Citrus Vinaigrette (recipe follows)
1   cup shaved Asiago cheese
¼   cup chopped Italian parsley
35   to 40 yellow petite pear tomatoes
2   navel oranges, sliced into half rings
2   lemons, sliced into half rings

1. Toss the spring mix lightly with vinaigrette dressing, being careful not to overcoat the lettuce. You will have extra dressing. Place the tossed salad on serving plates.

2. Sprinkle with shaved Asiago cheese and chopped Italian parsley. Garnish with 4 to 5 pear tomatoes on each salad, and scatter orange and lemon rings on the outside edge of the salad plates. Voila!

SERVES 8+

Citrus Vinaigrette

1   tablespoon chopped shallots
1   6-ounce can frozen limeade concentrate, thawed
1   6-ounce can frozen lemonade concentrate, thawed
1   6-ounce can frozen orange juice concentrate, thawed
1   teaspoon salt
½   teaspoon white pepper
1   cup seasoned rice wine vinegar
1   cup canola oil

1. In a blender combine the shallots, concentrates, salt, pepper, and vinegar. Blend at medium speed for 30 to 40 seconds.

2. Increase the speed to high, and slowly add the canola oil, allowing the dressing to emulsify.

SERVES 8+

JJ's Chicken Fajitas

2 tablespoons olive oil
3 pounds boneless/skinless chicken, sliced
(thigh meat is best)
1 teaspoon salt
1 teaspoon coarse black pepper
1 tablespoon chili powder
1 tablespoon finely chopped fresh garlic
2 medium red bell peppers, cleaned and juli-
enned
2 medium green bell peppers, cleaned and
julienned
1 large red/Bermuda onion, sliced
1 bunch cilantro, cleaned and chopped
(no stems)
  fresh flour or corn tortillas
  fresh salsa

1. In a large skillet heat the olive oil over medium high heat. Add the sliced chicken, salt, pepper, and chili powder. Sauté for approximately 4 ½ to 5 minutes, until three-fourths cooked.

2. Increase the heat to high and add the fresh garlic, peppers, and onions. Toss together vigorously approximately 5 minutes, until the peppers are slightly softened yet still firm.

3. Remove the pan from the heat, add the fresh cilantro, and toss well.

4. Serve with fresh flour or corn tortillas and fresh salsa.

SERVES 8

CHAPTER 8

~~~

HARRY CONNICK JR.

Connick is a sincere individual who honestly cares about his fans. He always enjoys angel hair pasta with marinara in his dressing room prior to the show, and sometimes he's not alone.

Harry Connick Jr., a New Orleans–born musician, rose to fame with his big band style jazz tunes. Sometimes referred to as the next Frank Sinatra, Connick has carried his popularity from the music stage to television (with a guest appearance on *Cheers*) and on to the silver screen (portraying a serial killer opposite Sigourney Weaver, in *Copy Cat,* and playing a small but memorable role in the blockbuster hit *Independence Day*).

Harry married former model Jill Goodacre, of Victoria's Secret catalog fame, in 1994. Since their marriage, work hasn't changed too much for the couple. Ms. Goodacre left modeling to pursue a career in photography and directing, and finally motherhood. Harry travels, playing concert halls, jazz clubs, and the occasional movie role.

Harry's style of music has changed each year. His first major tour was a sellout, and it had the southern musician jazzing up the stage with his big band style tunes. Most recently, the artist has ventured into a new genre of music best described as "funk." This was a sharp departure from the original style that his fans were accustomed to.

Along this music sensation's career path, Behind the Scenes has had the opportunity to cook for him and his wife on several occasions. In doing so, we have become accustomed to his tastes. For example, Harry always enjoys angel hair pasta in his dressing room before performing. Sometimes his wife Jill joins him at his customary table for two, while other times it is his manager or just an empty second chair.

In 1994, Harry and his orchestra appeared at the Hollywood Bowl. During this performance he was joined backstage by his beautiful wife. It is important to note that privacy is critical backstage. Everyone is credentialed and access to the artist's dressing room, the stage, and hospitality area is limited. As the caterer and backstage hospitality provider, we are almost always allowed free access to

dressing rooms and the stage, simply because they need to be set up and serviced by our staff.

This particular night at the Hollywood Bowl, it was time to deliver the pasta dinner to Harry's room. Initial food and drink requirements were already set in the room prior to Harry's arrival to minimize later interruptions. (Also, during the performance, the rooms are typically refreshed with additional food and beverages and fresh ice.) Harry always requested his customary pre-performance angel hair pasta about an hour or so before show time. We carried the dinner to the dressing room and knocked on the door several times, but there was no answer. Typically, if no one answers, the artist is on stage or elsewhere in the venue. That's the assumption we made. Upon entering the room to set up the din-

ner, however, we discovered quite the contrary. Mr. and Mrs. Connick were getting ready for the show. They had both just gotten out of the shower—thus the lack of response to our knocking. Needless to say, towels were frantically flying everywhere. In the end, everyone was a good sport about the interruption. With towels in place, they both smiled and thanked us for the dinner.

Two days later, Harry and Jill were in San Diego for the same show. He asked that we make the same pasta: "It was fabulous. Maybe even [make] some extra to take on the tour bus. Oh, and wait till I answer the door before you set it up," he said with his contagious smile.

Harry Connick Jr. Dressing Room Requirements:

- Diet Snapple Iced Tea—Lemon
- Evian water
- Knudsen fruit juices
- coffee service
- tea service, including Earl Grey
- Peanut M&Ms
- fresh fruit tray
- orange juice
- cranberry juice
- Diet Coke
- Ginger ale
- 6 bottles non-alcoholic beer

Dinner:
- fresh angel hair pasta with a meatless red sauce for two
- mixed salad or caesar salad for two

```
╔══════════════════════════════╗
║          The Menu            ║
║  ──────────────────────────  ║
║  Angel Hair Pasta with Red & Sassy  ║
║         Pomodoro Sauce        ║
║                              ║
║  Chopped Salad with Mustard   ║
║          Vinaigrette          ║
╚══════════════════════════════╝
```

RED & SASSY POMODORO SAUCE

¼	cup olive oil
2	tablespoons peeled, chopped fresh garlic
1	cup chopped white onion
2	28-ounce cans whole peeled tomatoes
2	28-ounce cans ground tomatoes with purée
1	teaspoon salt
1	teaspoon black pepper
¼	cup sugar
¼	cup chopped fresh parsley
4	bay leaves
1	tablespoon ground oregano
½	cup chopped fresh basil

1. In a medium saucepan heat the olive oil over medium-high heat and sauté garlic and onions until lightly browned.

2. Add the whole tomatoes and continue to sauté for approximately 10 minutes. Mash the tomatoes with a hand masher.

3. Add the ground tomatoes, salt, pepper, and sugar. Reduce the heat and simmer for 20 minutes.

4. Add the parsley, bay leaves, oregano, and basil, and simmer over low heat for 30 minutes, stirring occasionally. Be careful to keep the heat low to prevent scorching the sauce.

SERVES 8

HOW TO COOK HARRY'S ANGEL HAIR PASTA (HARRY PREFERS ANGEL HAIR PASTA!)

	water
¼	cup olive oil
1	teaspoon salt
	pasta

1. In a large stock pot over high heat, bring water, oil, and salt to a rockin' boil. Add the pasta and stir well, to keep the pasta from sticking. Cook the pasta for 6 to 11 minutes, depending upon the type of pasta. Pasta is cooked when it is firm but not chewy (al dente). Angel hair pasta requires the shortest cooking time.

2. Remove the pot from the heat, and drain the pasta through a colander. Lightly oil the pasta with olive oil if it is to be set aside awaiting preparation of a sauce. Pasta may then be brought back to temperature by dipping it in boiling water for 5 to 10 seconds just prior to serving.

Note: Cooking times vary for different pastas. Remember, al dente pasta is still somewhat firm. Fresh pastas cook in about half the time of dry pastas.

CHOPPED SALAD WITH MUSTARD VINAIGRETTE

2   medium heads romaine lettuce, with out-
side leaves removed, cleaned and chopped
small

2   medium heads of iceberg lettuce, with
outside leaves removed, cleaned and chopped
small

1   medium head of green leaf lettuce,
cleaned and chopped small

2   cups diced Roma tomatoes

1   cup diced green onions

1½   cups cubed (½") dry italian salami

1½   cups cubed (½") mozzarella cheese

1½   cups peeled and diced cucumber

1   cup shredded fresh parmesan cheese
     Mustard Vinaigrette (recipe follows)
     cracked black pepper

1. In a large mixing bowl combine all of the ingredients except ½ cup of Parmesan cheese. Toss well. Slowly add the Mustard Vinaigrette and continue to toss until the salad appears well coated. Be careful not to overdo the dressing, as the salad will quickly wilt.

2. Portion equal amounts of salad on serving plates or place in a large serving bowl. Garnish with the remaining Parmesan and cracked black pepper if desired.

SERVES 8

MUSTARD VINAIGRETTE

¾   cup red wine vinegar

1½   tablespoons whole grain mustard

1   teaspoon finely chopped shallots

½   teaspoon ground black pepper

½   teaspoon salt

½   teaspoon ground oregano

¼   cup lemon juice

1   tablespoon sugar

1   cup olive oil

1. In a blender, combine all of the ingredients except the olive oil. Blend on medium high for approximately 1 minute.

2. Continue blending, slowly adding oil until the dressing emulsifies. Chill and serve.

9/14
KENNY LOGGINS
AR leap of faith
TOUR
LOCAL CREW

CREW
Tracy Lawrence
CAT

CHAPTER 9

YANNI

The artist's soulmate, Linda Evans, was ever present on Yanni's tours. They were a genuine couple who had no trouble dining with their band and crew members. (You might be surprised at how uncommon this is.)

Roasted Tuscan Chicken
Tuscan Balsamic Sauce
Mediterranean Pasta
Grilled Assorted Vegetables

Yanni is a master of "new age" music or "instrumental music," as he prefers to call it. Yanni was born in Greece, but came to the United States to study psychology at the University of Minnesota, graduating in 1976. While growing up, the musician discovered that he possessed the rare gift of "perfect pitch." In other words, he is able to hear the music first in his mind before translating it for the ear.

Yanni's music has been described as soothing, uplifting, and energizing. With such song titles as "Desire," "Swept Away," and "The Rain Must Fall," there is a definite sense of passion and sincerity in his work. It is this passion that is felt by his fans who flock to buy his albums and "experience" his live performances. His album *Live at the Acropolis* has sold over seven million copies worldwide.

In 1990, *Reflections of Passion* went platinum and stayed at the top of the adult alternative charts for forty-seven consecutive weeks, setting a new record. Another album, *Dare to Dream* (1992), went gold after only two months.

While on tour, the artist's soulmate, the actress Linda Evans, was ever present. He and Ms. Evans spent a great deal of time together before and after his performances. As a musician, he is very genuine and friendly, yet still very passionate about his work. He is very talkative to not only his band and crew, but also to "outsiders," like the caterer. Yanni and Ms. Evans often dine with the band and crew members, a rare experience among famous musicians. Often, artists separate themselves from the band or crew members. Backstage at Yanni's concerts, the atmosphere is very casual, but energetic. There's a job to be done, but Yanni is devoted to making it an enjoyable experience.

Over dinner, the band and crew spent time teasing each other and sharing jokes. In fact, just in time for their dining and reading pleasure, the latest issue of the *Greek Gazette* was distributed. The *Greek Gazette* is a newsletter of sorts created by some road crew members. It contains humorous stories, jokes, and information related to those on tour. Several bands circulate such "publications," such as Reba McEntire's *Reba Record*. The newsletters boost morale for the bands' members, who spend months on the road away from home. It takes a great sense of humor to make the best of that situation. Much of the comedy that arises backstage is centered around the experience of moving forty to fifty people around the globe for months on end. The excerpt on the following page was taken from the *Greek Gazette*.

After dinner was served, Yanni and Ms. Evans personally offered their compliments to the chef. The curtain rose a few short hours later, and Yanni, pounding on his keyboard, brought down the house.

Yanni Dressing Room Requirements:

- coffee service
- tea service including peppermint and chamomile
- 1 jar honey
- 6 1.5-liter bottles Evian
- 6 cans Coke
- 6 cans Canada Dry ginger ale

- 1 jar unsalted or lightly salted mixed nuts
- 1 bag low salt tortilla chips and your best salsa
- cheese and cracker tray
- fresh fruit basket

Top Ten Reasons Why Yanni Is Smiling So Much:

10. Can now buy his father that new Ferrari.
9. Negotiating a deal with NBC to replace Donahue.
8. Finally put that weasel Tesh in his place.
7. Two words: Yanni mugs.
6. Recently achieved a higher state of consciousness by finding the perfect EQ . . . yeah, right!
5. His mustache constantly tickles his upper lip.
4. Secretly knows the words to all of his songs.
3. Making more money than Kitaro.
2. Linda, Linda, Linda!!!

. . . and the number one reason why Yanni is smiling so much:

1. **Finally has a crew he can trust!**

The Menu

Roasted Tuscan Chicken

Tuscan Chicken Balsamic Sauce

Mediterranean Pasta

Grilled Assorted Vegetables

ROASTED TUSCAN CHICKEN

1	cup balsamic vinegar
¼	cup Worcestershire sauce
1	tablespoon chicken base
1	small red bell pepper, cleaned and chopped
¼	cup diced red/Bermuda onion
1	tablespoon cracked black pepper
2	tablespoons finely chopped fresh garlic
2	tablespoons chopped fresh rosemary
½	cup olive oil
2	whole chickens, quartered
	Tuscan Chicken Balsamic Sauce (recipe follows)

1. In a medium mixing bowl whisk together the vinegar, Worcestershire sauce, chicken base, red pepper, onion, cracked pepper, garlic, and rosemary.

2. Slowly add the olive oil and continue whisking. Place the quartered chickens in a shallow dish. Pour the marinade over chickens, cover, and refrigerate for 8 to 10 hours (overnight).

3. Preheat the oven to 350°. Remove the chicken from the refrigerator and place on a nonstick baking sheet. Save the excess marinade for sauce. Roast the chicken uncovered for approximately 50 to 60 minutes or until browned and cooked through.

4. Serve with Tuscan Chicken Balsamic Sauce. This is also wonderful with Tomato and Herb Risotto!

SERVES 8

TUSCAN CHICKEN BALSAMIC SAUCE

½	cup sugar
1	cup balsamic vinegar
2	cups Demi-Glace (see index)
2	tablespoons French Roux (see index)
2	sprigs rosemary
	drippings and marinade from Roasted Tuscan Chicken

1. Skim the oil the from marinade. Skim the oil from the drippings.

2. In a medium saucepan combine the skimmed marinade, skimmed drippings, sugar, and balsamic vinegar. Bring to a boil over high heat. Add the demi-glace and stir well. Reduce the heat to medium and simmer for approximately 30 minutes.

3. Whisk in the French Roux to thicken. Garnish with rosemary and serve atop Tuscan Roasted Chicken.

MEDITERRANEAN PASTA

¼	cup olive oil
2	tablespoons fresh garlic, finely chopped
½	cup julienned red/Bermuda onion
½	cup dry white wine
1½	cup chicken or vegetable stock
1	tablespoon chopped fresh oregano
2	tablespoons chopped fresh basil
3	tablespoons chopped Italian parsley
1	teaspoon salt
1	teaspoon ground black pepper
1	cup julienned marinated sun-dried tomatoes
½	cup kalamata olives, pitted and chopped
1	cup artichoke hearts
¼	cup capers
2	pounds Penne, cooked al dente

1	cup dry feta cheese
¼	cup toasted pine nuts

1. In a large saucepan heat the olive oil and sauté the garlic and onion over medium high heat for approximately 5 minutes. Reduce the heat to medium.

2. Add the white wine, stock, oregano, basil, parsley, salt, and pepper. Stir and simmer for approximately 5 to 7 minutes. Add the sun-dried tomatoes and simmer for an additional 3 to 5 minutes. Add the olives, artichoke hearts, and capers. Stir well.

3. Remove the pan from the heat and gently toss with the piping hot pasta. Serve with crumbled feta cheese and toasted pine nut garnish.

SERVES 8

GRILLED ASSORTED VEGETABLES

¼   cup dry white wine

¼   cup lemon juice

2   tablespoons finely chopped fresh garlic

1   tablespoon chopped fresh oregano

1   tablespoon chopped fresh basil

1   tablespoon cleaned and chopped fresh rosemary

1   teaspoon salt

½   teaspoon black pepper

2   tablespoons garden herb seasoning (Lawry's Salt Free 17 is ideal)

2   tablespoons diced white onion

1½   cups olive oil

1   pound thin asparagus, bottoms removed

1   pound portabella mushrooms, sliced after grilled, if necessary

¾   pound zucchini squash, sliced to ⅛-inch thick lengths (top to bottom)

¾   pound yellow squash, sliced to ⅛-inch thick lengths (top to bottom)

1   large eggplant, sliced to ¼-inch rings

2   medium red/Bermuda onion, quartered

2   medium red bell peppers, cleaned and quartered

2   medium yellow bell peppers, cleaned and quartered

1. In a large mixing bowl combine the wine, lemon juice, garlic, oregano, basil, rosemary, salt, pepper, herb seasoning, and onion. Whisk together well. Add the olive oil and continue whisking until well blended.

2. Preheat the grill to medium-high. Place the prepared vegetables on a sheet pan and brush with the marinade mixture. Place the marinated side of each vegetable face down on the grill. Baste the other side of each vegetable as it is grilling. Continue to rotate and turn the vegetables on the grill to prevent burning. Each type of vegetable has a different cooking time. Asparagus cooks the fastest, and the peppers will take the longest. Use your judgment on cooking times. Vegetables are done when nice even grill marks are apparent on both sides.

3. Remove from the heat and serve. Some larger vegetables may need to be cut down to a serving size.

SERVES 8

THE DOOBIE BROTHERS
REUNION TOUR '87
Backstage

CHAPTER 10

MICHAEL BOLTON/ CELINE DION

He travels with a personal chef to—literally—cater to his every whim.
She was more amenable to the menu offered to the crew.

Vermicelli with Fruits of the Sea

Saffron and Porcini Risotto

Grilled Radichio and Parmesan
with Balsamic Vinaigrette

Michael Bolton's "World Tour 1994" rolled into San Diego on June 19. Michael's career was launched by his inspirational love ballads. Many of his female fans also loved Bolton's long, naturally curly hair. However, while in San Diego, the audience was evenly mixed. Why? He was touring with one of the hottest up and coming stars of 1994, Celine Dion. Celine is a beautiful, vivacious Canadian-born singer who began her career mostly in Europe and Asia, earning a gold record in France and a gold medal at the Yamaha World Song Festival in Tokyo. Her career accelerated into high gear with the help of Sony Music, then hit new highs in the United States with such songs as "If You Asked Me To," and "When I Fall In Love," from the box office hit *Sleepless in Seattle*. And of course, since that time Celine has recorded the Academy Award–winning song from the film *Titanic*, "My Heart Will Go On."

The double-headliner tour arrived at the Sports Arena around 7:00 A.M. The venue soon came alive with hundreds of road cases being rolled off the trucks. In the process, three or four large cases were rolled into our hospitality area. Not knowing the contents, we pushed them off into a corner. At around midday, a pleasant lady appeared and introduced herself as Michael Bolton's personal tour chef. After a brief conversation, she proceeded to unpack the giant road cases, creating a makeshift kitchen. The chef spent the rest of the day and evening, about eight hours, cooking. She prepared a lovely country French meal. At the end of the concert, Michael returned to his dressing room to find the beautiful meal set out for him. He literally took two bites, changed his clothes, and left for the hotel. The chef stood there somewhat disappointed. She explained to us that sometimes he eats and other times not, depending on his mood.

Michael's crew, Celine, and her staff and crew all enjoyed their full meal in the hospitality area. The backstage area was very mellow at this show. The stage and equipment weren't too complex: mostly lots of lights.

After dinner, the artists had a brief break before they took their turns on the stage.

After Celine and Michael left the venue, a pair of guys from the road crew, knowing Michael often doesn't eat his specially prepared meal, raided the dressing rooms looking for scraps, a little "late night snack." During a ten-minute break, they sat and enjoyed some exquisite French cuisine. As they sat and ate they laughed at each other with their napkins tucked into their T-shirt collars, "Pass the Grey Poupon, James," one said. "Why certainly, sir," the other responded.

mm

Michael Bolton/Celine Dion Dressing Room Requirements:

MICHAEL BOLTON DRESSING ROOM REQUIREMENTS:
- coffee service including one pound gourmet coffee
- tea service including Celestial Seasonings Lemon and Red Zinger teas
- 1 gallon fresh-squeezed orange juice
- 6 1-liter bottles Evian
- 6 cans Cherry 7Up
- 6 cans raspberry ginger ale
- 6 cans assorted soft drinks
- deli tray including swiss cheese, tomatoes, dill pickle chips and lettuce
- whole wheat and white bread
- fresh fruit tray
- Peanut M&Ms
- 1 squeeze honey bear

CELINE DION DRESSING ROOM REQUIREMENTS:
- room must be free of air conditioning
- assortment of sandwiches including egg salad and chicken
- small plate watermelon
- 6 cans Diet Coke
- 6 spring water on ice
- 10 spring water at room temperature
- 1 package of Clorets gum
- 1 bottle vinegar
- fresh flowers

The Menu

Vermicelli with Fruits of the Sea

Saffron and Porcini Risotto

Grilled Radichio and Parmesan with
Balsamic Vinaigrette

VERMICELLI WITH FRUITS OF THE SEA

½   cup olive oil

4   tablespoons finely chopped fresh garlic

4   tablespoons finely chopped shallots

1½ pounds fresh shrimp (U21/25), cleaned
and deveined

1   pound sea or bay scallops

1   pounds whole baby calamari, cleaned

1   teaspoon salt

1   teaspoon black pepper

3   tablespoons chopped Italian parsley

1   cup white wine

2   small red chilies, seeded (optional to spice
up recipe)

4   cups sea clam juice

4   cups Red and Sassy Pomodoro Sauce
(see index)

½   cup shredded fresh basil

1½ pounds green lip or Eastern black mussels,
cleaned thoroughly

1½ pounds little neck clams, cleaned
thoroughly

2   pounds vermicelli, cooked al dente

1. In a large skillet heat ¼ cup of olive oil over medium heat and sauté 2 tablespoons of garlic and 2 tablespoons of shallots for approximately 5 minutes, or until the shallots appear translucent.

2. Add the shrimp, scallops, and calamari. Increase the heat to high. Add ½ teaspoon of salt, ½ teaspoon of black pepper, and 1 tablespoon of Italian parsley. Toss the seafood thoroughly for approximately 4 to 5 minutes until seared but not fully cooked. Splash with 1 cup of white wine. Remove from the heat and set aside.

3. In a large saucepan heat ¼ cup of olive oil, 2 tablespoons of garlic, 2 tablespoons of shallots, and the red chilies if desired over medium-high heat for approximately 5 minutes. Add the clam juice, Pomodoro Sauce, residual juices from the sautéed seafood, fresh basil, ½ teaspoon of salt, and ½ teaspoon of pepper. Stir well. Increase the heat to high and bring to a rockin' boil.

4. Reduce the heat to medium and simmer for approximately 10 more minutes. Add the mussels and clams, cover, and simmer for an additional 10 minutes or until the mussels and clams are cooked and open. Drop in the sautéed seafood and simmer for an additional 3 to 4 minutes. Remove from the heat and serve atop a bed of piping hot vermicelli. Garnish with chopped Italian parsley.

SERVES 8+

SAFFRON AND PORCINI RISOTTO

½   cup olive oil
2   tablespoons finely chopped shallots
1   tablespoon finely chopped fresh garlic
1   cup chopped, reconstituted porcini
mushrooms
2   cups risotto (short grain rice)
1   cup white wine
8   cups chicken or vegetable stock
½   teaspoon whole saffron
2   tablespoons Italian parsley
4   tablespoons butter
    salt to taste
    black pepper to taste
1½ cups shredded Parmesan cheese

1. In a medium stock pot heat the olive oil over medium heat and sauté the shallots and garlic for approximately 2 to 3 minutes. Add the mushrooms and sauté for an additional 4 to 5 minutes. Add the risotto and sauté an additional 2 to 3 minutes, stirring constantly. Splash with white wine.

2. Add 4 cups of chicken or vegetable stock and the saffron, increase the heat to high, and cook until the liquid begins to boil. Reduce the heat to medium-low and simmer for approximately 20 minutes, stirring occasionally. Add additional stock as needed every 5 to 8 minutes.

3. Add the parsley, butter, salt, pepper, and 3/4 cup of Parmesan. Simmer, stirring constantly, for an additional 5 minutes, or until the risotto begins to slightly thicken

but is still saucy. Serve and garnish with the remaining Parmesan.

SERVES 8

GRILLED RADICHIO AND PARMESAN WITH BALSAMIC VINAIGRETTE

½   cup olive oil
2   medium heads Radichio, quartered
    salt to taste
    Black pepper to taste
1½ cups Sweet Balsamic Vinaigrette
(see index)
1   cup shaved Parmesan cheese
2   tablespoons chopped Italian parsley

1. In a large mixing bowl lightly oil the radichio quarters and season with salt and pepper.

2. Spray the grill with nonstick spray. Preheat the grill to medium. (Remember, the nonstick spray can is under pressure and flammable.) Grill the radichio on both sides, only to mark and slightly warm. Do not cook; this will wilt the radichio.

3. Place the grilled radichio on a serving platter, drizzle with Sweet Balsamic Vinaigrette, and top with shaved Parmesan. Serve garnished with chopped Italian parsley.

SERVES 8

CHAPTER 11

—⁓⁓—

GRATEFUL DEAD

This tour was an "unGrateful" nightmare of logistics. The band traveled with dude ranch chefs from their past to cater to their desires. However, it was our menu that was the real hit! Oh yes, don't forget the Twinkies!

Roast Leg of Lamb with Apple Chutney
Thai Shrimp Salad with Spicy Peanut Vinaigrette

The Grateful Dead tour of 1993–94 was a memorable one. The band's North American tour was one of the last for the group whose fans are extremely devoted. Two days prior to the artists' arrival, San Diego's Sports Arena parking lot, as well as nearby parking lots, became makeshift campsites for anxious fans. VW buses, converted camper trucks, and station wagons were filled with tie-dyed blankets, pillows, yarn work, and the like. It was as if you had stepped back in time to the 1960s. The Grateful Dead has had one of the largest cult followings of any modern day band. Their fans were famous for going on the road with the band, following the music from town to town. Some fans worked odd jobs on the road to make enough money to support this activity. Others simply saved money from their regular jobs and spent sometimes up to 6 months, or even longer, on the road with the band.

As if this ragtag group of fans huddled in every corner of the parking lot weren't enough, the band members themselves, headed up by Jerry Garcia, had their own idiosyncrasies. The group required the local promoter to install additional dressing rooms and office space. To accommodate this request, large office trailers were dismantled and reassembled within the cement tunnels under the arena seating platforms. Anything the band wanted it received.

The band traveled with a group from Avery Ranch. This group of people was from a dude ranch of sorts in Northern California. The story goes that members of the Grateful Dead were relaxing at the ranch a few years back, making friends with the ranch owners. The band asked if the ranch owners would like to come on tour to help provide food services. Avery Ranch agreed.

Upon the band's arrival, Behind the

Scenes constructed an outdoor kitchen facility in the arena parking lot. The kitchen was complete with refrigerators, tables, mixers, pots, pans, utensils, plates, microwaves, ovens, stoves—anything that might possibly go in a "real" kitchen, right down to the Tupperware containers. The Avery Ranch staff prepared a hand written menu each of the two show days. The menu consisted of what was referred to as "traditional" selections and "nonfat" offerings. The fare was nothing terribly spectacular: hamburgers, "showdogs," steak, fish kabobs, and pita sandwiches. These menus were distributed to the band and select members of the production staff.

Everyone carried Motorola radios, including a member of our staff. Throughout the day, starting at 9:00 A.M., at no specific interval, people holding menus would radio their requests and whims to the makeshift parking lot kitchen. The funny part of this routine was how they would order items not on the menu—not even close. The Avery Ranch "runners" ended up spending more time in line at the grocery store across the street from the arena, than at the venue. More than half the orders required a grocery store run. For example, "Kitchen: I feel like a sirloin sandwich, with the meat grilled medium and sliced thin, on a sourdough roll, with two thin slices of tomato, one leaf of romaine lettuce, and a bit of whole grain mustard. Also, a bag of Cheetos and two Twinkies." It was a game of indulgence

and the Grateful Dead always won. The three days of catering were long and exhausting. "The Dead" crew members were a bit more ungrateful than courteous, at times. The backstage motto was "They are the Grateful Dead, they can have anything they want!" They certainly did.

Avery Ranch would always include on the menu the meal we were serving to the band and crew. Without dispute, our Roast Leg of Lamb with Apple Chutney and Thai Shrimp Salad were the most popular items served.

Once the staging, lighting, and sound equipment was loaded in and setup, the backstage atmosphere changed. Security became extremely tight. The band was literally sneaked into the arena via several decoy caravans. The large crowd of "deadicated," pot-smoking fans was oblivious to the band's arrival at the venue due to the number of decoy vans used.

Before the show, the band settled into the dressing room, which would best be described as a 1960s time capsule. The arena locker room was converted into a "hippie" hideout with tie-dyed fabrics draped from the walls and ceiling. Several overstuffed chairs and couches were placed in the room, sitting flat on the ground—no legs. The lighting was soft and muted. Incense burned in all corners of the room. The floors were covered with soft carpets and pillows. It was quite a transformation from the ice hockey locker room that normally occupies the space.

As show time approached, the band casually made its way to the stage and began to play to a crowd of 13,000+ fans. The music was received with cheers, chants, and enthusiasm. The crowd remained standing throughout the concert beneath a cloudy haze of smoke that hovered above the arena floor.

This routine continued for two days. At the conclusion of the second show, the band exited the venue under the same security blanket used for their entrance. The trucks were quickly loaded and we were left with a hazy, empty arena. It took a good twelve hours to clear the parking lot of the wayward fans. The arena and parking lot looked like a tornado had hit it. Clothing, trash, cigarettes, and other remnants from the concertgoers littered the area. "The Dead" were again off on their journey and San Diego returned to its version of normalcy.

Jerry Garcia Dressing Room Requirements:

- 1 quart tonic water
- 1 quart milk
- 1 quart fresh orange juice
- 1 quart fresh carrot juice
- 12 bottles Beck's beer
- 2 bottles cabernet wine
- 2 quarts Knudsen lemonade
- 6 liters Evian
- 1 gallon spring water
- vegetable soup (no oil/no salt)

- fresh fruit
- mixed nuts
- fresh vegetables with dip
- coffee service
- tea service (including Earl Grey and Constant Comment)

The Menu

Roast Leg of Lamb with Apple Chutney

Thai Shrimp with Spicy Peanut Vinaigrette Salad

ROAST LEG OF LAMB WITH APPLE CHUTNEY

1   5-pound boneless, domestic, leg of lamb (Colorado)

2   tablespoons chopped fresh rosemary

1   tablespoon chopped fresh garlic

1   teaspoon salt (kosher if possible)

1   teaspoon coarse pepper

1   teaspoon chopped mint

½   teaspoon ground cumin

1   tablespoon dried onion

1. Preheat the oven to 450°.

2. In a small mixing bowl, mix the rosemary, garlic, salt, pepper, mint, cumin, and onion together.

3. Coat the lamb with the herb mixture and place in a roasting pan with the fatty side up.

4. Cook the lamb at 450° for 15 minutes. Reduce the heat to 350° and continue cooking for approximately 90 minutes or until the lamb reaches an internal temperature of 180°.

SERVES 8+

APPLE CHUTNEY

2 tablespoons butter

1½ cups white onion, chopped

5 cups clean, peeled, and sliced medium apples (New Zealand Enza apples are best, however, domestic Granny Smith apples will also work well)

1 teaspoon ground cinnamon

1 cup granulated sugar

⅛ teaspoon powdered allspice

1 teaspoon salt

pepper to taste

½ cup brandy

½ cup apple cider vinegar

2 cup chicken stock

½ cup golden raisins

1 teaspoon fresh mint, finely chopped

1. In a 4-quart saucepan melt the butter over medium heat and sauté the chopped onions until they appear translucent.

2. Add the apples, cinnamon, sugar, allspice, salt, and pepper. Continue stirring.

3. Add the brandy and flambé.

4. Add the vinegar and chicken stock, stirring delicately to prevent breaking up the apples. Simmer over low heat for approximately 8 to 10 minutes, until the apples are cooked but still somewhat firm.

5. Add the golden raisins and fresh mint. Stir gently, and continue to simmer for approximately 5 minutes. Thicken with cornstarch liquid, if necessary. Glaze the leg of lamb or serve as a side accompaniment.

THAI SHRIMP WITH SPICY PEANUT VINAIGRETTE SALAD

Marinade:

¼ cup seasoned rice wine vinegar

¼ cup oyster or fish sauce

½ cup soy sauce

1 teaspoon ground ginger

1 tablespoon sesame oil

1 teaspoon chili oil

1 teaspoon fresh garlic, finely chopped

1 teaspoon fresh cilantro, finely chopped

1 teaspoon fresh mint, finely chopped

1 teaspoon toasted sesame seeds

2 pounds fresh shrimp (U21/20), peeled, deveined, and skewered

1 head Napa cabbage, cleaned and coarsely chopped

1 pounds mixed baby greens

1½ cups bean sprouts

¼ cup seasoned rice wine vinegar

1 large red bell pepper, cleaned and julienned

1 large yellow bell pepper, cleaned and julienned

1 cup fried Chinese crispy noodles

½ cup chopped green onion

½ cup peeled and julienned carrots

Spicy Peanut Vinaigrette (recipe follows)

½ cup fresh cilantro, cleaned whole leaves, no stems

1. In a medium mixing bowl whisk together all of the marinade ingredients. Place the

skewered shrimp in the marinating dish and coat with marinade. Cover and refrigerate for 30 to 45 minutes.

2. Preheat the grill to medium high. Grill the shrimp skewers for 3 to 4 minutes on each side. Remove from the grill, remove from the skewers, and set aside.

3. In a large mixing bowl toss the Napa cabbage, mixed greens, and bean sprouts with seasoned rice wine vinegar. Place even portions on serving plates or in a large serving bowl. Top the salad(s) with red and yellow peppers, Chinese noodles, green onion, and carrots. Place 5 to 6 shrimps atop each salad and drizzle salad with Spicy Peanut Vinaigrette. Garnish with cilantro and serve.

SERVES 8

SPICY PEANUT VINAIGRETTE

¾ cup peanut butter

¼ cup sesame oil

½ cup seasoned rice wine vinegar

¼ cup coconut milk

1 teaspoon cleaned and finely chopped fresh ginger

¼ cup soy sauce

¼ teaspoon cayenne pepper

½ teaspoon chopped fresh garlic

1. In a blender, combine all of the ingredients and blend on medium high for approximately 1½ minutes or until smooth.

2. Transfer to a container with a lid and refrigerate, or serve immediately with Thai Shrimp Salad.

CHAPTER 12

~~~

MELISSA ETHERIDGE

Put your canine teeth away, this tour goes strictly veggie! This is one down-to-earth lady whose menus are as natural as she is.

Grilled Herb Polenta
Sautéed Wild Mushrooms
Tabbouleh
Tuscan Pasta Salad
Sweet Balsamic Vinaigrette

Put your canine teeth away, because the Melissa Etheridge tour goes strictly veggie. This is one down-to-earth lady whose menus are just as natural! Having catered for this artist on several occasions, from the Open Air Theater on a college campus to Symphony Hall in San Diego, California, Behind the Scenes knows that the backstage environment tends to be a bit more casual with this performer when compared to others.

At a local appearance, Melissa arrived at the venue in the late afternoon, with her partner, Julie Cypher. She was not followed by a lengthy entourage or escorted by multiple security guards. She carried her own bag, stopped to say hello to fans waiting to meet her, and eventually made her way to the dressing room. After settling into her dressing room, Melissa came on stage to survey the set. She stopped to chat with crew members and venue personnel. After about 45 minutes of

wandering around the stage and venue, Melissa made her way to the microphone with guitar in hand to begin her sound check. Forty-five minutes later, the artist, her band, and the crew retired to the hospitality area for dinner.

Most of the crew were vegetarians like Melissa. However, there were a few die-hard meat and potato men that were appropriately attended to. Melissa, along with Julie, who is the ex-wife of actor Lou Diamond Phillips, and the crew feasted on vegetarian salads and entrees. All our dinner guests were very complimentary. So often a vegetarian dish served to artists on tour consists of sautéed vegetables with brown rice. No creativity, no flavor, and hardly appetizing! Melissa, the band, and the crew have always been very complimentary of our selections. "This is great, so much flavor, I can't believe it is actually a vegetarian dish," commented the singer during a San Diego appearance.

After dinner, naturally comes dessert. What is Melissa's favorite? Rice Dream Cookies and Cream Ice Cream. A true vegetarian delight! The artist and her crew polished off five quarts of this dessert on that one night.

After dinner, the playful banter of the band and crew subsided and all returned to their respective posts for last minute concert preparations. Melissa moved into a room to meet and greet guests prior to the show. Such guests are typically radio contest winners, band or crew guests, and venue personnel. After about thirty minutes, the singer returned to her dressing room.

Showtime soon arrived and Melissa took the stage with hit songs from her album *Yes I Am*. Hit songs such as "I'm the Only One" and "Come to My Window" entranced the audience. She was true to her fans and to her music. Without fail, Melissa plays her heart out every show.

After the show, the band returned to the dressing room to shower and change for the road trip to Los Angeles, and to enjoy a light pasta meal. The dressing room hospitality area was set up with Pasta Primavera with Sundried Tomatoes, a small green salad, and some fresh bread: just a light snack before boarding the bus. This is typical of vegetarian musicians. They tend to eat smaller meals and snacks more frequently throughout the day.

Melissa Etheridge Dressing Room Requirements:

- 4 1.5-liter bottles spring water
- lemon
- honey
- tea service including Celestial Seasonings

  Red Zinger and Peppermint
- lemon recharge

The Menu

Grilled Herb Polenta

Sautéed Wild Mushrooms

Tabbouleh

Tuscan Pasta Salad

Sweet Balsamic Vinaigrette

GRILLED HERB POLENTA

¼   cup olive oil

1   teaspoon finely chopped fresh garlic

1   cup diced white onions

1   teaspoon cleaned and chopped fresh rosemary

1   cup dry white wine

8   cups vegetable stock

4   cups cornmeal (for polenta)

     Sautéed Wild Mushrooms (recipe follows)

1½ cups shredded Asiago cheese

2   tablespoons chopped Italian parsley

1. In a medium saucepan heat the olive oil and sauté the garlic, onions, and rosemary over medium-high heat for 5 to 6 minutes. Splash with white wine. Add 2 cups of stock. Reduce the heat to medium.

2. Slowly whip in the cornmeal. The mixture will begin to thicken. Gradually add the rest of the stock and cornmeal.

3. Reduce the heat to low and simmer for 10 to 12 minutes or until the mixture becomes smooth, pasty, and creamy.

4. Spray a 9 x 13-inch baking pan with nonstick spray. Spread the polenta mixture evenly in the pan. Cover and chill for 1 to 2 hours.

5. Preheat the grill to medium. Remove the prepared polenta from the refrigerator. Cut into squares or triangles. Place on a nonstick-treated grill for 3 to 4 minutes per side to mark and heat, being careful not to burn. Remove from the grill and top with Sautéed Wild Mushrooms or other vegetables. Garnish with shredded Asiago cheese and chopped parsley and serve.

SERVES 8

SAUTÉED WILD MUSHROOMS
(SERVE WITH GRILLED HERB POLENTA)

2   tablespoons olive oil

1½ tablespoons finely chopped fresh garlic

8   cups chopped assorted wild mushrooms, reconstituted or fresh

    pinch salt

    pinch black pepper

¼   cup brandy or dry sherry

1   tablespoon chopped Italian parsley

4   tablespoons butter

1. In a large sauté pan heat the olive oil and sauté the garlic, mushrooms, salt, and pepper over medium-high heat for 5 to 7 minutes or until the mushrooms become tender.

2. Add the brandy or dry sherry and flambé.

3. Stir in the parsley and the butter, and simmer until the butter is melted. Spoon over grilled polenta.

TABBOULEH

2	pounds bulk tabbouleh grains
4	cups spring water, boiling (estimate, depends upon type of tabbouleh used)
¾	cup diced celery
1	cup diced roma tomatoes
¾	cup diced red/Bermuda onion
¾	cup diced pickled carrots
2	tablespoons black currants
1	tablespoon whole/dry oregano
2	tablespoons chopped fresh Italian parsley
½	teaspoon ground cumin
½	teaspoon salt
½	teaspoon ground black pepper
¾	cup olive oil
½	cup lemon juice
1	cup dry goat cheese

1. In a mixing bowl place the tabbouleh grains and slowly add boiling water, stirring constantly. Continue to add water until tabbouleh reaches a wet, pasty consistency (not runny).

2. Stir in the celery, tomato, onion, pickled carrots, currants, oregano, parsley, cumin, salt, and pepper. Stir in the olive oil and lemon juice.

3. The tabbouleh at this point will appear oversaturated. Cover and refrigerate for 1 hour. Remove from the refrigerator and toss. The tabbouleh should be moist. If it appears slightly dry, toss with a bit more olive oil and lemon juice to taste. Sprinkle with crumbled goat cheese and serve.

SERVES 8 +

TUSCAN PASTA SALAD

1	pound tri-color fusilli (cooked al dente, chilled, lightly olive oiled)
¼	cup julienned red bell pepper
1	cup sliced marinated artichoke hearts
½	cup pitted, coarsely chopped kalamata olives
½	cup poached, julienned sundried tomatoes
¼	cup shredded fresh basil leaf
2	tablespoons chopped Italian parsley

1. In a large bowl combine the fusilli, bell pepper, artichoke hearts, olives, sundried tomatoes, and basil.

2. Toss with Sweet Balsamic Vinaigrette. Chill in the refrigerator for at least 1 hour prior to serving.

3. Toss the salad upon removing from the refrigerator to refresh the pasta. Drain any excess dressing before serving. Garnish with chopped Italian parsley.

SERVES 8

SWEET BALSAMIC VINAIGRETTE

1	cup balsamic vinegar
½	cup red wine vinegar
2	cloves garlic, peeled
2	tablespoons dry whole oregano
1	tablespoon dry chopped basil
1	teaspoon salt
¼	cup sugar
1½	cups olive oil

1. In a blender, combine the vinegars, garlic, oregano, basil, and salt. Blend at medium-high speed.

2. Slowly add the olive oil through the top of the blender and continue to blend approximately 30 to 45 seconds until the dressing has emulsified.

CHAPTER 13

OINGO BOINGO

You probably know Danny Elfman has a talent for writing film scores, but did you know that he also writes and sings songs about sandwich condiments?

Penne Arrabiata

Pasta and White Bean Soup

As time passes, caterers often get to know a band and its management pretty well, and this was one of those bands. Boingo was an eclectic band from Southern California. While they toured worldwide, home is the Golden State. The band's names, Oingo Boingo, Boingo, Mystic Nights, and Mystic Nights of the Oingo Boingo, are all essentially the same. Mystic Nights of the Oingo Boingo was the original name of the band conceived by Richard Elfman, Danny Elfman's brother and lead vocalist.

The band consisted of several members: Danny Elfman (songwriter, lead vocalist, rhythm guitar, co-arranger), Steve Bartek (lead guitar, and co-arranger), John Avila (bass and vocals), Johnny "Vatos" Hernandez (drums), Sam "Sluggo" Phipps (horns), Leon Schneiderman (horns), Dale Turner (horns), George McMulden (horns), Warren Fitzgerald (guitar), Marc Mann (keyboards), Doug Lacy (accordion and rhythm), and Katuran Clarke (rhythm).

Boingo's best selling album, *Dead Man's Party*, was released in 1985. The band's best-selling single, which brought national notoriety, was "Weird Science," used in the soundtrack of the motion picture of the same name. The band enjoyed great success releasing thirteen albums in their career. Their final tour ended in 1995, on Halloween. Throughout the band's years of success, Danny Elfman continued to pursue a separate career. He has become a prominent figure in the motion picture industry, providing musical scores for such films as *Batman, Batman Returns, Edward Scissorhands,* and *The Nightmare Before Christmas.* In addition, he has worked on several screenplays. Elfman's movie successes and all the band members' desire to move on to their own creative endeavors led to the group's dissolution.

During a 1990 concert tour, on New Year's Eve, Danny Elfman was giving an interview in his dressing room prior to the evening's performance. The interview was with a nationally syndicated entertainment network. During the videotaping, his production manager asked that Behind the Scenes finish up his dressing room setup and straighten the room. Trying to avoid camera cables and lighting pods erected for the interview, John accommodated the request.

Unfortunately, the hospitality table was set up right by the door. Owing to the configuration of the cameras, lighting and furniture in the room, John was perched at the end of the table attempting to clear the tabletop. A band member entered the room, swinging the heavy door open and striking John in the lower back with the inside door handle. Without thinking, John blurted out, "*%#@!" Danny burst into laughter. The reporter was furious and stopped the interview to loudly berate John. Danny kindly asked the reporter to relax and apologized for the accident. She persisted until Danny explained that the interview would be over if she continued her complaining.

He explained that John had a job to do, just like everyone else in the room.

During a concert stop on Boingo's final tour, in 1995, Danny began waxing poetic about the sandwich he was constructing in his dressing room, not realizing that he wasn't alone. When our presence in the room dawned on him, Danny turned and finished his performance of the impromptu chorus regarding the "mayo" he was spreading on his sandwich. Amid laughter, we realized the chorus was making everyone hungry!

The atmosphere backstage at an Oingo Boingo concert was always very casual, with lots of guests and fans present. The ardent fans were willing to stand in the pouring rain for two and a half hours to hear Oingo Boingo play their entire show during a stormy evening at the San Diego Outdoor Amphitheater. The crowd came to hear a concert, and Oingo Boingo wasn't about to disappoint them. While Oingo Boingo may no longer exist, their music and memories left behind will always remain.

Oingo Boingo Dressing Room Requirements:

- 8 liters Evian
- 1 case Calistoga sparkling water
- 1 gallon milk
- 12 bottles IBC root beer
- 6 quarts assorted fruit juices
- 12 cans Coke
- 6 Diet Coke or Diet Pepsi
- 12 bottles Panax ginseng extract
- 1 case Sundance Sparklers (grapefruit, orange, cranberry, lemon)
- 1 case Crystal Geyser juice squeeze (ruby grapefruit and pink lemonade)
- 1 case Snapple (kiwi strawberry and assorted)
- 1 bottle red wine
- 1 bottle white wine

- 2 cases beer including 6 Bud—the rest imported
- 6 Yoplait yogurts assorted
- 6 Kit Kat bars
- snacks including chips and dip, mixed nuts, assorted granola bars
- 1 fresh fruit tray
- 1 deli tray with fresh turkey, ham, roast beef, assorted cheese and either turkey salad, chicken salad or tuna salad
- mustard and mayo

The Menu

Penne Arrabiata

Pasta and White Bean Soup

PENNE ARRABIATA

2   tablespoons olive oil

2   tablespoons finely chopped shallots

2   tablespoons finely chopped fresh garlic

1   teaspoon chili pepper

8   cups Red and Sassy Pomodoro Sauce (see index)

2   tablespoons chopped Italian parsley

2   tablespoons shredded fresh basil leaf

2   pounds penne, cooked al dente

3   tablespoons crushed red chilies

1   cup shredded Parmesan cheese

1. In a large saucepan heat the olive oil and sauté the shallots, garlic, and chili pepper over medium-high heat for 4 to 5 minutes until the garlic appears golden.

2. Add the Pomodoro Sauce and continue cooking for 3 to 4 additional minutes. Reduce the heat to medium-low and

simmer for an additional 10 minutes, stirring frequently.

3. Stir in the Italian parsley and basil. Toss with piping hot pasta. Serve with sprinkled crushed red chilies and Parmesan cheese.

SERVES 8

PASTA AND WHITE BEAN SOUP

2 tablespoons olive oil

1 tablespoon finely chopped fresh garlic

1½ cups diced white onions

1 pound prosciutto, diced

1 cup diced celery (approximately 2 stalks)

3 cups uncooked white beans, presoaked overnight

12 cups chicken stock or vegetable stock

1 28-ounce can ground Roma tomatoes in purée

1 tablespoon cleaned and chopped fresh rosemary

1 tablespoon chopped fresh sage

½ tablespoon dry whole oregano

2 bay leaves

2 teaspoons salt

1 teaspoon coarse black pepper

¼ teaspoon cayenne pepper

½ cup peeled and diced carrots

2 cups small elbow macaroni

1¼ cups shredded Parmesan cheese

2 tablespoons chopped Italian parsley

1. In a large stock pot heat the olive oil and sauté the garlic, onions, and prosciutto over medium heat for 5 to 7 minutes. Add the celery, beans, chicken stock, tomatoes, rosemary, sage, oregano, bay leaves, salt, black pepper, and cayenne pepper. Increase the heat to medium-high and bring to a rockin' boil.

2. Reduce the heat to low and simmer for 40 to 45 minutes, stirring occasionally. Stir in the carrots and simmer an additional 20 minutes. Stir in the uncooked macaroni and simmer an additional 15 to 20 minutes.

3. Serve topped with Parmesan and Italian parsley.

SERVES 8 +

115

CHAPTER 14

REBA McENTIRE

Ms. McEntire packs arenas across the nation with her unique style and grace. Reba isn't just a flashy smile and a smooth voice, she is a business executive as well.

Kick Ass Meat Loaf

Homestyle Ketchup

Roasted Garlic Mashed Potatoes

Tomato and Herb Risotto

Reba McEntire was born in McAlster, Oklahoma, in 1955. Her talents were discovered in 1974, at age 19, at a National Rodeo Competition in Oklahoma City, while singing the national anthem. Little Reba has come a long way from those humble beginnings. Over the years, this talented musician and performer has continued to win American Music Awards as Favorite Female Country Vocalist, and for Favorite Country Album, as well as Grammy Awards, Academy of Country Music Awards, Country Music Association Awards, People's Choice Awards, and TNN Viewer's Choice Awards.

Reba has released more than two dozen albums over the years. Some topped the charts while others attained moderate success. However, much of Reba's success is due to her devotion to her fans and her savvy business style. It is these attributes that have allowed this country diva to build her entertainment conglomerate, Starstruck Entertainment. Starstruck's new headquarters occupies a prominent place on Nashville's Music Row.

Reba and her husband and manager, Narvel Blackstock, have mastered the art of concert tours. Starstruck not only owns the tours it produces, but the company owns its own trucks, equipment, and custom tour buses/coaches—which glimmer a beautiful turquoise green, one of Reba's favorite colors. The singer has been able to pull off one successful and consistent tour after another because of the faithful crew she employs year round, from truck drivers to lighting/sound technicians to wardrobe staff. With Starstruck owning the tour, Reba is able to cut out the middleman, for example a local promoter, in most markets.

The backstage atmosphere during a Reba McEntire concert is very businesslike. Everything is done according to a strict schedule: *Artist's dressing room ready time: 3:30 p.m.; Artist's arrival: 4:30 p.m. ; Sound check: 5:00 p.m.; Dinner served: 6:00 p.m., and so on.*

At a typical concert, the opening act, which is usually an up and coming country sensation, takes the stage at 8:00 P.M. sharp. They whip the crowd into a toe-stomping frenzy. By the time Reba takes to the stage at 9:00 P.M., the crowd is ready for some good old country music.

Reba McEntire certainly is a showgirl, as each song in her concert takes on its own look. Her performances are like video presentations of her music. Using such props as a taxi cab driving onto the stage, an on-stage elevator, and a cherry picker to hoist the artist high into the air above the crowd are commonplace at a Reba concert. With each new tour, fans wonder What will she do next?

After the curtain fell at this particular concert, Reba was still hard at work. She made a quick stop in her dressing room for a quick change into a pair of black leggings and a bright green blazer to meet a group of elated fans backstage. These lucky fans were beside themselves as Reba took the time to greet each of them one by one, taking pictures and signing autographs. These fans were guests of Frito-Lay, the tour's sponsor that year. Fans can also get backstage passes from radio stations. At many concerts these listeners are disappointed because they are ignored or not given the opportunity to really meet the musicians. Not at a Reba McEntire concert! Like many country artists, she has an acute understanding that she is where she is because of her fans. At the end of the Meet & Greet, Reba stopped briefly to talk with John. She grasped his hand with both of hers and offered a big thank you for all the wonderful service and attention provided to her and her crew. Later, as she left her dressing room to board the tour bus, she stopped to thank the dressing room security guard. She gave him a big hug and kiss on the cheek. The guard said he had a smile on his face all the way home.

Reba McEntire Dressing Room Requirements:

- 6 Diet Coke
- 6 Caffeine Free Sprite
- 9 Evian—individual size bottles
- tea service including Celestial Seasonings

Sunburst C, Red Zinger, Tropical Escape and the sampler pack

The Menu

Kick-Ass Meatloaf

Homestyle Ketchup

Roasted Garlic Mashed Potatoes

Tomato and Herb Risotto

KICK ASS MEATLOAF

3	pounds lean ground beef
2	pounds lean ground turkey
1	pound ground sweet Italian sausage
6	whole eggs
2	cups diced white onion
¾	cup peeled and finely chopped carrots
2	tablespoons finely chopped fresh garlic
2	tablespoons soy sauce
4	tablespoons Worcestershire sauce
2	tablespoons dry whole oregano
2	tablespoons dried leaf basil
1	tablespoon chopped parsley
1	teaspoon salt
1	tablespoon ground black pepper
2½	cups seasoned bread crumbs
	Homestyle Ketchup (recipe follows)

1. Preheat the oven to 350°.

2. In a large mixing bowl combine all of the ingredients except the bread crumbs. Blend together by kneading the meat mixture with your hands. (Don't forget to wash your hands first!). Continue to knead until well blended.

3. Continue blending, slowly adding the bread crumbs. This will eliminate lumping and make for a very consistent blend. The mixture should appear moist and solid in nature.

4. Divide the mixture in half and place into two nonstick 4 x 9 x 3-inch loaf pans, or similar. Roast uncovered for one hour to 1 hour and 15 minutes. Check the meatloaf while cooking, as some ovens cook unevenly. If the meatloaf begins to turn dark brown before fully cooked, cover loosely with foil for the remaining cooking time.

5. Option: After one hour of cooking, top the meatloaf with Homestyle Ketchup and return to the oven for 15 minutes.

SERVES 8+

HOMESTYLE KETCHUP

1	cup tomato paste
1	cup tomato sauce
1	tablespoon whole grain mustard
1	tablespoon Worcestershire sauce
½	teaspoon seasoning salt
½	teaspoon lemon pepper
1	tablespoon honey
1	teaspoon paprika
2	teaspoons red wine vinegar
1	teaspoon sugar

1. In a small mixing bowl combine all of the ingredients and blend well.

2. Use the ketchup on Kickass Meatloaf or simply as a side to fried potato fritters or homestyle fries. If not using immediately, transfer to a container with a cover and refrigerate until needed.

ROASTED GARLIC MASHED POTATOES

¾	cup olive oil
1	cup whole cloves garlic, peeled
8	pounds red potatoes
1	cup butter
1	cup sour cream (some artists prefer we use lowfat or nonfat sour cream)
1½	cups whole milk (again lowfat/nonfat substitutions may be made)
2	tablespoons salt
1	tablespoon black pepper, regular grind
¼	cup Italian parsley, finely chopped

1. In a medium sauté pan heat the olive oil, and sauté the garlic over medium heat for 5 minutes or until the oil is hot. Reduce the heat and simmer on low for 20 to 30 minutes, occasionally stirring, until the garlic turns golden brown and soft in texture. Drain the oil and set it aside to use in other dishes.

2. Let the garlic cool. Purée in a food processor. Set aside.

3. Quarter the potatoes and boil (with the skins on) until easily mashed with a fork. Remove from heat and drain.

4. In a large bowl combine the potatoes, garlic purée, butter, sour cream, milk, salt, and pepper. Mash preferably with a hand masher or whisk with a hand mixer until creamy with some chunks. Whip in the Italian parsley. Serve garnished with a sprig of Italian parsley.

TOMATO AND HERB RISOTTO

½   cup olive oil
¼   cup finely chopped shallots
1   tablespoon finely chopped fresh garlic
2   cups risotto (short grain rice)
1   cup white wine
2   cups chopped and drained Italian peeled
tomatoes
8   cups chicken or vegetable stock
1   tablespoon Italian parsley
1   tablespoon fresh basil
1   teaspoon oregano
4   tablespoons butter
     salt and black pepper to taste
1½ cups shredded Parmesan cheese

1. In a medium stock pot, heat the olive oil
   and sauté the shallots and garlic over
   medium heat for approximately 2 to 3
   minutes. Add the risotto and sauté an
   additional 2 to 3 minutes, stirring con-
   stantly. Splash with white wine.

2. Add the tomatoes and 4 cups of chicken
   or vegetable stock. Increase the heat to
   high and cook until the liquid begins to
   boil. Reduce the heat to medium-low and
   simmer for approximately 20 minutes,
   stirring occasionally. Add additional stock
   every 5 to 8 minutes, as needed.

3. Add the parsley, basil, oregano, butter,
   salt, pepper, and 3/4 cup of Parmesan. Stir
   well and continue to simmer for approxi-
   mately 5 minutes or until the risotto
   begins to thicken slightly but is still saucy.

4. Garnish with the remaining Parmesan
   cheese and serve.

SERVES 8

CHAPTER 15

~mm~

WHITNEY HOUSTON

This woman has a voice! She was back on tour just weeks after the birth of her child. With little extra weight to shed after becoming a mother, the songstress fed her band and crew a traditional southern meal.

Southern Style Fried Chicken
Orange Mustard Sauce
Shrimp and Andouille Gumbo
Tomato Cucumber Salad

CHAPTER 15

"**W**hitney Houston Live World Tour" hit the road in late 1993. The tour was an instant success. Whitney had already enjoyed sales of over eighty-six million copies of her first four albums with Arista Records. The soundtrack from the film *The Bodyguard* was at the time the biggest selling motion picture soundtrack, selling over thirty-three million copies worldwide. In 1994, Whitney earned three Grammy Awards, as well as accolades from the American Music Awards, NAACP Image Awards, People's Choice Awards, and the Soul Train Awards.

Whitney has been exposed to music since birth. Her mother, Cissy Houston, an R&B/Gospel singer, was the minister of music for the New Hope Baptist Church in Newark, New Jersey. Whitney was a member of the junior choir while growing up and also performed with her mother in local New York clubs. In 1985, she signed her recording deal with Arista Records. That relationship launched her musical career, with hit songs like "Saving All My Love for You," "How Will I Know," and "The Greatest Love of All" topping the charts soon after their release.

The "Whitney Houston Live" tour was long anticipated by her fans, and followed the birth of her first child with pop music star Bobby Brown. The pregnancy certainly didn't slow her down. Whitney belted out tunes at the Hollywood Bowl in a skin tight, plum-colored, velvet dress. She showed few signs that she had given birth just four weeks earlier.

Whitney has earned a reputation of demanding the best of herself during a performance or public appearance and she surrounds herself with similar people. Her tour management and crew are very demanding of themselves as well as those they work with. To maintain these high standards, everyone is accountable for something on the tour and everyone is required to be in radio contact throughout the load-in, concert, and load-out to assure everything is properly taken care of.

The first items off the trucks bright and early in the morning were the radios. Everyone put on a Motorola radio before breakfast, including the backstage caterer. The day progressed rather smoothly considering the 110-plus crew members involved in load-in and setup of this fantastic show. Then in the late afternoon, prior to the singer's arrival, we received our most urgent call. The fruit basket in Whitney's dressing room was not covered with plastic wrap. Although someone went over immediately to rectify this emergency, the radio calls persisted for twenty minutes: "We need plastic wrap in Whitney's Room now!" "Is anyone listening to me?!"

The requests became more and more intense: "Catering, come in, are you understanding that this plastic wrap is a priority?" Finally, Teresa walked over to the dressing room/wardrobe manager for the tour and personally walked with her to the dressing room to show her that the fruit had been covered as requested long ago. The manager quickly apologized, saying she hadn't bothered to check the status of the fruit after her original request. This may seem like a ridiculous incident, but someone was in charge of the fruit in the dressing room and Whitney does prefer that it be covered upon her arrival. It goes to show how important it is to fulfill the stars requirements to a T, and how everyone works together to do just that.

All requests aside, Whitney performed for the crowd on time and on cue. This singer has a voice filled with passion and strength, which delighted fans on this tour.

After the Hollywood Bowl performance, the crew packed up and moved the show to San Diego. Our second team was waiting for them with a hot breakfast at 6:00 A.M. at the Embarcadero Marina Park Symphony Pops venue. The trucks rolled onto the seaside peninsula and the crew slowly disembarked the buses after only three or four hours sleep.

Behind The Scenes was simultaneously serving breakfast to the local union crew at the Hollywood Bowl in Los Angeles since the load-out had taken longer than expected.

The day in San Diego progressed as expected until about one hour before dinner. Whitney's management decided to use the normal hospitality/dining tent for a Meet & Greet. Therefore, dinner was to be served on another secluded portion of the peninsula overlooking the yacht harbor. It was a bit of chaos as we moved tables, chairs, plants, flowers, buffet tables, and beverage stations about 200 feet away. The chaos subsided, the palms were illuminated with spotlights, candles on the dining tables glowed and a traditional southern style menu was served, right down to the cracker-coated fried chicken and gumbo.

Whitney Houston Dressing Room Requirements:

- coffee and tea service
- 8 boxes assorted herbal teas
- natural honey (this is a must)
- 1 fresh fruit basket
- 1 platter of grilled chicken breasts
- 1 cheese and fruit tray
- 1 liter apple juice
- 1 liter orange juice
- 1 liter grape
- 1 liter cranraspberry
- 1 liter cranstrawberry
- 1 liter pineapple
- 1 liter crangrape
- 4 liters spring water
- 8 cans root beer and ginger ale
- M&M candies
- assorted cookies

- 24 hard boiled eggs
- 1 jar mayonnaise
- 6 cinnamon buns, salt bagels and sourdough rolls
- large colorful floral arrangements

The Menu

Southern Style Fried Chicken

Tangy Orange Mustard Sauce

Shrimp and Andouille Gumbo

Tomato Cucumber Salad

SOUTHERN STYLE FRIED CHICKEN

4	whole eggs
1	teaspoon salt
2	teaspoons white pepper
1	heaping tablespoon poultry seasoning
2	cups buttermilk
4	cups cracker meal
8	6-ounce chicken breasts, pounded flat
3	cups canola oil

1. In a 3-quart mixing bowl combine the eggs, half of the pepper, half of the salt, and half of the poultry seasoning, and beat with a whisk until creamy. Whisk in the buttermilk. Set aside.

2. Place the cracker meal in a medium pan or bowl and add the remaining seasonings. Mix well.

3. Dip the chicken in the buttermilk-egg mixture, then into the cracker meal mixture. Place the coated breasts on a dry platter. Repeat this step until all breasts are well coated.

4. In a large skillet, preheat the oil to medium to medium-high heat. Add the coated chicken breasts to the oil and cook, rotating often, for 8 to 10 minutes or until golden brown.

5. Remove from the oil and let drain on a tray or plate lined with a dry paper towel to absorb excess grease.

6. Serve with Tangy Orange Mustard Sauce (recipe follows), Country Chicken Gravy (see index), or Homemade Barbecue Sauce (see index).

SERVES 8

TANGY ORANGE MUSTARD SAUCE

1	cup orange marmalade
½	cup dijon mustard
2	tablespoons honey
1	tablespoon finely chopped orange zest
½	teaspoon lemon pepper
1	tablespoon sugar
1	tablespoon seasoned rice wine vinegar
½	teaspoon salt

1. In a small mixing bowl combine all ingredients, and mix well.

2. Use immediately or transfer to a container with a cover and refrigerate until needed.

SHRIMP AND ANDOUILLE GUMBO

½   cup olive oil (Cajun roux)

½   cup flour (Cajun roux)

1   cup cleaned and diced celery

3   tablespoons finely chopped fresh garlic

2   cups chopped white onion

2   medium cleaned and chopped green bell peppers

1   teaspoon cayenne pepper

½   teaspoon white pepper

½   teaspoon black pepper

1½   teaspoons salt

1   tablespoon chopped fresh basil

1   tablespoon dry whole oregano

1   tablespoon chopped fresh thyme

3   tablespoons Worcestershire sauce

2   tablespoons Tabasco sauce

10   cups chicken stock

1   28-ounce can ground tomatoes with purée

1½   pounds andouille sausage, sliced into rings

2   cups sliced okra (fresh or frozen)

1½   pounds fresh shrimp (U40/50), cleaned and deveined

---

1. In a large stock pot, combine the olive oil and flour. Heat on low for approximately 15 to 20 minutes or until golden brown, whisking constantly. Be careful not to burn!

2. Add the celery, garlic, onion, and bell pepper to the Cajun roux mixture. Increase the heat to medium-high and add the cayenne pepper, white pepper, black pepper, salt, basil, oregano, thyme, Worcestershire sauce, and Tabasco sauce. Stir

well. Continue to sauté the peppers and celery for approximately 4 to 5 minutes.

3. Add the chicken stock and tomatoes and stir well. Bring to a medium boil, add the sliced sausage, and reduce the heat to low.

4. Simmer for approximately 40 minutes, stirring occasionally. Add the okra and simmer an additional 10 minutes. Add the shrimp and simmer an additional 5 minutes. Remove from the heat, cover, and let stand for 5 minutes. Remove the cover and stir. It ready to dish up over a bed of steaming white rice.

SERVES 8+

TOMATO CUCUMBER SALAD

---

16   Roma tomatoes, sliced into thick rings

4   cucumbers, medium, peeled and sliced into half rings

1   cup julienned red/Bermuda onion

½   cup shredded fresh basil

1½   cups Sweet Balsamic Vinaigrette (see index)

8   sprigs fresh basil leaf for garnish

---

1. In a large mixing bowl gently toss all ingredients until well coated. Refrigerate for 1 hour and thirty minutes to marinate and chill.

2. Remove from the refrigerator and lightly toss. Drain any excess liquid. Garnish with fresh basil leaf and serve.

SERVES 8

LORRIE MORGAN

CREW

U2 ZOO TV
OUTSIDE BROADCAST
WORKING PERSONNEL

CATERING
24

CHAPTER 16

~

MOODY BLUES

The marvels of electronic wizardry allow the band to travel the country playing with different symphony orchestras sounding as clear as if they were in the studio. It was a sold-out show once again, and that means the usual: Cristal and caviar!

Halibut Atop Braised Spinach

Champagne Tarragon Sauce

Low Fat Purée of Broccoli Soup

Lime Ginger Shrimp

It was a late September evening, one of the last outdoor venue concerts of the season. Even in California, fans move to indoor concert venues, to avoid the "frigid" winter temperatures—which hover around the low sixties. The Moody Blues, consisting of Justin Hayward (lead guitar, lead vocalist); John Lodge (bass guitar, vocalist); Ray Thomas (flute, vocalist); and Graeme Edge (drums), filled the evening sky with their popular, mesmerizing music.

Having served the band throughout Southern California for several years, we have learned a great deal of insight about the group and its members. For instance, the band has an affinity for green Gatorade, rare and premium wines, and expensive imported cigarettes. With one week's notice of their concert appearance, we ordered their special Rothmans and Silk Cut cigarettes at a cost of $6 a box.

The Moody Blues has had a place in the world of rock since the introduction of the band's first album in 1967, *Days of Future Passed.* The band created their own unique sound, combining rock music with classical orchestral arrangements. Since that time, the band has gone on to release more than fifteen additional albums, but that first album contained two songs the band has become best known for, "Tuesday Afternoon," and "Knights in White Satin." The band still receives a

standing ovation today when those songs are played. Thanks to the marvels of electronic wizardry, the band can play with regional orchestras on tour and still mix the sound to a level as good as their studio recordings.

Hollywood in late September found the band setting the stage for another blockbuster concert. The backstage atmosphere was a bit different than usual, simply because they were to play that night with the Los Angeles Philharmonic. By midafternoon the venue was filled with musicians in shorts, T-shirts and sundresses. Orchestra members arrived at the venue in typical California summer garb. The musicians separated into small groups and began to practice their scripts for the evening. The backstage area resembled a high school band room in sound and appearance.

At 4:00 P.M., the French burgundy and chardonnay wines were corked to allow them to breathe before dinner. The band's manager sauntered into our hospitality area to approve the evening's meal and wine selections. Dinner was served under canopies in the warm, late-summer evening. It became almost a surreal experience. At 5:00 P.M., dinner was served and we received notice that the show was officially sold out. The band traditionally celebrates sold-out concerts with five tins of Beluga caviar and six bottles of Cristal champagne. Our catering runner was immediately sent out to scour Hollywood for the celebration items. It took about two hours and three specialty stores to gather the goods. By the time the show was over, the dressing room was set with crystal champagne glasses, Beluga caviar with all the trimmings, and six icy bottles of Cristal champagne.

During the dinner hour, the production crew was busy maneuvering twelve high-power event spotlights in the backstage area. The stage backdrop of the Hollywood Bowl is a half dome shape. The lights were positioned and wired to shine bright at the peak of the song "Knights in White Satin." The lighting engineer cued the lights on key thereby illuminating the outline of the dome. It was a breathtaking sight, to the tune of $12,000 for the special effect.

The band's faithful fans packed the Hollywood Bowl, for a sellout numbering over 18,000. Moody Blues repeated the performance days later in San Diego selling out two nights with over 13,000 fans. During the Hollywood Bowl performance, John visited with the sound engineer who revealed how the band members sounded so great after all these years. Each orchestra instrument, band instrument, and vocal microphone was separately wired. The real artist for the evening was the sound engineer. In mid-concert, he demonstrated how he could literally tune out an off-key violinist or tone down the entire flute section. He could even make the Moody Blues a little softer or higher pitched depending on the song. Now that's some inside information.

Moody Blues Dressing Room Requirements:

- 12 Corona beers
- 12 Beck's beer
- 6 long neck Budweisers
- 6 Molson Golden
- 6 O'Doul's non-alcoholic beer
- 6 Snapple Iced Tea
- 6 Diet Coke
- 6 Diet 7Up
- 6 7Up
- 12 Perrier bottles 8oz.
- 24 quarts Green Gatorade
- 16 liters Evian
- 12 Clearly Canadian—Raspberry and Peach

- coffee and tea service
- potato chips
- mixed nuts
- chocolate candies
- vegetable tray
- fresh fruit basket
- limes
- 6 packs Silk Cut Cigarettes—purple pack
- 6 Rothmans Blue Cigarettes

The Menu

Halibut atop Braised Spinach

Champagne Tarragon Sauce

Low Fat Purée of Broccoli Soup

Lime Ginger Shrimp

HALIBUT ATOP BRAISED SPINACH

¼   cup lemon juice

¼   cup olive oil

¼   cup dry white wine

½   teaspoon salt

½   teaspoon ground black pepper

1   teaspoon chopped Italian parsley

8   6-ounce halibut fillets

Braised Spinach (recipe follows)

Champagne Tarragon Sauce (recipe follows)

1. In a medium bowl, whisk together the lemon juice, olive oil, wine, salt, pepper, and parsley. Place the halibut fillets in a baking dish and cover with the marinade. Refrigerate for 1 hour.

2. Preheat the oven to 375°. Remove the marinated halibut from the refrigerator and place on a baking sheet. Roast in the oven for approximately 12 to 15 minutes.

3. Remove from the oven and serve atop a bed of Braised Spinach, finished with Champagne Tarragon Sauce.

BRAISED SPINACH

1   tablespoon olive oil

1   teaspoon finely chopped fresh garlic

¼   teaspoon salt

¼   teaspoon ground White Pepper,

2   bunches fresh spinach, washed thoroughly, stems removed

1. In a large sauté pan heat the olive oil over medium-high heat and sauté the garlic, salt, pepper, and spinach for approximately 5 minutes (Do not overcook!)

2. Place ⅛ portion of spinach onto each plate, top with a halibut fillet, and finish with Champagne Tarragon Sauce.

SERVES 8

Champagne Tarragon Sauce
(Best on Light Fish!)

1   tablespoon olive oil
2   tablespoons finely chopped shallots
¼   cup brandy
½   cup champagne
1½ cup fish stock or sea clam juice
½   teaspoon white pepper
1   tablespoon finely chopped fresh tarragon
1   tablespoon French Roux (see index)
1   cup heavy whipping cream

1. In a small saucepan heat the olive oil over medium heat and sauté the shallots approximately 5 minutes until translucent.

2. Add the brandy and flambé. Add the champagne, stir, and simmer for 5 minutes. Add the stock or clam juice, stir, and continue to simmer for an additional 15 minutes.

3. Add pepper and tarragon. Continue to stir over medium heat. Blend in the French Roux. Gradually stir in the whipping cream and simmer an additional 15 minutes, stirring occasionally, until the sauce reaches a creamy velvety texture. Remove from the heat and let stand 2 to 3 minutes. Ladle over the fish. This is a light and delicate sauce, so be careful not to overcook as the sauce will break.

Low Fat Purée of Broccoli Soup
(Can Be Vegetarian)

1   tablespoon olive oil
1½   cups chopped white onion
2   pounds broccoli crowns, chopped
10   cups chicken stock or vegetable stock, if you prefer a vegetarian soup
1   teaspoon salt
½   teaspoon white pepper
1½   pounds potatoes, peeled and chopped
     chopped fresh poached broccoli for garnish

1. In a large stock pot heat the olive oil and sauté the onions and broccoli over a medium heat for 5 to 7 minutes, stirring constantly.

2. Add the stock, increase the heat to high, and bring to a boil. Add the salt and pepper and stir well. Add the potatoes, reduce heat to low, and simmer for 45 to 50 minutes.

3. Remove from the heat and let cool. Fill a blender pitcher three-fourths full of the soup mixture. Blend at medium high for 3 to 4 minutes per batch or until the soup is completely puréed. Pour the soup into a fresh stock pot and continue to process until all ingredients have been blended.

4. Heat the puréed soup over medium heat until hot. Garnish with fresh chopped and poached broccoli.

SERVES 8+

LIME GINGER SHRIMP

1   cup lime juice

3   tablespoons cleaned and chopped fresh
ginger

1   tablespoon finely chopped fresh garlic

1   teaspoon salt

½   teaspoon white pepper

1   tablespoon chopped fresh cilantro (no
stems)

4   tablespoons soy sauce

2   tablespoons honey

2   tablespoons sesame oil

3½ pounds raw shrimp (U10/15), cleaned,
peeled, and deveined

½   cup olive oil

1. In a large mixing bowl combine the lime
    juice, ginger, garlic, salt, pepper, cilantro,
    soy sauce, and honey. Beat with a whisk.
    Slowly add the oils and continue to
    whisk.

2. Place the shrimp in a marinating dish and
    coat with marinade. Cover refrigerate for
    1 hour.

3. Preheat the grill to medium-high. Remove
    the shrimp from the refrigerator and grill
    3 to 4 minutes per side. (May want to
    skewer your shrimp depending upon the
    size used.) Remove the cooked shrimp
    from the grill and place over a bed of long
    grain and wild rice. Garnish with chopped
    cilantro.

SERVES 8

CHAPTER 17

~~~

PEARL JAM

This band played the small stage at a civic theater for three sold-out performances so that Eddie Vedder could play the stage where he saw the Nutcracker Ballet as a child.

Stuffed Italian Breasts

Fabulous Sage Sauce

Fettucine Contadina

Insalata De Caprese

Pearl Jam hit the alternative music scene in 1990. The band was formed in Seattle, Washington, a hotbed of alternative music in the early 1990s. Members include Eddie Vedder (lead vocals, rhythm guitar); Stone Gossard (rhythm guitar, backup vocals); Mike McCready (lead guitar, backup vocals); Jeff Ament (bass guitar, backup vocals); and now Jack Irons on drums and percussion. Jack officially joined the band in January of 1995. He is the fourth drummer for Pearl Jam since 1990. While the band got its start in Seattle, Eddie Vedder spent much of his adolescence in San Diego working as a gas station attendant and busboy at a local music bar.

Pearl Jam released its first album, *Ten,* in 1991. The first single released from the album "Alive," blazed up the charts. The popularity of the band flourished with further releases of songs like "Evenflow" and "Release." *Ten* sold over eight million copies by January 1995, in the United States alone. The band soon became the solid leader of the alternative rock scene. Pearl Jam released two more albums during the following two years with great success. *Vs.* was released in 1993 and *Vitalogy* hit music stores in December of 1994.

Pearl Jam continued to gain fans and attention, and Eddie's face even graced the cover of *Time* magazine. The band's albums continued to sell and their alternative music is now synonymous with the 1990s. The attention and responsibility were not the band's original goals.

Pearl Jam simply loves to make music. None of the band members expected to become icons in the music industry.

Pearl Jam soon became the mouthpiece for disgruntled fans over a controversial issue. Concert ticket costs had continued to rise, not due to the band's price but because ticket agencies added exorbitant service charges. Band members soon found themselves giving testimony before a government sub-committee on Capitol Hill regarding the escalating ticket prices for entertainment events. The band took the dispute as far as the Justice Department, eventually filing an antitrust lawsuit against Ticketmaster. The dispute forced the band to cancel a summer concert tour, leaving many fans disappointed. However, they rescheduled many of their tour dates and set up their own ticketing service to do so.

Pearl Jam's first San Diego visit was in November 1993, before all the controversy over ticket prices. They played two dates in San Diego at the Civic Theater, home of the San Diego Opera, which seemed a strange venue for the alternative rock band. The theater only held 2,300 fans and the interior was upscale with red velvet seats. There was, however, a specific reason the band had chosen that venue. As a child in San Diego, Eddie Vedder attended a performance of the "Nutcracker Suite" at the Civic Theater. Ever since then, he had always wanted to play that theater. The band could have sold out ten nights but they had to settle on two, due to their schedule. The show sold out in less than one hour. The lucky fans knew the tickets they had were priceless.

Security backstage was very tight. Theater personnel were nervous about holding an alternative rock show in the small venue with high balconies. Every possible precaution was taken. Pearl Jam arrived at the theater in a large passenger van. Fans who had waited at the stage door since early morning had a chance to secure a quick autograph before the band rushed into the theater. Eddie and the band appeared very humble. They took their music very seriously and appeared stunned by the devotion and of their fans.

With all the hype and security surrounding the concerts, Eddie quickly became bored backstage. His half-brother, Jason, who was working with our company at the time, went to visit with Eddie. While they talked, Jason presented him with a rubber mask he had purchased. Eddie was thrilled; he loved masks—especially the unusual and grotesque looking ones. The performer donned the new mask and made his way out of the theater and into the stage door crowd of about forty people. He joked and played around with the eager fans who had no idea who he was. People even snapped pictures with him. After about ten minutes of his little joke, Eddie removed the mask, revealing himself.

The crowd took a minute before they realized who he was. They went nuts—trying to grab at the performer as he scurried back through the stage door. Eddie and his brother got a good laugh, although the security guards found it a little less humorous.

Pearl Jam played for two nights, to rave reviews from fans

and local critics. After the concert, Eddie made his way back to his dressing room. There he sat for over an hour talking with two old friends from high school. He showed no signs of an inflated ego whatsoever.

The band returned to town in November 1995, selling out two nights at San Diego's 14,000+ seat Sports Arena.

While they haven't won their battle over high-priced concert tickets, they vow to continue the fight. For now, Pearl Jam continues to do what they love, playing their music for their fans.

Pearl Jam Dressing Room Requirements:

- 2 cases Evian
- 2 cases premium beer — 12 Beck's, 12 Corona, 12 Heineken, 12 micro
- 2 bottles red wine—Cabernet Sauvignon
- 6 quarts fresh fruit juice
- 36 cans assorted soft drinks
- 3 cases Snapple—2 lemon iced tea and 1 raspberry iced tea
- 2 bags tortilla chips with salsa
- 2 bags potato chips with dip
- 1 loaf multi grain sandwich bread
- 1 jar peanut butter
- 12 assorted bagels
- selection of candy bars, i.e. Mars, Snickers
- M&Ms
- vegetable and fruit platter with dips

- basket with fresh fruit
- assorted vegetables for juicing including ginseng root
- coffee and tea service including Throat Coat
- 1 carton of marlboro red cigarettes
- 1 carton camel lights cigarettes

VERY IMPORTANT: One five-gallon bucket of ice cubes to be in dressing room 15 minutes before scheduled end of show. The drummer soaks his wrists and elbows after the show.

The Menu

Stuffed Italian Breasts

Fabulous Sage Sauce

Fettuccine Contadina

Insalata de Caprese

STUFFED ITALIAN BREASTS

8	8-ounce boneless/skinless chicken breasts
½	pound fontina cheese, thinly sliced
2	tablespoons chopped fresh basil
¼	cup pine nuts, toasted
⅓	pounds prosciutto, thinly sliced
¼	cup olive oil
1	cup all-purpose flour
½	teaspoon salt
1	teaspoon black pepper
¼	cup dry white wine
	Fabulous Sage Sauce (recipe follows)

1. Slice the chicken breasts horizontally in the center, three-fourths of the way through, creating a cozy little pocket in the center of the breast. Insert equal amounts of cheese, basil, pine nuts, and prosciutto. Set aside.

2. In a large skillet heat the olive oil to medium. Dust the stuffed breasts with flour and place in the hot skillet. Sprinkle breasts with half of the salt and pepper. Sauté for approximately 5 minutes.

3. Turn the chicken over and continue to sauté for 3 to 4 minutes. Splash with white wine, and season with salt and pepper. Reduce the heat to low, cover, and simmer for 3 to 5 minutes. Remove from the heat and serve with Fabulous Sage Sauce.

SERVES 8

FABULOUS SAGE SAUCE

1	cup chicken stock
2	tablespoons lemon juice
½	cup dry white wine
1	tablespoon chopped fresh sage
½	teaspoon salt
½	teaspoon black pepper
½	cup butter, cubed

1. In a small skillet combine the chicken stock, lemon juice, and wine. Bring to a rockin' boil over medium-high heat. Reduce the heat to medium and simmer for approximately 8 minutes.

2. Add the sage, salt, pepper, and butter. Stir well. Increase the heat to medium-high. Reduce the sauce for 3 to 5 minutes, whisking constantly, until the consistency is velvety and smooth. Be sure not to overcook, as the sauce will break!

FETTUCCINE CONTADINA

2	tablespoons olive oil
2	tablespoons finely chopped fresh garlic
½	cup diced white onion
2	cups thick sliced mushrooms
¼	cup brandy
2	pounds sweet Italian sausage, cooked and drained
2	cups Red and Sassy Pomodoro sauce (see index)
1	quart heavy whipping cream
1	tablespoon chopped fresh Italian parsley
1	teaspoon salt
1	teaspoon coarse black pepper
2	medium red bell peppers, cleaned and julienned
2	cups artichoke hearts (not marinated)
2	tablespoons chopped fresh basil leaf
2	pounds fettuccine pasta, cooked al dente
½	cup shredded parmesan cheese

1. In a large saucepan heat the olive oil and sauté the garlic and onions over medium heat for about 5 minutes. Add the mushrooms and continue to sauté an additional 5 minutes. Add the brandy and flambé.

2. Add the sausage, Pomodoro Sauce, and heavy cream. Increase the heat to high and bring to a rockin' boil, stirring constantly. Reduce the heat to medium and add the parsley, salt, and coarse pepper. Continue to simmer and stir over medium heat until the sauce begins to thicken.

3. Add the bell peppers and simmer 5 additional minutes. Reduce the heat to low and add the artichoke hearts and basil. Simmer an additional 2 to 3 minutes. Toss the sauce with piping hot fettuccine and garnish with shredded Parmesan cheese.

SERVES 8

INSALATA DE CAPRESE

6	vine-ripened tomatoes, hothouse if available
1	fresh basil leaf, bunch
1	small red onion, thinly sliced (shaved)
1	pound fresh buffalo mozzarella
½	cup red wine vinegar
¼	cup balsamic vinegar
½	teaspoon salt
¼	teaspoon black pepper
½	cup extra-virgin olive oil
½	bunch fresh Italian parsley, chopped

1. Slice the tomatoes into ¼-inch thick rings.

2. Arrange the tomato slices on a serving platter or individual plates. Place whole basil leaves on top of the tomato slices. Sprinkle shavings of red onion over the basil leaves.

3. Top with sliced fresh mozzarella.

4. In a medium bowl combine the vinegars, salt, and pepper. Whisk in the olive oil until the mixture is emulsified. Drizzle the vinaigrette over the salad. Garnish with fresh Italian parsley.

SERVES 8

CHAPTER 18

~~~

BETTE MIDLER

Bette Midler's stage shows rival a Las Vegas revue. Meanwhile, the "Divine Miss M" and her band snack on kosher foods in her dressing room.

Grilled Salmon Fillet

Pink Peppercorn Lobster
   Sauce

Pasta Primavera

Bette Midler's 1993–94 tour, "Experience the Divine," was more than a run-of-the-mill concert tour. It was a theatrical and musical experience, staged more like a Broadway musical than a concert. Bette sold out venues coast to coast.

Born and raised in Hawaii, Bette Midler decided on a career in acting while in high school. She soon moved from her tropical roots to New York City and began to play roles on Broadway in hits such as "Fiddler on the Roof." In 1973, Bette earned a Grammy Award for best new artist for her debut album *Divine Miss M.* In 1979, Bette Midler portrayed a self destructive rock singer in the film *The Rose.* That role landed her an Oscar nomination, and the soundtrack from the film hit platinum and earned the singer and actress another Grammy. Bette's successes continued with album releases including *No Frills* in 1982, and *Mud Will Be Flung Tonight,* a comedy album released in 1985. In 1989, Bette starred in the movie *Beaches.* The movie's soundtrack earned the singer her fourth Grammy Award. Bette moved into the '90s with the release of the number one single "From a Distance." In 1993, Atlantic Records released a greatest hits collection, *Experience the Divine.* This release kicked off the nationwide sold out tour.

In a statement released by Atlantic Records regarding her long and varied career, Bette said, "Music is something that I just have always had to do and wanted to do and loved to do. I work hard, but I have a lot of fun, too. When it stops being a good time, that's when I'll throw in the towel." And a good time, indeed, was had by all on the "Experience the Divine" tour.

The stage show, backdrops, and props were fantastic. One of the numbers in the show had Bette Midler and the Harlettes (her dancers and backup singers) dressed as mermaids. In order to complete the routine and maneuver around the stage, specially designed wheelchairs were used. Those chairs sat, lined up nice and straight, idle all morning. Well, the temptation became too great. By the time sound check rolled around, crew members and staff, including us, were entering the semifinal rounds of the International Wheelchair Invitational. The competition was fierce yet full of laughter as a sound engineer tipped over mid-race and slid across the cement floor on his behind.

All those on a Bette Midler tour are well cared for. Truck drivers, dancers, and crew members are all treated with great respect. Truck drivers are able to order individual late night meals. The dancers, backup singers, and band are all provided with their individual desires. During this particular show, the request was for kosher foods—everything kosher.

As we were setting up the dressing rooms, we learned that Bette would be arriving early. We doubled our setup crew and her Tattinger and Dom Perignon champagne were chilled just in time for her arrival. The door to her dressing room was shut and the handle polished just as her limousine entered the venue via the loading ramp. Her personal requests were healthy and light foods.

There are some performers who are very casual with their needs and requests. Others require a bit more attention. When we received word of Bette's early arrival, panic struck the crew as they feverishly worked to finish the staging and dressing room setups. To assure the artist was well taken care of, we assigned a staff member to stand by throughout the evening to monitor her dressing room needs.

Dinner is typically served in a hospitality area adjacent to the stage. However this didn't provide quite enough intimacy and ambiance for the performer and her crew. We had the Arena Club (a lounge within the venue) close down so that dinner could be served in a more comfortable atmosphere.

Crew members were very friendly, as was the "Divine Miss M." It was the day after Christmas and everyone was in the holiday spirit. As the show continued into the evening the laughter from the crowd deepened. Bette Midler certainly is a crowd pleaser. During the show the backstage area was more active than usual. There were backdrops and props everywhere that were ushered onto the stage on cue, while other items rotated off the stage.

Due to the large number of props and staging items for the show, it promised to be a lengthy load-out. The crew was required to pack up the show and travel to the next venue by 7:00 A.M. The concert ended just past 11:00 P.M. Frustration soon mounted as crews found themselves unable to load trucks because of a Meet & Greet and limousines blocking the loading access. The Divine Miss M met with several backstage guests and local promotion staff after the show, taking time to sign autographs and pose for pictures. The crew asked that the limo be moved so they could begin the load-out. They were told that that wasn't an option, since Bette would need the limo ready as soon as she was through. This situation often occurs. The artist is obligated to meet and talk with fans and guests after a performance while the crew has a much different task to accomplish after the concert. It's an unfortunate combination, but the fans indeed come first, because without them where would the stars be?

Bette Midler Dressing Room Requirements:

- brown rice and steamed vegetables
- fresh hot soup containing no milk or cream
- 1 fruit tray
- 1 vegetable tray with dip
- 1 tuna or egg salad
- 1 large garden salad
- 1 bottle Tattinger Rose champagne (premium)
- 1 bottle of Dom Perignon champagne
- 6 1.5-liter bottles Evian
- 12 cans assorted soft drinks
- 1 quart fresh squeezed orange juice

- 1 quart cranberry juice
- 1 quart apple juice
- 6 Snapple iced tea—3 lemon, 3 raspberry
- coffee (decaf) and tea service

The Menu

Grilled Salmon Fillet
Pink Peppercorn Lobster Sauce
Pasta Primavera

GRILLED SALMON FILLET

¼ cup lemon juice
1 sprig fresh rosemary, stripped and coarsely chopped
1 teaspoon cracked black pepper
1 tablespoon finely chopped fresh garlic
1 teaspoon salt
¼ cup olive oil
2 whole bay leaves
8 6-ounce salmon filets
  Pink Peppercorn Lobster Sauce (recipe follows)

1. In a medium bowl combine the lemon juice, rosemary, cracked pepper, garlic, and salt. Whisk together well.

2. Continue beating, slowly adding the olive oil until the marinade emulsifies. Stir in the bay leaves.

3. Place the salmon fillets in a shallow baking dish. Pour the marinade over the fillets, being sure to cover the salmon thoroughly. Refrigerate for 1 hour.

4. Preheat the grill to medium-high heat. Remove the salmon from the refrigerator and place on the grill. Grill approximately 6 minutes per side, turning and rotating at least twice. Remove from the heat and serve with Pink Peppercorn Lobster Sauce.

SERVES 8

PINK PEPPERCORN LOBSTER SAUCE

1 tablespoon olive oil
2 tablespoons diced shallots
1 tablespoon finely chopped fresh garlic
1 tablespoon ground pink peppercorns
¼ cup brandy
2 cups Your Basic Shrimp Stock (see index)
½ cup tomato sauce
1 tablespoon lobster soup base
2 tablespoon French Roux (see index)
1 cup heavy whipping cream
1 cup whole milk

1. In a medium saucepan heat the olive oil and sauté the shallots, garlic and peppercorns over medium heat for approximately 4 to 5 minutes.

2. Add the brandy and flambé.

3. Add the shrimp stock, tomato sauce, and lobster base. Increase the heat to medium-high, bring to a boil.

4. Reduce the heat to low and simmer for approximately 20 to 25 minutes. Add the whipping cream and whole milk. Increase heat to medium-high. When mixture begins to boil whisk in Roux. Reduce heat to simmer, stirring until the sauce reaches a velvety creamy texture. Ladle over Salmon Fillets and serve!

PASTA PRIMAVERA

¼ cup olive oil

2 tablespoons finely chopped shallots

2 tablespoons finely chopped fresh garlic

½ cup dry white wine

2 cups vegetable stock

1 tablespoon shredded fresh basil leaf

½ teaspoon chopped fresh rosemary

1 tablespoon dry whole oregano

6 cups Assorted Grilled Vegetables

(see index)

2 pounds fusilli, cooked al dente

1½ cup shredded Parmesan cheese

chopped fresh Italian parsley for garnish

1. In a large sauté pan heat the olive oil and sauté the shallots and garlic for approximately 5 minutes or until the shallots are golden. Splash with white wine. Add the vegetable stock, basil, rosemary, and oregano. Reduce the heat to medium-low and simmer for an additional 10 minutes.

2. Stir in the Grilled Vegetables and sauté another 3 to 4 minutes.

3. Lightly toss the piping hot pasta with the sauce, being careful not to break up the pasta. Garnish with fresh Parmesan and chopped Italian parsley.

SERVES 8+

ESPN TV

June 19–28, 1997
San Diego, CA

LOCAL CREW

heart,
soul
&
a voice
Jon Secada
world tour 1994

SAN DIEGO

FEB 16 95

k.d. lang

INGÉNUE TOUR 1992

LOCAL
CREW

35

CHAPTER 19

―〰〰〰―

SANTANA

These artists deliver consistent soul and music to their audience.
Santana's intoxicating music draws crowds from across the border.

Ancho Chili Skirt Steak
Southwestern Stir-Fry

Carlos Santana filled the azure evening sky at San Diego's Embarcadero Marina Park on opening night of the Symphony Pops summer season with his electrifying sounds. Santana's band includes Chester Thompson on keyboards, Benny Rietveld on bass guitar, Karl Perazzo on timbales and percussion, Raul Rekow on congas and percussion, Horatio "El Negro" Hernandez on drums, and Tony Lindsay with vocals.

Carlos Santana was first introduced to music at the age of five by his father, Jose. Jose was a mariachi violinist and accomplished musician. Though he learned the basics of music from his father, Carlos Santana was left with the desire to pursue the new music of the day: rock and roll. And that he did. Santana became entrenched in the music scene of Tijuana, Mexico, during the late 1950s. Eventually the musician left Tijuana for San Francisco to join the rest of his family. It was in San Francisco in 1966 that Carlos formed the Santana Blues Band. This group took the stage before 500,000 fans at Woodstock in 1969. Since that historic concert, at which he shared the stage with Jimi Hendrix, Santana has enjoyed great successes. Santana's unique style of music has earned the performer fourteen gold and nine platinum albums, with sales of over thirty million.

Santana has traditionally opened the summer pops season in San Diego. His sold-out concerts draw crowds of young and old fans to see the talented guitarist and his unique style of rock and roll jazz.

The atmosphere backstage at a Santana show is very mellow. The musician requires very little special treatment. There is no big lighting display or stage props. His concerts take place on a simple stage with standard concert lighting and sound. There is Santana with his guitar and his band to back him up. It is his spirit and dedication to his music that is often cited by fans as the reason for their appreciation of his sound. His concerts are intense, yet enlightening.

Santana's appearances in San Diego paled in comparison to his show at the bullring in Tijuana, Mexico. Having spent much of his childhood in Mexico, Santana was excited about the opportunity to play music in his hometown. Logistically, the concert was a nightmare. The bullring arena wasn't equipped for a major rock concert. Dressing rooms had to be constructed and all the staging materials had to be driven across the border from the United States.

Backstage at the Tijuana show resembled a family reunion. Many friends, guests, and Mexican dignitaries attended the show and came backstage. Since there were limited food preparation facilities, much of the food served for this show was grilled and served Santa Mar-garita style with lots of fresh fruits and vegetables, marinated meats, and seafood. It was a rustic menu perfect for the setting.

Santana considered his band and crew family. He ate meals with them and socialized with them. Striking a healthy balance between an artist and his public is essential to longevity in the music industry; Santana has almost effortlessly accomplished this task. This balance, and of course his amazing talents, contribute greatly to his devoted following and long career.

Santana Dressing Room Requirements:

- 14 assorted regular soft drinks
- 6 cans assorted diet soft drinks
- 4 liters fresh squeezed orange juice
- 24 bottles assorted Snapple fruit and iced tea
- assorted chocolate bars
- 1 case Heineken beer
- 4 liters apple juice
- 10 liters spring water
- coffee and tea service

After Show Hospitality:
- 3 bottles of red wine
- 1 bottle white wine
- 24 premium beers
- buffet of hot hors d'oeuvres; may include BBQ, Thai, Indian, Chinese, pasta, but always include vegetarian options.

The Menu

Ancho Chili Skirt Steak

Southwestern Stir-Fry

ANCHO CHILI SKIRT STEAK

4   pounds skirt steak, cleaned and skinned, separated into 8-ounce portions

1   tablespoon chopped fresh garlic

1   small red/Bermuda onion, cleaned and stripped

½   cup achiote concentrate (spiced annato seed paste/powder)

1   bunch fresh cilantro, cleaned, no stems

2   dried ancho chilies, remove stems

2   tablespoons beef base concentrate

2   tablespoon dry whole oregano (Mexican)

1   cup lemon juice, fresh-squeezed if possible

¾   cup lime juice

1   tablespoon chili powder

1. In a blender, combine all of the ingredients except the skirt steaks. Blend on medium-high for 1½ minutes, until thick and emulsified.

2. Place the portioned beef into a 6-quart container and pour the blended marinade over the beef. Coat the meat well. Refrigerate for 6 to 8 hours.

3. Preheat the grill to medium-high heat. Place the marinated steaks on the grill for approximately 4 to 5 minutes on each side for rare to medium steaks. Continue to grill longer if desired. Remove from the grill and serve!

SERVES 8

SOUTHWESTERN STIR-FRY
(A FAVORITE ON THE ROAD!)

¼   cup olive oil

2   tablespoons chopped fresh garlic

1   teaspoon salt

½   teaspoon black pepper

¼   teaspoon ground cumin

1   tablespoon chili powder

½   teaspoon cayenne pepper

1   cup diced red/Bermuda onion

1   cup peeled, julienned carrots

1   cup julienned red, green, and yellow bell peppers

½   cup mushrooms (preferably shiitake or portabella), sliced

1   cup julienned zucchini squash

1   cup baby corn stalks

½   cup roma tomatoes, chopped

3   cups prepared brown rice

½   cup dry goat cheese

½   cup pine nuts

¼   cup chopped fresh cilantro

1. In a wok or large sauté pan heat the olive oil to medium-high heat and sauté the garlic, salt, pepper, cumin, chili powder, and cayenne pepper until the garlic begins to brown.

2. Add the onion, carrots, and peppers, and sauté for approximately 1 minute.

3. Add the mushrooms, stirring constantly, and sauté for approximately 1 minute.

4. Add the zucchini and corn, stirring constantly, and sauté for approximately 45 seconds.

5. Add the chopped tomatoes, and continue to toss carefully, so as to not mash the corn and tomatoes.

6. Serve over the brown rice. Sprinkle with goat cheese, pine nuts, and chopped cilantro. Finish with a sprig of cilantro at the side of each dish.

SERVES 8

CHAPTER 20

mmm

TINA TURNER

Amazing stage, amazing performance, and a loose hairpiece. While her crew enjoyed Cajun cuisine, Tina dined on ham, white bread, Hellman's mayonnaise, and chicken wings in her dressing room.

Down-Home Carolina Oven-Fried Catfish
Louisiana Style Creole Sauce
Cajun Roux
Mama's Vegetarian Gumbo

Anyone who has seen a Tina Turner concert knows she is a performer who gives it all she's got. At fifty-something, Tina continues to sell out arenas around the country with her sultry and dynamic music. Tina Turner, born Anna Mae Bullock in 1939 in Nutbush, Tennessee, was raised by her grandparents after her mother left her, moving out of state. Tina met her first husband, Ike Turner, in 1956. She was married to him for seventeen years until she left the abusive relationship in 1976.

In her solo career, Tina Turner was initially a greater success in Europe. Her first solo hit "Let's Stay Together," was released in Europe in 1983. The single reached number six in the United Kingdom but wasn't released in the United States until 1984, where it reached number twenty-six. The turning point in Tina's solo career came with her album *Private Dancer,* released in 1984. The album only took about two weeks to put together and ended up selling over ten million copies worldwide. Following the success of *Private Dancer* came six more albums: *Break Every Rule* (1986), *Tina Live in Europe* (1988), *Foreign Affair* (1989), *Simply the Best* (1991), *What's Love Got to Do With It/Soundtrack* (1993), and *Wildest Dreams* (1996). Her biggest solo hits include: "We Don't Need Another Hero," "Private Dancer," "Better Be Good to Me," and "What's Love Got to Do With It."

Since 1984, Tina Turner has embarked on at least five tours. The "What's Love" tour of 1993 and the recent "Wildest Dreams World Tour" (1996–1997) have been the best received since the "Private Dancer World Tour" in 1984–1985. All of Tina's concert tours are well received by the fans. In fact, she has made it into the Guinness Book of World Records for the largest paying audience assembled by a solo artist: 182,000 people at Moroccan Stadium in Rio De Janeiro, Brazil in 1988. Now that's a lot of dedicated fans!

During a stop in San Diego in 1991 on the Pepsi-sponsored "Simply the Best" tour, Tina noticed a brightly lit Dr. Pepper machine backstage. In fact, the arena was covered with Coca-Cola signs, machines, and decals. As a Pepsi spokesperson, Tina felt it was inappropriate to play a venue with such signage. To alleviate the problem, every sign, machine, decal, and poster was covered during her performance. The concessionaire even served the beverages in nondescript cups. There were so many Coca-Cola signs in the venue that it took a crew of four men about five hours to cover them all. They even were asked to cover the sign on the parking entrance marquis.

In 1991, the then-unknown Chris Isaak, donning a suit of mirrors, took the stage as Tina's opening act. Today Chris headlines his own tours with hit songs like "Somebody's Cryin'" and "Walk On Down." This 1991 concert was one of the most memorable concerts we have had the opportunity to cater. Tina's performance lit up the arena. She strutted her stuff on every corner of the stage. The staging and lighting were "Simply the Best." At one point during the show, Tina came charging straight at the audience from the back of the stage. As she reached a railing at center stage, she was lifted by a mechanical arm out twenty feet over the audience. The catapult–style contraption simply rose out of the stage, to the amazement of the fans. After the arm returned her to the stage, Tina began her closing number, "Proud Mary." As she was singing the song, the entire tier of lighting trusses slowly dropped from the rafters of the arena. The front of the lighting contraptions dropped faster and faster, revealing a staircase on the back side. Tina Turner sashayed all the way up the 100+ stairs to the roof of the arena as she closed the show. It was an incredible sight!

Backstage the atmosphere was very casual. Wardrobe and makeup readied the performer's wigs, costumes, and makeup for the show. Yes, it is a wig, and it actually became askew during the San Diego performance. The consummate professional just continued singing on her cordless microphone, ducked backstage for about twenty seconds, adjusted the wig in the quick change room, and continued the performance.

We had the opportunity to again cater to Tina and her band in 1997 during the "Wildest Dreams World Tour." Tina's dressing room was draped with black curtains to disguise the fact that is was actually a locker room. Floor and table lamps were brought in to create an intimate mood. A relaxed atmosphere was created with the six-foot couch and easy chairs, four large green plants, and a large arrangement of white flowers. Dark carpets were added as a finishing touch, making the room cozy and warm. Also, the tables were filled with candles throughout the room to provide a soothing ambiance.

Tina slipped into her private dressing room after sound check and spent the next two hours in wardrobe and makeup while enjoying a private dinner. Her special request that evening was our Garden Primavera Pasta.

As she hit the stage with a bang, the back of the set opened to reveal a 25-foot Jumbotron video screen. The crowd wouldn't miss a single moment of her incredible show. That tour was appropri-

ately sponsored by Hanes Hosiery. At almost sixty, Tina still has the legs to fit the bill.

Prior to her final encore, Tina took the time on stage in front of 14,000+ fans to introduce and thank her band members, dancers and backup vocalists, her lighting and sound engineers, her crew, and even our staff.

Tina Turner Dressing Room Requirements:

- 1 platter of fresh ham
- 1 loaf fresh white bread
- 1 jar Hellman's mayonnaise
- 1 plain yogurt
- 1 bowl cherry tomatoes
- 1 platter chicken wings or pieces
- fresh fruit basket
- 1 quart grape juice
- 1 bottle San Pellegrino sparkling water
- 1 bottle Evian
- 1 bottle dry white wine
- 6 cans Pepsi
- plain popcorn
- plain potato chips
- floral arrangements (white flowers only)
- Oven-baked sweet or regular potato should be available upon request as well as a fresh pasta dish

Special Requests: Tina's touring bus is stocked each night with: 3 hard-boiled eggs; fresh strawberries, grapes, and bananas; plain cottage cheese; plain yogurt; 1 pint Häagen-dazs strawberry ice cream; 3 tuna sandwiches; watermelon; 2 sweet potatoes; and 2 plain potatoes.

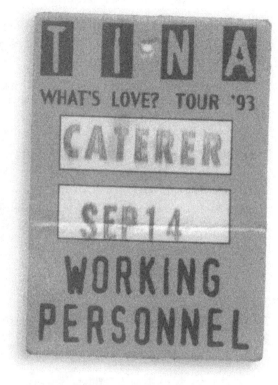

3. Moisten each portion of catfish in the egg mixture, then dip into the bread crumbs, making sure to completely cover with crumbs.

4. Place the breaded fillets on a baking sheet treated with nonstick cooking spray. Bake for 12 to 18 minutes until catfish appears golden brown. Top lightly with Louisiana-Style Creole Sauce.

SERVES 8

DOWN-HOME CAROLINA OVEN-FRIED CATFISH

2   cups seasoned bread crumbs
1   teaspoon ground thyme
1   teaspoon granulated garlic
1   teaspoon granulated onion
½   teaspoon salt
½   teaspoons black pepper
4   large eggs
¼   cup heavy whipping cream
4   pounds fresh catfish fillets (8-ounce portions)
    Louisiana Style Creole Sauce (recipe follows)

1. Preheat the oven to 425°. In a shallow mixing bowl combine the bread crumbs, thyme, garlic, onion, salt, and black pepper. Mix well and set aside.

2. In a small mixing bowl whisk the eggs and heavy cream until smooth.

LOUISIANA STYLE CREOLE SAUCE

2   tablespoons olive oil
2   cloves chopped fresh garlic
¼   cup diced white onion
¼   cup diced green bell pepper
½   cup Your Basic Shrimp Stock (see index)
1   28-ounce can ground peeled tomatoes with purée
½   teaspoon dry whole oregano
½   teaspoon ground thyme
½   teaspoon salt
½   teaspoon black pepper
3   dashes Tabasco Sauce (add more for spicier sauce)
3   dashes Worcestershire sauce
    Cajun Roux (recipe follows)

1. In a saucepan heat the olive oil and sauté the chopped garlic and onion over high heat until tender.

2. Reduce the heat to medium-low and add the bell pepper, shrimp stock, tomatoes, and remaining seasonings. Simmer the

sauce approximately 25 to 30 minutes until reduced and thickened.

3. If necessary, thicken with 1 tablespoon Cajun Roux (recipe follows).

4. Ladle the sauce lightly over the catfish fillets, and garnish with sprigs of thyme. The sauce is also excellent over white or brown rice as a side dish or vegetarian treat!

Cajun Roux

½ cup olive oil, extra-virgin if possible
½ cup all-purpose flour

In a skillet combine the olive oil and flour and blend well. Cook over low heat until the mixture reaches a pasty texture. Be careful not to brown or burn.

Mama's Vegetarian Gumbo

½   cup olive oil
½   cup all-purpose flour
½   cup diced celery
¾   cup chopped white onion
½   cup chopped carrots
¾   cup diced green bell pepper
¼   cup chopped fresh garlic
10 cups spring water
1   28-ounce can diced tomatoes
1   28-ounce can ground tomatoes with purée

1   tablespoon dry whole oregano
1   tablespoon dry whole thyme
1   teaspoon cayenne pepper
1½   teaspoons salt
3   tablespoons Worcestershire sauce
2   tablespoons Tabasco sauce
¾   cup chopped zucchini squash
¾   cup chopped yellow squash
¾   cup chopped mushrooms
¾   cup frozen or fresh cut okra
½   cup cooked black-eyed peas
     steamed white, wild, or brown rice

1. In a stockpot combine the olive oil and flour over low heat and cook for approximately 20 minutes, stirring constantly to prevent burning.

2. Add the celery, onion, carrots, bell peppers, and garlic. Continue to stir to coat the vegetables with the roux mixture.

3. Add the spring water and increase the heat to medium-high. Add the tomatoes, oregano, thyme, pepper, salt, Worcestershire sauce, and Tabasco sauce. Bring to a boil, stirring constantly.

4. Add the zucchini, yellow squash, mushrooms, okra, and black-eyed peas. Reduce the heat to medium-low and simmer the gumbo an additional 10 minutes. Serve over steamed white, wild, or brown rice. (Bonnie Raitt prefers hers over brown rice and cooked without oil.)

SERVES 8+

CHAPTER 21

~~~~

HOOTIE & THE BLOWFISH

The threat of rain in the forecast couldn't keep this band's die-hard fans away. With their sell-out tour, you'd think caviar would be on the menu. Nope, just a hell of a turkey sandwich!

Smoked Turkey, Green Chile, and Jalapeño Jack with Chili Cilantro Mayo

Hootie Chowder

Hootie & the Blowfish came on the national scene in 1994 with their first album produced by a major record label (Atlantic Records), *Cracked Rear View.* That album remained at the top of the charts with such songs as "Hold My Hand," "Only Want to Be With You," and "Let Her Cry." The band, consisting of Darius Rucker (lead vocals and guitar), Mark Bryan (guitar and background vocals), Jim "Soni" Sonefeld (drums and percussion), and Dean Felder (bass guitar and vocals), was formed originally at the University of South Carolina. The four band members were all attending the college when circumstances brought the group together. They started the band more for enjoyment and recreation at first, never anticipating their phenomenal rise to stardom. Their first major album continued to sell millions of copies as they took to the road for their first major tour in 1995. Hootie & the Blowfish sold out concerts coast to coast. They have won several awards for their work including an American Music Award for Favorite Band, Duo, or Group. Their second album release *Fair Weather Johnson* hit record stores in 1996 to rave reviews.

The band's rise to centerstage indeed came quickly. Fortunately, their fame is kept in perspective and the band members maintain a sense of normalcy. Backstage, there wasn't a security guard posted outside their dressing room, and they ate dinner with the crew. If you weren't aware of who the band members were, you'd have a difficult time picking them out of the backstage crowd. At one point in the evening, we lost track of one of our staff members only to find Darius Rucker talking with her and other guests as if they were long lost friends. This group of college buddies definitely earned their break into the music industry spotlight. The hard work put in by this band prior to their success is what many feel prepared them for their seemingly instant fame.

After dinner, Darius sat in the dining room of the hospitality house adjacent to the stage just talking with those in the room. Everyone was enjoying the conversation so much that the time had quickly slipped by. The tour manager emerged from his office and reminded the crew and band members that they had a show to do in ten minutes, and they might want to get ready. Everyone looked at their watches and scattered.

The band's low-key attitude backstage was also evident in the phrase that appeared above their dressing room requirements on the rider. "Hootie & the Blowfish are not a difficult bunch. We are very easy to please and don't consider ourselves to be very demanding. However, we would appreciate the following items prepared for us prior to our performance."

Looking at their dressing room requirements, you would think the band had taken the "college" parties on tour with them. However, the popular college drinks like Jaegermeister are more for backstage guests than the band. Their fresh, unadulterated image is what attracts their broad base of fans. Darius said during dinner "It was important to keep this all in perspective and have fun with it. . . ." in reference to the tour. The band took to the stage and brought the crowd to their feet for the duration of the show. Hootie enjoyed their time onstage; it was apparent by the smiles on the band members' faces.

Hootie & the Blowfish Dressing Room Requirements:

- 1 fresh fruit basket
- 5 submarine sandwiches (including 2 turkey, 1 ham, 1 roast beef, and 1 veggie)
- 2 cases Budweiser in bottles
- 2 cases Budweiser Light in bottles
- 3 fifths Jim Beam bourbon
- 1 fifth Absolut vodka
- 1 fifth Jaegermeister
- 1 half gallon Tropicana orange juice
- 24 liters spring water
- 24 cans Mountain Dew
- 24 cans Coke

- 24 cans Diet Coke
- 4 quarts Gatorade
- variety of chips
- 1 CD any artist
- 6 pairs athletic socks
- 9 pairs boxer shorts 3 size 32, 3 size 34, 3 size 36

SMOKED TURKEY, GREEN CHILE, AND JALAPEÑO JACK WITH CHILI CILANTRO MAYO

3½ pounds smoked turkey breast, sliced thin

1 16-ounce can mild green chilies, julienned or chopped

1 pounds jalapeño Jack cheese, grated

8 torta rolls

Chili Cilantro Mayo (recipe follows)

16 slices grilled beefsteak tomatoes (optional)

1 cup radicchio, shredded (optional)

1. Preheat the oven to 375°. On a nonstick sheet pan place 8 even amounts of turkey (approximately 6 ounces each), into oval-shaped piles. Top each pile with green chilies and grated cheese. Place in the oven for approximately 5 to 7 minutes or until the meat is warm and the cheese is melted.

2. Griddle-toast the torta rolls. Spread Chili Cilantro Mayo on the bread. Place the hot sandwich fixings on the rolls. Garnish with grilled tomatoes and radicchio (optional) and serve!

SERVES 8

CHILI CILANTRO MAYO

2 egg yolks

¼ teaspoon dry mustard

pinch cayenne pepper

1 tablespoon chili powder

1 tablespoon lime juice

pinch salt

½ teaspoon chopped roasted garlic

1 cup olive oil

2 tablespoons chopped fresh cilantro

1. In a clean blender process the egg yolk at low speed to stir.

2. Add the mustard, pepper, chili powder, lime juice, garlic, and salt, and blend on medium-high. Slowly add the olive oil and blend until it reaches a mayo-like consistency.

3. Scrape into a small bowl, fold in the fresh cilantro, and spread.

HOOTIE CHOWDER
(POTATO & CORN CHOWDER)

4 cups canned whole kernel corn

1½ tablespoons olive oil

1 cup diced celery

1½ cups finely chopped white onion

1 tablespoon chopped fresh garlic

½ pounds bacon, chopped, cooked crispy, and drained

10 cups chicken or vegetable stock

1 teaspoon salt

½ teaspoon white pepper

2 pounds red potatoes, cubed small, skin on

¼ cup French Roux

2 cups heavy whipping cream

chopped Italian parsley for garnish

1. In a food processor purée 3 cups of corn. Set aside.

2. In a large stock pot heat the olive oil and sauté the celery, onions, and garlic over medium heat for approximately 5 min-utes. Stir in the corn kernels, corn purée, and bacon. Continue to sauté for 3 to 4 minutes.

3. Stir in the stock, salt, and pepper. Increase the heat to high and bring to a boil. Reduce the heat to medium and simmer for approximately 30 minutes. Add the potatoes, increase the heat to medium-high, and cook for an additional 15 to 18 minutes.

4. Thicken the soup by whipping in the Roux gradually. Reduce the heat to low, stir in the cream, and garnish with fresh chopped Italian parsley.

SERVES 8

CHAPTER 22

ROBERT PLANT AND JIMMY PAGE

This partial Led Zeppelin revival packed the house. Backstage, the band made themselves right at home with baby cribs and laundry duties.

Pasta with Roasted Eggplant and
   Fresh Mozzarella

Gardens of India Salad

Moroccan Rice Salad

Led Zeppelin consisted of four members, Robert Plant, Jimmy Page, John Paul Jones, and John Bonham. The band was formed back in June 1968, and they played their first concert on October 17, 1968, at Surrey University near London. The band's popularity ignited and created a cult-like following throughout the 1970s. In September 1980, John Bonham died in an alcohol-related incident. Soon after his death, Led Zeppelin announced their breakup. Many young fans wore black armbands to school as their way of mourning the death of the band member and of Led Zeppelin itself.

When Plant and Page announced plans for a world tour in 1995, almost fifteen years later, their devoted fans came out in droves to purchase tickets. The fans were not in for Led Zeppelin tunes, as originally thought, but a convoluted mix of Egyptian folk sounds with talented rock and guitar tunes blended to create their own rock

symphony of sorts. The crowds loved it. Plant and Page played songs like "Friends," "Rumble On," and "Black Dog." The crowd watched, almost mesmerized by the sounds of the duo on stage. Some fans were surprised by Plant's voice. Many had doubted his singing abilities before the tour started.

The 1995 "Zoso Jimmy Page Robert Plant World Tour" featured Jimmy Page on guitar, Robert Plant on vocals, Charlie Jones on bass, Michael Lee on drums, Ed Shearmer on keyboards (and as musical director), Nigel Eaton on hurdy-gurdy, Purl Thompson on guitar and banjo, and the Hussam Ramzy Egyptian Ensemble as backup. It was certainly a different assortment of musicians than that of Led Zeppelin.

The "Zoso" tour lasted about a year. Added years had not diminished the band members. They were full of life and sounds on and off the stage.

The 1995 tour was much hyped and long awaited by Plant and Page fans. While the music differed a great deal from Led Zeppelin, the fans simply enjoyed the opportunity to see the artists perform. The artists' actions backstage were also different from what one would expect from such legendary performers. The atmosphere was rather light and many of the band and crew members spent the afternoon joking around with each other as they set the stage for the performance.

Laundry anyone? Part of the glamour of owning your own hospitality business is getting involved in every aspect of an event. Sometimes this involves exciting tasks like dumping trash or laundering towels and linens. John took advantage of a break in the day during the "Zoso" tour to wash some linens and towels in the San Diego Sports Arena's laundry facilities. This laundry room was located between two locker rooms, which doubled as dressing rooms for concerts.

In an effort to escape the crowds in front of the dressing rooms, Robert Plant and Jimmy Page ducked into the laundry room to gain access to the adjacent locker room/dressing room. Startled by the surprise guests in the laundry room, John attempted to quickly move the piles of dirty linens out of the walkway, not realizing who the visitors were. The artists found humor in the piles of laundry strewn on the floor. John soon realized who the pair was when he looked up from the front load washer he was filling.

"Look, it's laundry time," said Robert. Both jumped in to help, Jimmy with the Tide and Robert throwing the towels in the machine. "Anything else boss?" quipped Robert. John smiled and said, "No, that's all for now, thank you, I'll come get you when we're ready to switch the loads into the dryer." Everyone enjoyed a good laugh and the pair slipped out the back door to the adjoining dressing rooms.

Soon after the laundry was done, John gathered the folded linens and returned to the hospitality area. The band members decided to eat in their dressing room that evening to avoid the backstage crowd. A cart with their dinners in hot boxes was rolled into the dressing rooms. A table was set for about twelve guests and the dinner was served. The band raved over the Indian food that we served. They were getting tired of chicken, or "yardbird" as they referred to it with a chuckle. (Jimmy was a member of "The Yardbirds" in 1966 prior to the formation of Led Zeppelin.) Robert looked up from the table and remarked how fresh the linens smelled. Jimmy, Robert, and John smiled at the comment and the band finished their dinner.

Robert Plant/Jimmy Page Dressing Room Requirements:

ROBERT PLANT'S DRESSING ROOM REQUIREMENTS:
- 6 liters Evian
- 6 Miller Genuine Draft
- 4 quarts green Gatorade
- 6 bottles Perrier
- honey

JIMMY PAGE'S DRESSING ROOM REQUIREMENTS:
- 6 bottles of tonic water
- 6 bottles Perrier
- 4 quarts fresh orange juice
- 6 liters Evian
- 1 quart whole milk

The Menu

Pasta with Roasted Eggplant and
Fresh Mozzarella

Gardens of India Salad

Moroccan Rice Salad

PASTA WITH ROASTED EGGPLANT AND FRESH MOZZARELLA

2	medium eggplant, cubed (½")
2	tablespoons chopped fresh oregano
1	cup olive oil
2	teaspoons salt
1	tablespoon coarse black pepper
3	tablespoons finely chopped fresh garlic
½	cup shredded fresh basil
¼	cup red/Bermuda onion
½	cup dry red wine
2	tablespoons sugar
6	cups Red and Sassy Pomodoro Sauce (see index)
2	pounds penne, cooked al dente
2	cups cubed fresh mozzarella (½")
8	sprigs Italian parsley for garnish

1. Preheat the oven to 375°. In a large mixing bowl combine the cubed eggplant, 1 tablespoon of oregano, ¾ cup of olive oil, 1 teaspoon of salt, ½ tablespoon of pepper, 2 tablespoons of garlic, and ¼ cup of basil. Toss well. Place the coated eggplant in a single layer on a nonstick roasting pan. Roast in the oven for 12 to 15 minutes or until lightly browned. Set aside.

2. In a large saucepan heat the remaining olive oil over medium-high heat and sauté the garlic and onion for about 5 minutes until the onions appear translucent.

3. Reduce the heat to medium and add the red wine, black pepper, salt, and sugar. Stir well and simmer for an additional 5 to 7 minutes. Add the Pomodoro Sauce

and 1 tablespoon of oregano and stir well. Reduce the heat to medium-low and simmer, stirring occasionally, for 10 to 15 minutes.

4. Reduce the heat to low, add the remaining basil and the roasted eggplant, and stir well. Add the piping hot pasta and lightly toss. Add the fresh mozzarella, again lightly toss, and garnish with a sprig of Italian parsley.

SERVES 8

GARDENS OF INDIA SALAD

1½ pounds roasted red potatoes

2 cups Roasted Eggplant (see previous recipe)

1 cup chopped red/Bermuda onion

1½ cups julienned hearts of celery

1½ cups peeled and cubed cucumber

¼ cup cleaned and julienned fresh ginger root

1 cup seasoned rice wine vinegar

¼ cup lime juice

¼ cup lemon juice

1 cup olive oil

½ teaspoon ground cumin

¼ teaspoon ground coriander

1½ cups quartered roma tomatoes

2 tablespoon chopped fresh cilantro

1 tablespoon chopped fresh mint

salt to taste

black pepper to taste

1. In a large mixing bowl, combine the potatoes, eggplant, red onion, celery, cucumber, and ginger. Toss lightly and set aside.

2. In a separate mixing bowl combine the vinegar, lime juice, lemon juice, olive oil, cumin, and coriander. Whisk together. Pour the dressing over the salad mixture and toss. Lightly toss in the tomatoes, cilantro, and mint, being careful not to break up the tomatoes.

3. Add salt and pepper to taste. Cover and refrigerate for at least 1 hour. Remove from the refrigerator, lightly toss, and serve.

SERVES 8

MOROCCAN RICE SALAD

8   cups cooked long grain and wild rice
mixture
1   cup diced red/Bermuda onion
1   cup cleaned and diced celery
1   cup sliced mushrooms (marinated or
sautéed)
1   cup diced pickled carrots
1   cup diced roasted red bell pepper
2   tablespoons chopped Italian parsley
1   tablespoon whole leaf thyme
1   cup seasoned rice wine vinegar
2   cups marinated artichoke hearts
1½   teaspoons ground cumin
½   teaspoon cayenne pepper
1   tablespoon minced fresh garlic
½   cup lemon juice
2   tablespoons sugar
1   teaspoon salt
1   tablespoon coarse black pepper
1   cup olive oil
     sliced, pitted black Greek olives for
garnish

1. In a large mixing bowl combine the rice, red onions, celery, mushrooms, carrots, peppers, parsley, thyme, vinegar, and artichoke hearts. Mix well.

2. In a blender combine the cumin, cayenne pepper, garlic, lemon juice, sugar, salt, and black pepper. Blend on medium-high for 30 seconds. Slowly add the olive oil until the dressing emulsifies.

3. Toss the dressing with the salad mixture and serve on a bed of baby greens or as a side dish. Garnish with sliced, pitted black Greek olives.

SERVES 8+

CHAPTER 23

TOM PETTY AND THE HEARTBREAKERS

With a full police escort and entourage, the band escaped the crowds after their sold-out dates at the Hollywood Bowl. No time to even touch the expensive champagne requested in the dressing rooms.

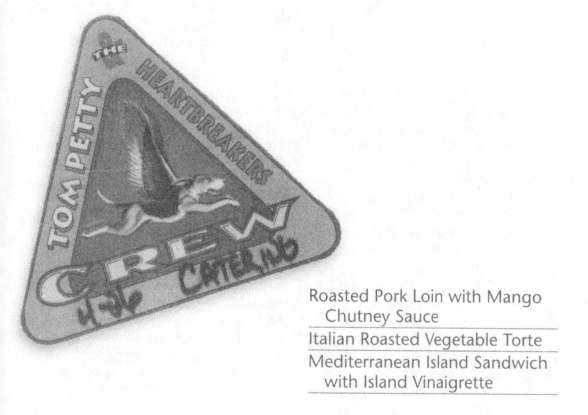

Roasted Pork Loin with Mango
  Chutney Sauce

Italian Roasted Vegetable Torte

Mediterranean Island Sandwich
  with Island Vinaigrette

Tom Petty and the Heartbreakers have been on the music scene for decades. Since their first self-titled album release in 1976, the band has ridden a roller coaster of success. The band's most successful tour came in 1995, to promote the album *Wildflowers* (released in 1994).

Welcome to Hollywood! Tom Petty and the Heartbreakers sold out two performances at the Hollywood Bowl in Los Angeles. Tom produced a record gross figure for a multi-night engagement by a single artist at the Bowl. When Tom takes the stage in Hollywood, the stars are bound to turn out. It was a warm day in June. The 18,000+ seat venue nestled in the Hollywood Hills was packed with fans of all ages. The VIP guest list changed by the minute. Dinner, originally planned for 75, jumped to 165 in a matter of minutes. Our crew scrambled to accommodate the additional guests for the first evening of Tom's two-day engagement. The backstage area was packed with guests and friends. The musician's daughter was present with several friends as well.

Tom feels very strongly about supporting humanitarian efforts such as AmFar (American Foundation for AIDS Research), Greenpeace, the National Veteran's Foundation, and USA Harvest. Many representatives from these groups were spotted backstage. The crowd scene made finishing the staging difficult for the crew, but you make do—this is Hollywood after all. The performer and his band arrived at the venue in what looked like a presidential caravan. The train of vehicles escorted by motorcycle officers of the Los Angeles Police Department included vans with the band members, limousines, Mercedes, and Lincoln Town cars with record company executives, managers, family members, and agents. It was quite an entourage.

Dressing rooms, staircases, and hallways were filled with friends and family throughout the night. The hospitality beverages and foods constantly needed to be replenished.

While the band and guests enjoyed the Roasted Pork Loin with Mango Chutney, Tom requested two separate meals be ready for him in his dressing room at 6:00 P.M. The requested meals consisted of ". . . a chicken breast (not a whole roasted chicken) served with mashed potatoes and gravy and cooked peas or carrotts (no broccolli or cauliflower, etc.) bread or roll. The pasta dinner should be served with a red sauce. Have two dinners ready with silverware and napkins." Obviously, whoever drafted this request wasn't the best speller, but he or she got the point across.

As the band began its encore, the police-escorted caravan moved into place backstage. We quickly stocked the vehicles with beverages. The engines were running and doors wide open. The band played their final tune and literally ran into the waiting vehicles directly behind the stage. They were whisked away into the warm night with lights and sirens blazing. All hopes of the Hollywood elite to meet the famous musician were dashed. The VIPs were escorted backstage following the performance only to discover the road crew packing up the stage gear for the night.

Tom Petty Dressing Room Requirements:

- coffee and tea service
- 1 gallon milk
- 1 jar honey
- 1 box sugar
- 18 bottles of Coke
- 12 cans Caffeine Free Diet Coke
- 24 natural soft drinks
- 4 quarts orange juice
- 8 quarts green Gatorade
- 6 Knudsen spritzer
- 8 quarts Recharge
- 8 bottles of sparkling water (not Perrier)
- 12 1.5-liter bottles Evian
- 6 Corona
- 6 Budweiser long necks
- 6 Miller Lite
- 1 vegetable tray including spinach, 2 large tomatoes, sprouts and parsley
- 1 fresh fruit basket
- 1 fruit tray
- 1 tuna salad
- 1 egg salad
- 1 loaf of wheat bread
- 1 loaf of protein bread
- 1 box melba toast
- 6 Yoplait yogurts
- 1 bowl raw unsalted almonds
- 1 bowl raw unsalted cashews
- 1 bowl mixed nuts

The Menu

Roasted Pork Loin with
Mango Chutney Sauce

Roasted Italian Vegetable Torte

Mediterranean Island Sanwich

Island Vinaigrette

ROASTED PORK LOIN WITH MANGO CHUTNEY SAUCE

1   4- to 6-pound whole pork loin, cleaned
(leave some fat to seal in juices)

3   tablespoons kosher salt

4   tablespoons cracked black pepper
fresh mint or rosemary for garnish

1. On a sheet pan place the pork loin dusted with salt and pepper.

2. Roast in a 375° oven for approximately 35 to 45 minutes until golden brown.

3. Remove from the oven, slice thin, and fan three or four slices on each plate. Drizzle with Mango Chutney Sauce, and garnish with a fresh mint leaf or rosemary sprig.

SERVES 8

MANGO CHUTNEY SAUCE

1   tablespoon olive oil

1   medium white onion, chopped

½   cup brandy

1   cup red wine vinegar

½   cup sugar

½   teaspoon white pepper

1   quart Demi-Glace (see index; may substitute prepared "Bisto" gravy)

2   tablespoons French Roux (see index)

10   to 12 ounces Major Grey's Mango Chutney (or comparable brand)

1. In a medium saucepan heat the olive oil and sauté the onions until translucent.

2. Add the brandy, vinegar, sugar, and white pepper. Let simmer for 5 minutes over medium heat. Add the Demi-Glace or Bisto mixture, and continue to simmer for 30 minutes over low heat.

3. Thicken the sauce with the French Roux. Add the chutney and cook, stirring constantly, for approximately 5 minutes to incorporate the flavors.

ROASTED ITALIAN VEGETABLE TORTE

1	cup sliced portabella mushrooms
1	medium zucchini squash, sliced
1	small eggplant, sliced
¼	cup olive oil
1½	teaspoon salt
½	teaspoon black pepper
4	cloves fresh garlic, peeled and diced
1	red bell pepper
6	large eggs
¼	cup heavy whipping cream
½	teaspoon dry basil
½	teaspoon dry whole oregano
1	tablespoon chopped fresh parsley
½	cup shredded mozzarella cheese
½	cup shredded Provolone cheese
½	cup fresh grated parmesan cheese
2	butter pastry pie shells (plain)
½	cup sautéed sliced onion

1. On a lightly oiled sheet pan arrange the mushrooms, zucchini, and eggplant (sliced ⅛ inch thick). Sprinkle with olive oil, a pinch of salt, a pinch of pepper, and finely chopped garlic. Roast in a 375° oven for 10 minutes. Set aside to cool.

2. While the vegetables are roasting in the oven, lightly oil the outer skin of the red pepper. Place on a grill or the open flame of a gas stove, continually turning, until the skin is completely charred. While still hot, place in a 1-quart Ziploc bag. The skin will steam off in the bag. Peel the pepper under running water, clean, and julienne.

3. In a blender, combine 6 eggs, the heavy cream, remaining salt and pepper, basil, oregano, and parsley. Blend on low speed (to prevent frothing) for 8 to 10 seconds.

4. In a medium bowl combine all shredded cheeses and set aside.

5. In each pie shell place ¼ cup of egg mixture. Sprinkle lightly with cheese. Next, add a single layer of roasted eggplant. Layer ¼ cup of egg mixture, more cheese, then a layer of mushrooms, then egg mixture, then cheese, then zucchini, then egg mixture then cheese, then onion and peppers, the remaining egg mixture, and the remaining cheese. Be careful not to overfill the shell to prevent quite a messy scene in the oven.

   If you have vegetables left over, seal them in an airtight bag or container and store in the refrigerator. They will make an excellent sandwich (serve on squaw bread with some light cream cheese) for a healthy late night snack!

6. Bake at 325° for approximately 20 to 25 minutes until the crust is golden and the torte is firm to the touch. If the torte appears too brown before fully cooking, cover it loosely with foil.

SERVES 8

MEDITERRANEAN ISLAND SANDWICH

8　torpedo rolls, cut three-fouths through lengthwise

1½ cups quartered artichoke hearts

1　cup sundried tomatoes (poached or marinated)

1 ½ cups peeled and cubed cucumber

1　cup red/Bermuda onion

¼　cup chopped black olives

¼　cup capers

2　tablespoons chopped fresh Italian parsley

8　large leaves green leaf lettuce, washed

2　cups crumbled dry feta cheese

　　Island Vinaigrette (recipe follows)

1. Line the inside of each torpedo roll with lettuce. Fill the rolls with equal amounts of artichoke hearts, sundried tomatoes, cucumber, red onion, black olives, capers, and some feta cheese.

2. Top with Island Vinaigrette and additional feta cheese. Garnish with chopped Italian parsley.

SERVES 8

ISLAND VINAIGRETTE

¼　cup lemon juice

½　cup red wine vinegar

1　teaspoon dry basil

1　teaspoon dry whole oregano

½　teaspoon finely chopped fresh garlic

1　tablespoon Dijon or whole grain mustard

　　pinch salt

　　pinch black pepper

¾　cup olive oil

1. In a blender combine all of the ingredients except the olive oil. Blend at medium-high for 1 minute.

2. Continue blending, slowly adding the olive oil until the dressing emulsifies. Refrigerate until chilled.

CHAPTER 24

——

LUTHER VANDROSS

Ever had one of those days when none of your clothes seem to fit? It's not a problem for this talented musician. He travels with a complete wardrobe to accommodate his fluctuating waistline.

Fettuccine Alfredo
Chicken Cordon Bleu
Spicy 7, 8, 9, 10 Bean Soup

Luther Vandross' career began on New York's lower east side while he was in high school. He was an accomplished pianist and devout fan of Aretha Franklin and Diana Ross. His first big break was in 1972, when a song he composed was chosen for use in the Broadway musical *The Wiz*. Two years later, Vandross teamed up with David Bowie as an arranger and to sing backgrounds. It was his relationship with Bowie that led to his meeting with actress and singer Bette Midler. Luther sang backup vocals for Bette on an album, as well as on tour. Luther's talents as an arranger and vocalist began to get noticed, and he was soon singing with the likes of Barbra Streisand. In 1975, Luther formed his own group, "Luther." However, it wasn't until 1981 that his solo career really got moving. He released his debut solo album with Epic Records, *Never Too Much*. Since that time, Luther has toured and continued to produce and write songs artists including Whitney Houston, Aretha Franklin, and Teddy Pendergrass.

Luther Vandross took to the road in 1991 on the "Power of Love" tour. That tour grossed over $15 million in ticket sales, selling out venues from coast to coast. While on tour and throughout his career, Luther has struggled with his weight, as do many busy musicians who spend long periods of time on the road and performing. Because of this, wardrobe can become quite a problem as an artist's weight fluctuates. Luther solved that problem by traveling with three complete sets of wardrobe (that is about ten rolling wardrobe road cases). He always wears the finest clothes and his seamstress never gets a break.

The *Power of Love* album not only preceded the 1991 tour, but contained such chart-topping hits as "Power of Love/ Love Power." This song and album earned the performer two Grammy Awards.

While serving the popular songwriter and musician along with the crew of "Divas" that grace the stage with him, we were careful to offer both hearty and healthy cuisine. While the Fettucine Alfredo and Chicken Cordon Bleu weren't exactly low in fat and calories, Luther's dressing room food (carrots, peaches, grapes and other tropical fruits and juices) was a bit more healthy.

The "Power of Love" tour found Behind The Scenes catering to this artist both in Hollywood and San Diego. A Luther Vandross concert resembles a piece of artwork, from the wardrobe to the choreographed stage performance. Not only does the artist and his entourage dress well, but he travels with an Ambiance Coordinator to take care of all the details like setting the dressing room, ordering food for after the show, and any other special requests. Luther was traveling at this time with quite an entourage, including his band, an orchestra, his backup vocalists and the dancing divas. They all required separate dressing rooms and separate hospitality food and beverage service.

During the show our staff delivered two bottles of Piper Heidsieck champagne to Luther's dressing room. These were chilled and ready for a toast after each performance. The dressing room decor included several soft velvet couches and oversized chairs. The room was lit with two table lamps, one shade covered with a colorful scarf to help set the mood of the room. The room was kept at a comfortable, yet slightly warm, temperature to protect the artist's vocal cords. Candles were lit to add to the ambiance. All of Luther's dressing room requirements were displayed just as he likes them on a side table. And on an end table to the right of the couch was a bowl of fresh rose petals that brightened the room with their light scent.

Under normal circumstances, prior to the end of his performance, all the tour buses would be stocked with late night snacks. In Hollywood, however, there were no buses. The tour entourage opted to drive or fly to San Diego for the next performance. So the snacks, including chicken strips, quesadillas, spare ribs, popcorn shrimp, and loads of Buffalo wings, were delivered to the production office. The band and crew stopped by and picked up to-go containers with their preferred snack selections. Health conscious cuisine was definitely not on the menu! Many band members and crew had families in Los Angeles so they returned to their homes after the performance and made their way to San Diego the following day.

Luther Vandross Dressing Room Requirements:

- 1 plate of carrot sticks
- 1 fresh fruit tray
- 10 peaches
- red seedless grapes
- tea service including Celestial Seasonings Apple Orchard and Apple Cinnamon
- 4 cans Crystal Light assorted flavors
- 2 boxes Crystal Light Popsicles or diet Popsicles
- 24 bottles Evian (small bottles)
- 4 cans Caffeine Free Diet Coke
- 4 cans Diet 7Up
- 4 cans Caffeine Free Diet Shasta — root beer, peach, cherry, raspberry
- 4 cans Diet Rite Kiwi Strawberry or Passion Plum
- 4 cans Diet Orange Slice
- 4 quarts assorted Gatorade
- 1 quart fresh-squeezed orange juice

- 1 bottle red wine
- 1 bottle white wine
- tea service
- 2 bottles Piper Heidsieck champagne with glassware

The Menu

Fettuccine Alfredo

Chicken Cordon Bleu

Spicy 7, 8, 9, 10 Bean Soup

FETTUCCINE ALFREDO

8	cups heavy whipping cream
2	cups shredded parmesan cheese
1	teaspoon salt
1	teaspoon black pepper
2	pounds Fettuccine, cooked al dente
1	tablespoon Italian parsley

1. In a large stock pot bring the heavy cream to a boil over medium high heat. Be careful not to let the cream boil over. Reduce the heat to medium-low and simmer for 10 to 15 minutes or until the cream slightly thickens into a rich texture.

2. Whip in 1 cup of Parmesan cheese, salt, and pepper. Add the piping hot fettuccine and toss thoroughly. Garnish with the remaining Parmesan cheese and chopped Italian parsley.

Can be served as an entrée or side dish. Use nonfat milk to replace half of the cream to lighten the fat and calorie content. You will have to thicken the sauce with a water and flour roux if you choose this lighter option. Lemon zest also makes a beautiful garnish atop this rich dish!

SERVES 8

Chicken Cordon Bleu

8	6- to 8-ounce skinless boneless chicken breast halves
½	pound black forest ham, thinly sliced
1	pound French Swiss cheese, sliced
1	teaspoon salt
1	cup all-purpose flour
1	tablespoon black pepper
6	large eggs
4	cups seasoned bread crumbs
2	cups canola oil

1. Slice each chicken breast sideways, three fourths through, to form a pocket in the center of each breast.

2. Stuff each breast evenly with ham and cheese.

3. In a shallow dish combine the flour, salt, and pepper. Dust each breast lightly with the flour mixture and set aside.

4. In a separate bowl whisk or blend the eggs until well stirred. Dip each floured breast into the egg mixture, then roll in seasoned bread crumbs. Set aside.

5. Preheat the oven to 375°. In a large sauté pan heat the canola oil to medium-high heat. Be sure not to overheat the oil or the chicken will cook unevenly.

6. Cook the breaded chicken breasts in oil until golden brown on both sides, approximately 4 minutes. Remove from the oil and drain on a paper towel. Place the partially cooked breasts on a nonstick coated sheet pan.

7. Bake the chicken for an additional 7 to 10 minutes.

8. Remove from the oven and serve atop a bed of tossed baby greens.

SERVES 8

SPICY 7, 8, 9, 10 BEAN SOUP
(VEGETARIAN)

¾   tablespoon ground cumin

1   teaspoon ground fennel

½   teaspoon ground coriander

12   cups vegetable stock

½   teaspoon cayenne pepper

1   teaspoon coarse black pepper

1   teaspoon salt

1   tablespoon finely chopped fresh garlic

1   cup diced celery

2   cups chopped white onion

1   cup diced carrots

3   cups mixed beans, uncooked, presoaked overnight

1   tablespoon chopped fresh sage

1. In a large stock pot combine the cumin, fennel, and coriander. Toast the seasonings over medium-high heat stirring constantly, for 2 to 3 minutes.

2. Stir in the stock, cayenne pepper, coarse pepper, salt, garlic, celery, onion, carrots, and presoaked beans. Bring to a boil. Reduce the heat and simmer for 50 to 90 minutes (depending on size of beans).

3. Stir in the fresh sage and continue to simmer an additional 20 to 30 minutes.

Optional: Add fresh vegetables to make a stew. For example, in step 3 stir in julienned carrots, quartered potatoes, baby corn, cauliflower, or fresh green beans. This is a great soup to let your creativity flow.

SERVES 8+

CHAPTER 25

~~~~

JIMMY BUFFETT

Hollywood brings out the unusual on Friday nights. However, they were hard to spot in the crowd of "Parrotheads" who traveled from across the state to witness this legendary performer. The tailgaters were even greeted by the crew in a roving beverage cart that traveled with the band.

Bouillabaisse

Toasted Crostini with Roué

Chilled Asparagus Salad

Nestled in among the equipment travel-ing with Jimmy Buffett's tour was "the golf cart." As it coasted by, everyone would stop and stare. Now, this wasn't your ordinary golf cart. This was the "Domino College Summer Session Tour '95 Golf Cart." It came equipped with its own blender and six Corona bottle hold-ers (Corona was the tour sponsor). Palm trees, banners, parrots, and similar themed items flapped in the wind as the cart drove by. It was quite an eyeful!

The cart was used by Jimmy and his crew to cruise the "parrot head" picnics that covered the parking areas at concert sites. We would stock the cart with refreshments and off it would go, some-times returning with a lovely young lady on its makeshift hood. The crew would distribute Coronita bottles and other paraphernalia to anxious concert ticket holders gath-ered in the parking lot. Securing a ride was a real treat. "Parrot heads" would go nuts trying to snap a quick photo of the contraption as it zipped by.

This particular tour stop was in Holly-wood. Jimmy played to a sold-out crowd of 18,000+ in the Hollywood Bowl—fitting for such a leg-end. But Jimmy never intended to become the music legend he now is.

Born on Christmas Day in 1946, Jimmy grew up in Mobile, Alabama, and attended McGill Toolen Catholic School in his youth. He then attended Auburn Uni-versity and finished his degree in history at the University of Southern Mississippi in 1969. Jimmy signed his first record contract with Barnaby Records in 1970. At first, Jimmy would play solo acoustic shows and introduce a fictitious backup band he called the Coral Reefers.

The original Coral Reefer Band, as introduced in those early days, was Jimmy Buffett (vocals, guitar); Marvin Gardens (guitar, country maracas); Kay

Pasa (bass); Kitty Litter (background vocals), and Al Vacado (drums). The crowd always got a good laugh during the routine.

Jimmy later added real members to his touring entourage, and the Coral Reefer Band became a reality. Greg Taylor (harmonica) and Michael Utley (keyboards) were the first two members to join. On his *Christmas Island* album, there were 14 or 15 "real" band members playing percussion, bass, saxophone, trumpet, and singing backup vocals. In fact, Sheryl Crow sang backup vocals on "Off to See the Lizard," though she was never an actual band member.

Jimmy doesn't bask in the limelight of his success. Instead, he uses his popularity and resources to aid several environmental concerns. He heads the Save the Manatee Club and was a founder of Friends of Florida, a group dedicated to preserving the Florida ecostructure.

Much of Jimmy's charity work revolves around Florida's natural environment, since he makes his home there most of the year. While his primary residence is Palm Beach, Florida, he also has homes in Key West, Long Island, New Orleans, and a ranch near Orlando, Florida.

Jimmy tours year round. He packs the crowds in for every show, selling out every venue he plays. To date, Jimmy has released more than 30 albums. His fans flock to all his public appearances. It is with songs like "Margaritaville," and "Cheeseburger in Paradise," that the performer has earned such notoriety.

The 1995 Hollywood Bowl concert became a huge backstage party. With all the tour guests and inebriated fans one almost forgot there was a concert to be played. The tour sponsor Corona delivered 65 cases of Corona to be used backstage and for VIP guests. Two cases of Pinot Grigio wine were iced down for the artist and Coral Reefer Band. The menu we served was chic California from Bouillabaisse to Chilled Asparagus Salad. No, cheeseburgers were not on the menu, but the selections were a bite of paradise.

The sold-out show brought with it the many Hollywood elite. Many of these VIP guests were ushered off to a separate area backstage and served Corona and light appetizers prior to the performance. Jimmy made a brief appearance, but it was as if the crowd was there to be seen, rather than to meet the artist.

Jimmy himself was very friendly to all our staff. He loves what he does; you can see it in his performance and hear it when he talks. He is very devoted to all his fans and takes the time to thank them and his crew during his performance. After dinner, Jimmy took a moment to thank our chef for the dinner served that evening. This doesn't often happen, so when it does it means that much more.

The backstage festivities continued through the afternoon and evening. Fans and guests continued to party in the hospitality tent as well as in the parking lot adjacent to the backstage, after the concert had ended. In fact, as the last of our equipment was packed, parking lot revel-ers were starting to fade. Thirst and dehydration began to set in, as well as the reality of getting home from the Hol-lywood Bowl. We offered some ice cold bottled water to the fans which were quickly snatched up—all five cases. It was the least we could do. These same devoted fans had kept us entertained throughout the afternoon as we prepared meals for the band and crew.

Jimmy Buffett Dressing Room Requirements:

- 1 case Coronita beer
- 2 liters Evian

The Menu

Bouillabaisse
Toasted Crostini with Roué
Chilled Asparagus Salad

BOUILLABAISSE

2   tablespoons olive oil
¼   cup chopped fresh garlic
1   cup chopped white onions
4   cups Your Basic Shrimp Stock (see index)
2   cups diced Italian plum tomatoes, skinless and seedless
4   cups sea clam juice
1   cup white wine
½   teaspoon whole saffron
1   teaspoon white pepper
1   teaspoon salt
2   stalks fennel root with leaf
2   pounds white fish fillet (i.e. halibut, sea bass, etc.), cubed
1   pound green lip or black mussels, cleaned
1   pound little neck clams, cleaned
1   pound raw shrimp (U21/24), cleaned, peeled, and deveined
1   10-ounce lobster tail (optional)
2   tablespoons chopped Italian parsley
2   tablespoons chopped fresh basil

1. In a large stock pot heat the olive oil and sauté the garlic and onions over medium

heat until the onions soften. Add the shrimp stock, tomatoes, clam juice, and white wine. Increase the heat to high and bring to a boil.

2. Reduce the heat to medium-high. Add the saffron, white pepper, salt, and fennel. Stir well for 3 to 4 minutes. Increase the heat to high and add the fish, mussels, and clams. Bring to a rockin' boil. Reduce the heat to low, cover, and simmer for approximately 15 minutes. Remove the lid and add the shrimp and lobster (optional).

3. Increase the heat to medium and continue to simmer for 5 minutes or until the shrimp and lobster are cooked. Add the parsley and basil. Serve in a large tureen or in medium soup plates. Serve with Toasted Crostini with Roué (recipe follows).

SERVES 8+

TOASTED CROSTINI WITH ROUÉ

½   cup olive oil
1   tablespoon finely chopped fresh garlic
1   teaspoon dry whole oregano
1   teaspoon dry basil
½   teaspoon dry rosemary
½   teaspoon salt
    pinch black pepper
1   thin French baguette, sliced into ¼-inch angled ovals

1. Preheat the oven to 375°. In a small mixing bowl, combine the olive oil, garlic, oregano, basil, rosemary, salt, and pepper.

2. Place the bread ovals on a baking sheet in a single layer. Baste the tops of the bread with the oil-herb mixture. Bake for 8 to 10 minutes or until golden brown.

ROUÉ

1   cup roasted red bell pepper
1   teaspoon chopped fresh garlic
1/2 teaspoon salt
1/2 teaspoon cayenne pepper
2   tablespoons olive oil
2   tablespoons lemon juice

1. In a blender, combine all of the ingredients and blend approximately 1 minute on medium until the mixture appears creamy and pasty.

2. Spread on crostini and serve with Bouillabaisse.

CHILLED ASPARAGUS SALAD

1   tablespoon olive oil
1½ cups julienned red bell peppers
1   cup julienned red/Bermuda onion
½   teaspoon salt
½   teaspoon cracked black pepper
3   pounds fresh asparagus, cleaned and bottoms (1"-2") removed

Sweet Balsamic Vinaigrette (see index)
1   cup grated asiago cheese
1   tablespoon chopped Italian parsley

1. In a medium sauté pan heat the olive oil and sauté the peppers, onions, salt, and pepper over medium-high heat for approximately 5 minutes making sure that the vegetables maintain a medium crispness. Remove from the heat and set aside.

2. In a stock pot bring 6 quarts of water to a boil (add a pinch of salt to the water). Poach the asparagus in water approximately 3 minutes or until semi-cooked. Remove from the heat, drain in a colander, and rinse until cool with cold running water.

3. On a large white oval platter or on individual salad plates, place off center equal amounts of the pepper and onion mixture. Fan approximately 6 to 8 asparagus spears in the center of the peppers. Refrigerate for 45 minutes. Remove from the refrigerator, drizzle with Sweet Balsamic Vinaigrette, and sprinkle with Asiago cheese and parsley. You're ready to rock!

SERVES 8

CHAPTER 26

——⁓⁓⁓——

EARTH, WIND & FIRE

Step right up for your Winterfresh breath mint chicken!

Korean Chicken/Shrimp
Ginger Glazed Baby Carrots
Fruit Salad with Orange
   Amaretto Sauce

Thankfully, Behind the Scenes doesn't have many catering disaster stories to share, but this one sure makes up for it! We have had several opportunities to cater for the Earth, Wind & Fire over the years, so we decided to offer a different menu selection to add a bit of variety to the band's usual chicken or fish. So the production manager and Teresa decided on Korean Chicken and Shrimp. It sounded pretty innocent; it's an entrée we had prepared several times in the past. The band was looking forward to the change of pace.

Sean Fisher prepared the dinner entrée for the band. He was a big fan of the group and wanted to make sure the dinner was just right. As you will see, the recipe calls for fresh mint to be used. Well, in its absence, Sean took a bit of creative license and decided to substitute a drop of mint extract to intensify the flavor. What he didn't realize was he had grabbed the mint concentrate by mistake. Oops! Close your eyes and you were whisked away to a cool arctic island with your Behind the Scenes peppermint patty—I mean chicken! By the time Sean realized what had happened, it was too late. There was no time to prepare a new chicken entree. So, the staff set out the meal and served it, praying the band would enjoy it. The reaction was remarkably mixed. The other flavors of the meal complimented the chicken for the most part. Many remarked that they found the meal interesting and refreshing. Needless to say, do not substitute mint extract or concentrate for fresh mint. But if you do, you certainly will not need an after dinner mint breath freshener.

When Earth, Wind & Fire started out in 1972, they were called the Salty Peppers. The band went through three labels and several band members before signing with Columbia Records with their current lineup, in 1973. The band had their first gold single, "That's the Way of the World," in 1975. In 1976, Maurice White (Earth, Wind & Fire's band leader) formed Kalimba Productions and released the album *Spirit.* The name Kalimba came from the African thumb piano Maurice often played on stage. He used this instrument in much of the band's music as the connection between the African culture and the band's pop music influence.

Earth, Wind & Fire consists of Maurice White, Phillip Bailey (lead vocals and percussion), Larry Dunn (keyboards), Alan McKay (guitar, percussion, and sitar), Freddie White (drums), Verdine White (bass and percussion), and Andrew Woolfolk (sax and flute).

This band was one of the first groups to embrace their African-American heritage within their music. Their use of African instruments and the onstage robes they wore added to the blending of their ancestral culture and the pop music medleys they produced.

After the band ate their peppermint patty chicken, or rather, Korean Chicken, we uncorked bottles of Puligny Montrachet wine, as requested. After enjoying their after-dinner beverages for about an hour, the band retired to their dressing rooms to prepare for the show. At 8:00 P.M., Earth, Wind & Fire hit the stage for a sold-out crowd. Their disco-style tunes like "Shining Star," "All in All," and "Runnin'" dazzled the crowds more than fifteen years after their original release. The band's songs never seem to fade in popularity. Rhythm and blues artists and rappers continue to sample from the group's music. The band doesn't seem to mind though, viewing it as a compliment to their music and success.

Earth, Wind & Fire Dressing Room Requirements:

- 1 gallon apple juice
- 1 gallon grape juice
- 1 gallon orange juice
- 1 half gallon cranberry juice
- 2 bottles Evian
- 2 bottles Lynch Bages red (1982–1989)
- 2 bottles Poully Montrachet white
- 1 case Heineken
- 6 bottles St. Pauli Girl
- 1 case assorted soda
- tea service including natural ginseng and herbal teas
- coffee service
- hot vegetable soup
- 1 box red cayenne pepper
- raisins and assorted nuts
- 1 fruit tray
- 1 fruit basket
- 6 Dannon yogurt
- 1 deli and condiment tray
- 1 whole wheat bread

- 1 plain tuna salad
- 1 plain chicken salad
- 1 jar Jif peanut butter & grape jelly
- 1 bag pretzels and potato chips
- 1 bag trail mix
- 10 mixed granola bars
- 1 bag organic corn chips
- 1 bag sunflower seeds
- Hors d'oeuvres may include: shrimp, buffalo wings, crab cakes, turkey meat balls, egg rolls and dim sum, salmon croquettes, barbecue chicken, sushi, salads, pasta, southern fried chicken, fish sticks, Thai, or Mexican.

The Menu

Korean Chicken/Shrimp
Ginger Glazed Sweet Baby Carrots
Fruit Salad with Orange Amaretto
Sauce

KOREAN CHICKEN/SHRIMP

½   cup soy sauce
¼   cup hoison sauce
½   cup seasoned rice wine vinegar
2   tablespoons sesame seeds
1   tablespoon fresh garlic, finely chopped
¼   cup honey
2   tablespoons cleaned and chopped fresh
ginger
¼   cup diced green onion
1   tablespoon chopped fresh mint
2   tablespoons chopped fresh cilantro
(no stems)
1   teaspoon ground black pepper
½   teaspoon hot chili sauce
8   6-ounce boneless/skinless chicken breasts
or thighs or 3½ pounds raw shrimp (U10/15),
cleaned, peeled, and deveined
¼   cup sesame oil
    long grain and wild rice

Garnish
   chopped cilantro
   chopped scallions
   toasted sesame seeds

1. In a large mixing bowl combine all ingredients except the sesame oil and chicken or shrimp. Beat with a whisk. Slowly add the oil and continue to whisk.

2. Place the chicken or shrimp in a marinating dish and coat with marinade. Cover and refrigerate for 1 hour (shrimp), or 3 hours (chicken).

3. Preheat the grill to medium-high. Remove chicken or shrimp from the refrigerator and grill shrimps for 3 to 4 minutes per side or chicken for 6 to 8 minutes per side, rotating and turning twice. (May want to skewer your shrimp depending upon the size used.) Place atop a bed of seasoned long grain and wild rice. Garnish with chopped cilantro, scallions, and toasted sesame seeds.

SERVES 8

GINGER GLAZED SWEET BABY CARROTS

2 tablespoons olive oil

2 tablespoons chopped shallots

3 tablespoons ginger root, peeled and grated

1½ cups spring water

1 cup sugar

¼ teaspoon salt

¼ teaspoon white pepper

2 pounds peeled baby carrots

Garnish

fresh chopped parsley

toasted sesame seeds (Toast in oven for 6 to 8 minutes at 400°.)

1. In a medium sauté pan, heat the olive oil over medium-high heat and sauté the shallots and ginger root for 6 to 8 minutes until golden brown and translucent.

2. Add the spring water and sugar, and bring to boil.

3. Reduce the heat immediately to low and simmer for approximately 35 to 45 minutes until the liquid achieves a glazing texture. Stir in the salt and white pepper. While the glaze is simmering, in a separate stock pot boil the water and cook the carrots for 10 to 12 minutes until al dente.

4. Bring the carrots back to temperature by immersing for 30 to 45 seconds in boiling water. Toss the hot carrots in the glazing sauce. Serve garnished with fresh chopped parsley or toasted sesame seeds.

SERVES 8

FRUIT SALAD WITH ORANGE AMARETTO SAUCE

1 6-ounce can orange juice concentrate

1 cup Amaretto

2 cups spring water

1½ cups sugar

2 cups chunked cantaloupe melon

2 cups chunked honeydew melon

1½ cups chunked fresh pineapple

1 cup skinned and cubed pink grapefruit pieces

1 cup skinned and cubed orange pieces

1½ cups strawberries, tops removed and halved

1 cup fresh blueberries, washed and stems removed

1½ cups kiwi fruit rings

sprigs fresh mint

1. In a medium saucepan combine the orange juice concentrate, Amaretto, water, and sugar. Bring to a boil over high heat. Reduce the heat to low and simmer, stirring occasionally, for 20 to 25 minutes or until the sauce thickens. Remove from the heat and let cool to room temperature.

2. In a large mixing bowl toss the chilled fruit with the sauce. Garnish with sprigs of fresh mint.

SERVES 8+

ELVIS COSTELLO
AND THE
ATTRACTIONS

BRUTAL YOUTH
WORLD TOUR 1994

16. Mai 1994

CREW

local
crew

Tom Jones
world
tour '95

CHAPTER 27

~~~

R.E.M.

Backstage was a family affair with this seasoned touring group. And some of our Cajun favorites certainly spiced up the atmosphere.

Cajun Roasted Chicken
Cajun Sauce
Black Jack Peas

R.E.M., a band often associated with the 1980s, consists of Michael Stipe (lead vocals), Mike Mills (bass), Peter Buck (guitar), and Bill Berry (drums). The band, whose name was chosen from a dictionary because members felt it was so ambiguous, has released more than fourteen albums over their two-decade career. Their popularity never seems to wane. R.E.M.'s albums, including *Document, Green, Out of Time, Automatic for the People, Monster,* and *New Adventures in HiFi,* all seem to have their own unique sound. This sound is carried over to the band's live performances.

In 1995, on the "Monster" tour, R.E.M. dazzled fans with special concert renditions of many of their popular songs like, "Man on the Moon," and "What's the Frequency, Kenneth?" The band's success was brought to the music news front when they signed a five-album deal with Warner Brothers valued at $80 million.

With their success came sophistication. R.E.M. traveled with a tour wine list containing high quality bottles of red and white wines. The tour manager would make selections off this list to be provided in the artists' dressing room, "the family room," backstage and to the tour production office. In October 1995, in San Diego, the band consumed nearly $600 worth of wine. Labels as Kistler Vine Hill Vineyard, and Chateau Morguex Bordeaux Red were just a few of the choices.

The backstage atmosphere was casual because band members were traveling with family and friends. The artists had two dressing rooms set for them and one family/hospitality room. However, once the band hit the stage the tone was purely business. The near sell-out crowd of 14,000 enthusiastically grooved to the sounds of R.E.M. The band played a twenty-four song set, which is a rather lengthy show, but there were no complaints from the exhilarated crowd.

R.E.M. Dressing Room Requirements:

ROOM NUMBER ONE
- 4 liters Mountain Valley Water—NO Evian
- 1 bottle of exceptional red wine
- 1 bottle of exceptional white wine
- 1 witch hazel
- 1 fresh fruit bowl including organic bananas
- tabbouleh and pita bread
- coffee and tea service

ROOM NUMBER TWO
- 1 local daily paper
- 1 *USA Today*
- 2 cases Mountain Valley spring water—NO Evian
- 2 bottles Perrier or Pellegrino
- 1 liter fresh-squeezed orange juice
- 1 liter fresh apple juice
- 1 liter fresh pineapple juice
- 1 bottle exceptional red wine
- 1 bottle exceptional white wine
- 12 bottles microbrewery beer
- 12 cans Coke Classic
- 12 bottles Budweiser
- 6 cans Diet Coke
- 4 quarts green Gatorade
- coffee and tea service
- vegetable tray including red and green peppers
- assorted dips for vegetables including bleu cheese
- 1 package whole roasted sunflower seeds in the shell
- basket fresh fruit—no grapes
- assorted bagels including whole wheat and garlic
- assorted cheese and crackers

The Menu

Cajun Roasted Chicken

Cajun Sauce

Black Jack Peas

CAJUN ROASTED CHICKEN

1	tablespoon seasoned salt
½	teaspoon black pepper
½	teaspoon white pepper
1	tablespoon granulated garlic
1	tablespoon granulated onion
1	tablespoon whole dry oregano
1	tablespoon dry basil
1	tablespoon whole dry thyme
½	teaspoon cayenne pepper
1	tablespoon paprika
2	teaspoons salt
2	4- to 5-pound whole chickens
2	tablespoons olive oil

1. Preheat the oven to 350°. In a food processor, combine all of the ingredients except the chickens and olive oil, and blend well. Transfer the Cajun Rub Mixture to a bowl.

2. Place the chickens on a baking sheet or foil sheet. Thoroughly coat the chickens with the dry Cajun Rub Mixture. Place the chickens side by side in a roasting pan.

3. Roast in the preheated oven for approximately 2 hours. Baste the chickens with natural juices 2 or 3 times during second hour. Remove from the oven and let the chickens stand for 10 to 15 minutes. Remove from the roasting pan, quarter, and serve. Save the drippings for Cajun Sauce.

SERVES 8

CAJUN SAUCE

1	tablespoon olive oil
1	tablespoon finely chopped fresh garlic
¼	cup diced white onion
¼	cup cleaned and diced green bell pepper
	drippings from Cajun Roasted Chicken recipe
2	cups chicken stock
1	tablespoon Cajun Rub Mixture (see Cajun Roasted Chicken)
2	tablespoons Worcestershire sauce
¼	cup barbecue sauce
1	teaspoon dry basil
1	teaspoon dry whole oregano
1	teaspoon dry whole thyme
2	tablespoons French Roux (see index)

1. Skim the fat from the chicken drippings and discard. Set the drippings aside.

2. In a medium saucepan heat the olive oil and sauté the garlic, onion, and green peppers over medium heat for approximately 5 minutes.

3. Increase the heat to high and add the chicken drippings, chicken stock, Cajun Herb Mixture, Worcestershire sauce, barbecue sauce, basil, oregano, and thyme. Bring to a boil. Reduce the heat to medium and simmer for approximately 15 minutes, stirring occasionally. Thicken with French Roux. Serve over chicken or as a side dipping sauce.

BLACK JACK PEAS

¼ cup olive oil

¼ cup finely chopped white onion

¼ cup diced sweet red bell pepper

½ cup Jack Daniel's bourbon whiskey

5 cups cooked black-eyed peas (frozen or fresh)

½ cup chicken or vegetable stock

1 teaspoon salt

1 teaspoon coarse black pepper

¼ cup firmly packed brown sugar

¼ cup butter

¼ cup chopped fresh parsley

1. In a sauté pan, heat the olive oil and sauté the onions and peppers over medium-high heat.

2. Flambé the onion mixture with Jack Daniel's until the flame extinguishes.

3. Add the peas, stock, salt, pepper, and brown sugar. Stir until well coated and the liquid reduces. Add the butter and stir until melted. Garnish with fresh chopped parsley.

SERVES 8+

CHAPTER 28

BARRY MANILOW

This famous crooner melted the hearts of every woman in the audience. He even drew a few tears from their dates. How does Barry keep in shape on tour? Check out his special diet meal.

Shrimp, Artichoke, and Mushroom Salad
Wild Mushroom, Chicken, and Walnut Pasta
Mushroom Marinade

Barry Manilow hit the stage over twenty years ago as a talented piano player, songwriter, arranger, and composer. He is still as popular as ever with his fans—or "friends" as he refers to them.

Barry was born in 1946 in the Williamsburg section of Brooklyn, New York. When he was two, his father abandoned the family, leaving Barry to be raised by his mother and extended family. Barry's grandfather, Joe Manilow, invested a great deal of time in his grandson. Soon, like virtually every Jewish boy in his neighborhood, Barry was persuaded to take up the accordion. After high school Barry studied advertising in college, for lack of interest in any other area. Quickly losing interest in his studies, he entered the New York School of Music and Julliard. At the same time, he was working in the CBS mailroom. At this point, Barry's interests started to focus on his music career. First, he was asked to arrange music for an off-Broadway musical. Barry soon left the mailroom and became musical director for a CBS-TV series. Barry started working with Ed Sullivan Productions and singing for commercials. His career continued to progress and he started to perform, playing piano and singing his own music. Barry's popularity soon exploded in the late '70s with songs like "Can't Smile Without You," "Mandy," and "Copacabana." Crowds couldn't get enough of Barry Manilow.

Fan clubs began to form soon after his career took off. Barry has an extremely loyal and active fan club. Whenever he tours, a group of fans goes backstage to decorate his dressing room and hospitality area. They hang posters and ribbons and fill the room with flowers, stuffed animals, and home-baked cookies, brownies, and fudge. The group is usually made up of five or six giggling middle-aged women. They take their job seriously and consider it an honor.

Barry has performed in a variety of settings with distinctively different formats over the years. For example, he played with an entire choir as backup, he played show tunes with a big band orchestra, and he played solo with his piano as accompaniment. No matter the makeup of the show, the crowd goes wild, especially the women who pack the concerts to hear the crooner sing his love songs. Barry often chooses a lady from the audience to sing with him on stage. In Palm Desert, California, an excited female admirer was pulled up onto the stage and was beside herself. When he asked if she had seen his show before, she melted and answered "Yes, 70 times." The singer smiled, thanked his new friend, and began to sing "Can't Smile Without You" with her.

With all the snacks left backstage, it was surprising to find anyone hungry. Nevertheless, after sound check, Barry, his supporting band, and crew arrived for dinner. Barry, however, requested a special meal: one cup cooked noodles with fresh oregano, basil, salt, and pepper; one cup steamed zucchini; one French roll; a small tossed salad; one tangerine; and one piece of sponge cake. It was a somewhat simple meal for someone who can literally have anything he chooses while on tour.

The singer joked with one of our staff members, who was very concerned that the artist receive the special meal just as requested. As Barry entered the crowded dining room at Symphony Hall, the staff member tripped over an extension cord trying to get to the table to serve the artist, and landed on his knees next to Barry's seat. "Now that is service," responded Barry to the completely embarrassed waiter. "I'd like a small salad from the buffet while you're at it," he added. To try and find a bit of comedy in the embarrassing fall, the staff member walked on his knees over to the buffet line (six feet or so away) and proceeded to assemble a salad for the talented artist. Upon his humble return to the table amid laughter and cheers from those in the room, Barry responded, "I'll let you know when I am ready for dessert. Thank You!" Everyone in the room got a good laugh as the waiter got up and dusted off his knees.

After dinner, the musicians returned to the stage and finished tuning their instruments. This particular show was out-doors along the waterfront. The audience filled every seat and square inch of grass on the peninsula to hear Barry. Sailboats and motor yachts dropped anchor along the rocky coast to hear the sweet sounds of the singer/composer. The lights kicked on, the band came up, and Barry took to the stage in a bright green blazer. The crowd went crazy as he grabbed the microphone and greeted the crowd, including the seabound fans. He thanked his "friends" for coming and began the show. He played all the favorites, including "Somewhere in the Night" almost causing a female fan in the front to faint as he sang it gazing into her eyes.

The show came to a close and the curtain dropped. Satisfied fans slowly exited the venue and Barry exited the stage and made his way to his vehicle. As he did, he stopped along the way to thank our staff and the venue personnel.

Barry Manilow Dressing Room Requirements:

- 2 bottles Evian (large)
- 12 bottles Evian (small)
- 1 bottle Pouilly Fuisse
- 2 quarts orange Gatorade
- 1 quart fresh orange juice
- fresh fruit tray
- vegetable tray
- small bowl mixed nuts
- tea service

Special Requests: After the show two sandwiches were made up for Barry—turkey, Swiss, lettuce, and tomato on wheat bread.

The Menu

Shrimp, Artichoke, and
Mushroom Salad

Wild Mushroom, Chicken, and
Walnut Pasta

Mushroom Marinade

SHRIMP, ARTICHOKE AND MUSHROOM SALAD

3   cups marinated, drained, and quartered artichoke hearts

3   cups marinated and drained button mushrooms

3   cups shrimp (U51/60), peeled, cooked, and deveined

¼   cup diced red/Bermuda onion

1   tablespoon chopped Italian parsley

2   medium red bell pepper, cleaned and julienned

1   cup red wine vinegar

1   teaspoon finely chopped fresh garlic

1½   teaspoons dry whole thyme

1½   teaspoons dry basil

2   tablespoons sugar

salt to taste

black pepper to taste

1   cup olive oil

1. In a large mixing bowl combine the artichoke hearts, mushrooms, shrimp, onions, Italian parsley, and peppers. Toss thoroughly.

2. In a blender combine the vinegar, garlic, thyme, basil, sugar, oregano, salt, and pepper. Blend well on medium speed, approximately 1 minute. Continue blending, slowly adding the olive oil until the mixture emulsifies.

3. Toss the vegetables and shrimp with the dressing. Cover and refrigerate for 1 hour. Remove from the refrigerator, lightly toss, and serve garnished with a sprig of Italian parsley.

SERVES 8 +

WILD MUSHROOM, CHICKEN, AND WALNUT PASTA

¼   cup olive oil

1   tablespoon finely chopped fresh garlic

2   tablespoons finely chopped shallots

1½   pounds boneless, skinless chicken breast, cubed (¾")

½   cup brandy

1½   cups button mushrooms

1½   cups wild mushrooms (fresh or reconstituted)

½   cup chicken stock

1   teaspoon salt

½   teaspoon coarse black pepper

1   cup walnuts, crushed

4   cups heavy whipping cream

1   cup shredded parmesan cheese

2   pounds rigatoni, cooked al dente

2   tablespoons chopped fresh Italian parsley

1. In a large skillet heat the olive oil and sauté the garlic and shallots for 3 to 4 minutes over medium-high heat. Add the cubed chicken and continue to sauté for 5 to 7 minutes. Add the brandy and flambé. Add the mushrooms and chicken stock, and simmer for an additional 6 to 8 minutes, stirring constantly. Add the salt, pepper, and walnuts. Stir well.

2. Add the heavy cream and bring to a boil. Reduce the heat to medium and simmer for an additional 8 to 10 minutes or until the cream begins to thicken.

3. Add ½ cup of Parmesan cheese and the piping hot rigatoni and toss well. Garnish with the remaining Parmesan cheese and fresh chopped Italian parsley.

SERVES 8

MUSHROOM MARINADE

3   cups mushrooms

1   cup red wine vinegar

1   cup olive oil

1   teaspoon chopped fresh Italian parsley

1   teaspoon dry whole thyme

1   teaspoon finely chopped fresh garlic

2   tablespoons diced red/Bermuda onion

½   teaspoon salt

½   teaspoon black pepper

1. In a saucepan combine the vinegar and mushrooms, and bring to a boil over high heat. Reduce the heat to low and simmer for 7 to 10 minutes.

2. Remove from the heat and pour the mushrooms and vinegar into a bowl. Set aside and let cool to room temperature.

3. Add the remaining ingredients and toss well. Cover and refrigerate for 6 to 8 hours.

nine inch nails

CATERING
10/10

self destruct tour

SAN DIEGO

WORKING CREW

George
Strait

4/27/95 CATERING

WORKING
CREW

CHAPTER 29

~~~

FRANK SINATRA

Ol' Blue Eyes' dressing-room requirements didn't change one bit through his many years of performing live concerts. Must haves: A hot crock of Campbell's chicken and rice soup and cherry Lifesavers!

CREW

Grilled New York Steak with Wild
  Mushroom Sauce

Fusilli with a Peppered Vodka
  Sauce

Porcini Mashed Potatoes

What is there to say about this musical legend that hasn't already been said? Backstage at a Frank Sinatra concert was a journey back in time. Many of today's popular acts have young, sometimes inexperienced tour personnel. Not Sinatra! The gentlemen who controlled his tour were definitely seasoned. They had been with Sinatra for many years. They knew his likes, dislikes, and needs. Red carpet was a must for his trip to the stage in the round. A black limousine was required to transport him to and from the venue.

Sinatra's dressing room requirements filled more than a few tables and hadn't changed in years. Like many seasoned performers, he was very superstitious—remove a pack of Lifesavers and risk tampering with fate. Sinatra rarely touched the items in the room except for the bar, the tea service on occasion, and the cough drops or Lifesavers, once in a while. The Campbell's chicken soup was there just to make Mom happy. On this particular tour, Sinatra also requested several Dunhill cigars at the last minute, to be placed in his room.

Sinatra's last tour was in 1993. He came to San Diego at the beginning of December with Don Rickles as his opening act. It was just like the old days when a comedian would warm up the crowd before a concert. These days, up and coming bands tend to open a concert. Sinatra preferred the tried and true and a close friend to introduce him to the crowd. Sinatra moved a little slower than in past years and required a TelePrompTer on the corners of the stage to guide him through the show. The crowd still loved him though. The sighs were audible as fans recognized classic song after classic song.

When the show ended, Sinatra blew kisses to the crowd and thanked them for coming. He needed a little assistance getting off the stage and back to the backstage area. He was helped into his waiting limousine and whisked away with drink in hand. The show lasted little more than an hour, but the near sellout crowd didn't seem to mind. They were happy to share the time with their friend, "Ol' Blue Eyes."

Frank Sinatra Dressing Room Requirements:

- 1 color television, cable ready
- 1 upright piano
- 1 bottle Absolut or Stoli
- 1 bottle Jack Daniel's
- 1 bottle Chivas Regal
- 1 bottle Courvoisier
- 1 bottle Beefeater Gin
- 1 bottle premium white wine
- 1 bottle premium red wine
- 1 bottle spring water
- 1 bottle Perrier
- 24 cans Diet Coke
- 12 cans Coke
- 1 bottle club soda
- assorted mixers
- 1 fruit platter including watermelon
- 1 cheese tray including brie and assorted crackers
- dijon mustard
- 2 egg salad sandwiches

- 2 chicken salad sandwiches
- 2 turkey sandwiches
- 24 chilled jumbo shrimp
- 1 platter of Nova Scotia salmon
- 3 cans Campbell's Chicken & Rice soup (heated)
- 12 rolls Cherry Lifesavers
- 12 rolls assorted Lifesavers
- 12 boxes Luden's cough drops including cherry and honey
- 1 bag miniature Tootsie Rolls
- 1 bowl pretzels
- 1 bowl potato chips
- 6 bottles Evian
- tea service including Lipton or Tetley

The Menu

Grilled New York Steak with Wild
Mushroom Sauce

Fusilli with a Peppered Vodka Sauce

Porcini Mashed Potatoes

GRILLED NEW YORK STEAK WITH WILD MUSHROOM SAUCE

2	tablespoons butter or olive oil
2	tablespoons chopped shallots
4	cups assorted wild and domestic mushrooms
⅓	cup brandy or cognac
1½	cups Demi-Glace (see index)
½	teaspoon salt
¼	teaspoon coarse black pepper
1	cup heavy whipping cream
8	8- to 10-ounce boneless New York strip steaks

1. In a 3-quart saucepan melt the butter or olive oil over medium to medium-high heat. Add the shallots and mushrooms, and sauté for approximately 5 minutes.

2. Add the brandy and flambé until the flames have diminished. Add the Demi-Glace, reduce the heat, and simmer for approximately 15 to 20 minutes or until the sauce begins to thicken.

3. Add salt and pepper to taste. Add the cream, increase the to medium, and continue to heat and stir until the sauce has reached a nice velvety/creamy texture, approximately 4 minutes. Do not overcook, as the sauce will separate. Set aside. You might need to bring back to temperature after the steaks are cooked.

4. Preheat the grill to high heat. Place the steaks on the grill and cook each side for 5 to 6 minutes, rotating twice for rare to medium-rare steaks. Allow slightly more cooking time for medium to well-done steaks.

5. Remove the steaks from the grill, ladle generously with mushroom sauce, and serve.

SERVES 8

FUSILLI WITH A PEPPERED VODKA SAUCE

1½	cups chopped pancetta
1½	cups chopped white onions
2	tablespoons finely chopped fresh garlic
1	tablespoon olive oil
½	teaspoon chili pepper
1½	cups peppered vodka
4	cups Red and Sassy Pomodoro Sauce (see index)
4	cups heavy whipping cream
2	cups shredded Pecorino Romano cheese
2	tablespoons chopped Italian parsley
	salt to taste

black pepper to taste

2　pounds fusilli, cooked al dente

½　cup shredded Parmesan cheese

1. In a large saucepan sauté the pancetta over medium heat for 5 to 7 minutes or until crisp like bacon. Add the onions, garlic, olive oil, and chili pepper. Continue to sauté an additional 3 to 4 minutes.

2. Add the vodka and flambé.

3. Add the Pomodoro Sauce and heavy cream. Increase the heat to medium high and bring to a boil, stirring constantly. Reduce the heat to medium and simmer for 18 to 20 minutes until the sauce begins to thicken.

4. Stir in 1 cup of Pecorino Romano cheese, and 1 tablespoon of parsley. Season with salt and pepper. Toss the sauce with hot pasta. Serve promptly with Parmesan and Pecorino Romano cheese, garnished with Italian parsley.

SERVES 8

PORCINI MASHED POTATOES

1　cup olive oil

1　cup whole peeled cloves fresh garlic

1　cup butter

1½　cup porcini mushrooms, reconstituted

1　teaspoon salt

1　tablespoon black pepper

5　pounds red potatoes, chunked, skin on

1　cup sour cream

1½　cups whole milk

¼　cup finely chopped Italian parsley

1. In a saucepan heat the olive oil and sauté the garlic over medium heat for approximately 5 minutes. Reduce the heat to low, and continue to simmer for an additional 10 minutes or until the garlic appears golden and soft to the touch. Remove from the heat and let cool. Once cool, purée the mixture in a food processor and set aside.

2. In a medium sauté pan melt the butter over medium heat and sauté the porcini mushrooms, a pinch of salt, and a pinch of black pepper for approximately 8 to 10 minutes or until the mushrooms are fully cooked. Remove from the heat and let cool. Purée the mushrooms in a food processor or blender with the garlic mixture.

3. Quarter the potatoes and boil with skins on for 20 to 25 minutes until they are easily mashed with a fork. Remove from the heat and drain.

4. Add the mushroom and garlic purée, remaining butter, sour cream, milk, and remaining salt and pepper. Mash with a hand masher or whisk the potatoes with a hand mixer until they appear creamy with some chunks. Whip in half of the Italian parsley. Garnish with the remaining Italian parsley.

SERVES 8

CHAPTER 30

~~~~

NATALIE COLE

Too bad Ms. Cole didn't invite a few more guests backstage. You could have fed an army with the refreshments in her dressing room. Maybe that's how she stays in shape: She looks at the food rather than eating it.

Ultimate Greek Chicken Salad with Pesto Vinaigrette
Stuffed Pork Loin
Merlot Mission Fig Sauce

Natalie Cole, daughter of jazz and pop legend Nat "King" Cole, is truly a veteran in the entertainment industry. The singer made her stage debut at age eleven and went on to sing in college, hoping someday to follow in her father's footsteps. In 1973, Natalie Cole hooked up with the producing and writing team of Jackson and Yancey. Together, they launched her career with a string of hit singles and albums from 1975 to 1983. During the late 1970s Natalie had several number one hits including "This Will Be" and "I've Got Love on My Mind."

In 1987, Natalie hit the charts with more pop-style hits such as "Jump Start," "I Live for Your Love," and "Over You." In 1991, she released *Unforgettable With Love,* selling over five million albums and receiving a Grammy Award. The album was a compilation of many of the songs first performed by her father back in the 1950s. The title track even contained the artist singing a duet with her late father via electronic manipulation. With the huge success of this jazzy album, Natalie released similar sounds in 1993, with *Take a Look.* Since then, Natalie has continued to tour and play for television specials. We have had the opportunity to prepare meals for the artist on several occasions, including an appearance with the now-defunct San Diego Symphony Orchestra. The concert was a benefit for the symphony and crowds packed the seaside peninsula. More than 5,000 concert fans filled the venue to see Natalie Cole perform.

Having been in the music business for more than 25 years, Natalie was accustomed to being taken care of in a certain manner. She was very "specific" with her dressing room requirements, which rival that of a major rock band like Metallica. There were separate rooms set for musicians, backup vocalists, and symphony personnel.

The 1995 San Diego show almost didn't happen. The concert was a benefit for the Symphony; however, there was a snag: the artist hadn't been paid by the Symphony in a timely fashion. When her limousine arrived at the venue, Natalie refused to get out. As you might imagine, usually such problems are worked out before the day of the show. Natalie was on the car phone with her agent and was advised that they had yet to receive prepayment for the performance and therefore she was not to exit the vehicle. Symphony management panicked. They had a packed house and a performer unwilling to play. The reality was that the Symphony was in the midst of serious financial problems and they were using ticket sale moneys for cash flow purposes. Vendors often were not paid in a timely manner. The artist was finally paid with box office revenues from the evening. Once the payment terms were agreed to, Natalie emerged from her limousine and made her way to the dressing room.

We served a splendid dinner that evening backstage as the sun slowly set over the glistening water. A special dinner was brought to Natalie's dressing room so that she could dine separate from the other musicians and Symphony members.

At 8:00 P.M. the Symphony took the stage to open the concert. Shortly thereafter, Natalie took the stage in front of the sold-out crowd. With the crowd blissfully unaware of the last-minute negotiations, the evening ended and Natalie quickly made her way to the awaiting limousine. As we cleaned up the dressing rooms after the show, we that noticed not one item requested in Natalie Cole's dressing room was touched except a single bottle of Mountain Valley water.

—mm—

Natalie Cole Dressing Room Requirements:

- 1 deli tray for three including ham, turkey, corned beef, American and jack cheese, peppers, lettuce, tomatoes, and sliced avocado (please spray or dip avocados in lemon juice to keep them from browning)
- 1 small loaf of whole wheat bread
- 1 small jar of mayonnaise (keep chilled)
- 1 stick of butter (keep chilled)
- 1 small jar of yellow mustard
- 1 small jar of Dijon mustard
- 1 set of salt & pepper shakers
- 1 bowl plain tuna salad (just tuna & mayo)
- 1 bowl plain chicken salad (just chicken & mayo)
- 1 fruit tray for three including sliced cantaloupe, strawberries, FRESH pineapple, oranges, whole bananas, nectarines, plums, peaches, and grapes (green seedless)
- 1 quart apple juice
- 1 quart grape juice
- 6 32-ounce bottles Mountain Valley water (No substitutions/brand important)*
- 6 Yoo Hoo chocolate drink (very important)*
- 1 bottle chardonnay (Far Niente or Cakebread Cellars)
- 1 bottle Merlot (Good!)

- 6 assorted soda (1 Coke, 1 Diet Coke, 1 Root Veer, 1 7Up, 1 ginger ale, 1 orange, 1 Hawaiian Punch—noncarbonated)
- 1 hot tea service with honey and lemon wedges
- 1 small bottle of apple cider vinegar
- 1 medium bowl of Hershey's Kisses
- 1 box Grapenuts cereal
- 1 jar Jif creamy peanut butter
- 1 box black vine licorice
- 1 box red vine licorice
- 1 potato chips (plain—NO RUFFLES)
- 1 lightly salted popcorn
- 1 bag vanilla creme sandwich cookies
- 1 bag peanut butter sandwich cookies
- 1 bowl dry roasted, unsalted peanuts in the shell—NO MIX!
- Accessories: clean ice, corkscrew, cups with saucers, glassware, silverware, etc.

* If these items are not available, please inform production manager 2 weeks before the show!

The Menu

Ultimate Greek Chicken Salad with
Pesto Vinaigrette

Stuffed Pork Loin

Merlot Mission Fig Sauce

ULTIMATE GREEK CHICKEN SALAD WITH PESTO VINAIGRETTE

2½ pounds mixed baby greens

1   cup poached and julienned sundried toma-
toes

½   cup light vinaigrette (see index)

½   cup thinly sliced red/Bermuda onion

8   6-ounce Greek Chicken Breasts, sliced at
an angle (see index)

2   cups marinated artichoke hearts

1   cup whole black Greek olives

1   cup whole green Greek olives

     Pesto Vinaigrette (recipe follows)

1½   cup dry feta cheese

¾   cup toasted pine nuts

1. In a large mixing bowl combine the mixed
   baby greens and sundried tomatoes. Toss
   lightly with Light Vinaigrette.

2. Place equal amounts of salad on serving
   plates or a large serving bowl. Sprinkle
   the salad(s) with red onion. Fan out
   chicken breast slices in the center of the

salad. Decorate with artichoke hearts and
olives. Drizzle Pesto Dressing over the top
of the salad(s). Garnish with feta cheese
and pine nuts.

SERVES 8

PESTO VINAIGRETTE

¾   cup chopped fresh basil (no stems)

⅓   cup pine nuts

⅓   cup shredded parmesan cheese

½   cup red wine vinegar

1   tablespoon lemon juice

     pinch salt

     pinch black pepper

1   cup olive oil

1. In a blender combine all ingredients
   except the olive oil. Blend on medium
   high for approximately 1 minute.

2. Continue blending, slowly adding the
   olive oil until the dressing emulsifies. Chill
   and serve.

STUFFED PORK LOIN

1	4-pound pork loin roast
2	cups pork stuffing (refer to Stuffed Pork Chops)
½	teaspoon salt
½	teaspoon coarse black pepper
1	teaspoon chopped fresh thyme
	Merlot Mission Fig Sauce (recipe follows)

1. Preheat the oven to 450°.

2. Insert a boning knife through each end of the pork loin, creating an X pattern. Take a sharpening steel and push it through the X cut to other end of the roast. Continue to move the steel to create a stuffing cavity. When complete, remove the steel.

3. Stuff the pork loin with the stuffing mixture through both ends until completely filled. Place the pork loin in a nonstick roasting pan and season with salt, pepper, and thyme. Be sure to place the roast in the pan fatty side up, as this will help seal in the juices when roasted.

4. Roast the pork loin for 15 minutes to sear the roast and seal in the delicious juices. Reduce the oven temperature to 350° and continue to roast for an additional 45 to 55 minutes. Remove from the oven. Let the roast settle for 10 minutes, slice into ¼-inch slices, and serve with Merlot Mission Fig Sauce.

SERVES 8

MERLOT MISSION FIG SAUCE

2	tablespoons olive oil
4	tablespoons finely chopped shallots or white onions
⅓	cup brandy
1	cup merlot red wine
⅓	cup sugar
⅓	cup red wine vinegar
2	cups Demi-Glace (see index)
½	teaspoon salt
1	teaspoon cracked black pepper
1½	cup dried mission figs

1. In a 3-quart saucepan heat the olive oil and sauté the shallots over medium heat until translucent.

2. Add the brandy and flambé. Add the merlot, sugar, and vinegar, and stir well. Simmer over medium heat until the liquid begins to thicken.

3. Add the Demi-Glace, salt, and pepper to taste. Continue to simmer over medium heat for 5 minutes. Thicken with a roux mixture, if necessary.

4. Reduce the heat and poach the dried figs in the sauce for 5 to 7 minutes. Do not overcook or the figs will fall apart and detract from the presentation of the sauce.

This sauce is preferably served with pork; however, it is wonderful over mushroom wild rice or as a compliment to beef.

CHAPTER 31

SEAL

Seal's sharp intellect saved the performer from an attack by a local food critic who was invited backstage. Seal had whimsical yet appropriate responses and questions for this reporter, who had not prearranged the impromptu interview.

Thai Pasta with Spicy
  Peanut Sauce

Buttons and Snaps

Orzo and Caramelized
  Onion Salad

*S*eal released his self-titled debut album in 1991 including the hit single "Crazy." The album was impressive, but Seal himself admitted to its very young and idealistic sounds. His second album, also called *Seal* was far more successful than the first. The artist, whose full name is Sealhenry Samuel, polished his sounds and added a hint of realism. The single "Prayer for the Dying," from his second album, rose to the top of the charts pushing the artist quickly into the limelight. In 1994, he released the single "Kiss from a Rose" as part of the soundtrack from the movie *Batman Forever.* It soon rose to the top of the charts.

Seal was born in 1963. The scars on the 6' 4" artist's face were caused by Lupus, which he suffered from as a child. He grew up in Paddington, England, and started singing at a relatively young age.

We had the opportunity to serve Seal during his summer tour in 1995. The tour was long anticipated and followed the success his album was enjoying on the charts. The concert was held at an outdoor amphitheater on the San Diego State University Campus. The venue provided a multi-level hospitality house adjacent to the stage. The hospitality house contained dressing rooms on the lower level, an outdoor deck on a second level and a family room and kitchen on the top level. This family room is where all the meals were served to the band and crew throughout the day.

A good friend of ours and a beloved San Diego food critic had asked for back-stage access on the premise of writing a feature article on the food we were serving. We received permission from the local promoter and allowed the critic to join the dinner crowd. The dining tables were set with white cloths and votive candles. The room resembled a mountain lodge but felt quaint with the candles and dimmed light. The dinner was set up as a buffet on the outdoor deck. The crew all enjoyed dinner around 5:30 P.M., shortly after sound check was complete. Seal and the band made their way upstairs from their dressing rooms shortly thereafter.

We had warned our guest that she was to sit at the side of the room, eat her dinner, and simply observe. That course of action only satisfied the seasoned reporter for about five minutes. Seal filled his plate and sat on one side of the cozy room at a table by himself. One of our staff members got him a beverage, Evian water, at room temperature to protect his vocal cords. John had left the dining room to check the artist's dressing room while he was eating.

Upon returning to the hospitality area, John discovered the food critic seated at Seal's table grilling him with questions. Seal was unaware who the critic was and why she was there. He played along at first but then became a bit confused when she started to question his diet and eating habits. He turned to the critic and politely asked who she was and why she was asking so many personal questions. After about five minutes with the artist, she began to work the room asking everyone present questions not only about the dinner but other personal topics. Thoroughly embarrassed by the incident, our chef, Sean, who is close friends with the reporter, politely asked to speak with her outside the room. As she left Seal's table she told the artist, "Stay away from the bread, I've had better." That was the last straw. The impromptu interview was cut short and the critic was escorted to her car. We apologized profusely to Seal for the distraction, but he just smiled and said it was no bother. Then he remarked to John, "I don't know what she's talking about—I like the bread." We all had a little awkward chuckle and tried to put the incident behind us.

―――

Seal Dressing Room Requirements:

- 1 fresh fruit bowl
- 12 pounds raw carrots for juicing
- 5 pounds seedless grapes including both red and green
- 4 small baking potatoes
- 6 fat free Health Valley granola bars (assorted)
- 1 bag pre-mixed salad
- 1 jar Paul Newman's vinaigrette dressing
- 1 jar fat free mayonnaise

- 2 cans albacore tuna in water
- 1 jar organic honey
- 1 deli tray
- 4 bottles caffeine free fruit flavor drinks
- 8 liters Evian
- 1 box Celestial Seasonings Emperor Choice
- 6 non-alcoholic beers

THAI PASTA WITH SPICY PEANUT SAUCE

¼   cup olive oil
1½ tablespoons fresh garlic, finely chopped
½   cup vegetable stock
1½ cups sliced mushrooms
1   cup julienned red/Bermuda onion
½   cup hoisin sauce
½   cup soy sauce
¼   cup pure sesame oil
1   tablespoon hot chili oil
1   tablespoon fresh ginger puree
½   cup oyster sauce
2   cups bean sprouts
1   cup cleaned and julienned red bell pepper
1   cup snow peas, cleaned, ends snipped
2   pounds linguini, cooked al dente
1   cup chopped green onion
½   cup toasted unsalted peanuts
1   tablespoon chopped fresh mint
1   bunch fresh cilantro (reserve 8 sprigs for
garnish, chop the remainder)
    Spicy Peanut Sauce (recipe follows)

1. In a large skillet heat the olive oil and
   sauté the garlic over medium heat for

approximately 4 minutes. Splash with
vegetable stock, and add the mushrooms
and red onion. Sauté for an additional 5
minutes.

2. Add the hoisin, soy, sesame oil, chili oil,
   ginger, and oyster sauce. Increase the
   heat and bring to a boil. Reduce the heat
   to medium. Add the bean sprouts, pep-
   pers, and snow peas, and toss well. Add
   the piping hot pasta, cilantro, and green
   onion. Toss vigorously. Garnish with
   toasted peanuts, chopped mint, and a
   sprig of cilantro. Drizzle with Spicy Peanut
   Sauce.

SERVES 8+

SPICY PEANUT SAUCE

1½ cup peanut butter
⅔   cup coconut milk
2   tablespoons sesame oil
    pinch cayenne pepper
1   teaspoon ground ginger
2   tablespoons honey

1. In a small mixing bowl whisk together all
   ingredients until thoroughly blended.

2. Drizzle over Thai Pasta.

BUTTONS & SNAPS

1	tablespoon canola oil
4	cups small button mushrooms
1	tablespoon finely chopped fresh garlic
3	cups cleaned snap peas
1	teaspoon finely chopped fresh ginger
2	tablespoons pure sesame oil
2	tablespoons toasted sesame seeds
2	tablespoons soy sauce
	salt to taste
	black pepper to taste

1. In a large wok heat the canola oil to medium-high and sauté the button mushrooms and garlic, tossing vigorously, for 3 to 4 minutes.

2. Add the snap peas and ginger, continuing to sauté an additional 3 to 4 minutes. Add the sesame oil, sesame seeds, and soy sauce. Toss an additional 1½ to 2 minutes. Salt and pepper to taste, and serve.

SERVES 8

ORZO AND CARAMELIZED ONION SALAD

2	pounds orzo, cooked al dente, chilled and lightly oiled
¾	cup olive oil
	Caramelized Onions (recipe follows)
1	teaspoon salt
½	teaspoon ground black pepper
2	tablespoons chopped fresh Italian parsley

¼	cup seasoned rice wine vinegar
1	teaspoon chopped fresh thyme
3	tablespoons shredded radicchio

1. In a large mixing bowl combine all of the ingredients and toss well. Refrigerate for 45 to 60 minutes.

2. Remove from the refrigerator and garnish with shredded radicchio.

CARAMELIZED ONION

3	tablespoons olive oil
3	medium brown onions, coarsely chopped
⅓	cup brandy or sherry
½	cup chicken stock
1½	tablespoons brown sugar
½	teaspoon salt
½	teaspoons ground black pepper

1. In a medium saucepan heat the olive oil and sauté the onions over medium high heat for approximately 5 minutes.

2. Add the brandy or sherry and flambé. Add the chicken stock.

3. Reduce the heat to low. Add the brown sugar, salt, and pepper. Stir well. Simmer for approximately 20 to 25 minutes. The liquid will reduce, leaving a caramel-like coating on the onions.

SERVES 8

smashing pumpkins
rock invasion
**HOUSE
CREW**
DEL MAR 26

STEVE
WORKING
FOR THE LOVE OF
STRANGE MEDICINE
1994
PERRY
C 12-12

CHAPTER 32

KISS

This reunion tour was strictly '90s, with low fat meals, lots of special effects, and Kiss' trademark makeup and magic.

Apple Cream Cheese and Toasted
   Almond Bagel

Seasonal Vegetable Puff Pastry

Low Fat Purée of Carrot Soup with
   Pernod

Chicken, Grape, and Walnut Salad

The rock group Kiss was the brainchild of Gene Simmons, a former elementary school teacher. The band formed in 1973 and consisted of bass player Gene Simmons, singer and guitarist Paul Stanley, drummer Peter Criss, and guitarist Ace Frehley. This popular '70s rock group ranks third behind the Rolling Stones and the Beatles for consecutive gold records. The band released twenty-four albums in their career, capturing fans with their flamboyant costumes and black-and-white face makeup.

Kiss really made a name for themselves in 1975 with their fourth album, a double shot live release, *Alive.* The album was led by the hit single "Rock and Roll All Nite." Kiss had continued success with the release of *Destroyer* in 1976. The single "Beth" from that album went to number seven on the singles chart, virtually unheard of for a hard rock group. *Alive II* was released in 1977, and *Double Platinum* hit the record stores in 1978, containing the group's greatest hits. In 1980, the group began to come apart. Criss left the band in 1982. Frehley followed suit. Kiss replaced both and went on tour the following year without the costumes and makeup. While the band still attracted fans, the group quickly lost their mystique. Then the band began to gain momentum again in 1989 with the album *Hot in the Shade.* But it wasn't until the 1996 "Summer Reunion Tour" that the band would rise back to its earlier glory. Criss and Frehley rejoined the group for the tour and the band once again took the stage with costumes and makeup. The fans loved it, and Kiss was back on top selling out arenas coast to coast.

The costumes and makeup looked great, considering the age of the band members. The backstage area was filled with hundreds of road cases. The band decided that to truly do a reunion tour they needed to revert back to the staging, pyrotechnics, and fog machines of their past. Cases of sound, video, and special effects equipment lined the backstage space. The band arrived in the late afternoon for sound check. Simmons and his bandmates hardly looked like a group of rock and roll artists; they looked much more adult.

The artists preferred to eat dinner in their dressing room. A pasta and chicken dinner was setup in their hospitality room upon completion of sound check. The band soon began to prepare for the show with each taking his turn in the makeup chair.

John decided to check with the production office to see if they needed anything prior to show time. Upon entering, he was greeted by a gentleman with full face paint. Not recognizing this guy, John assumed he was a band member and apologized for the interruption. Just then the masked man said, "John, it is no interruption." John turned back, puzzled at how this band member knew his name. To prevent being further embarrassed, he engaged the masked gentleman in conversation, only to hear him reveal more personal information the band members wouldn't have known. John looked perplexed, and the gentleman asked if he was okay. John replied, "Yes, but how do you know my business partner Teresa?" He said, "John, it's me, David." The masked and wigged man was the local promoter whom John has known for years. As part of the band's contract, a representative from the local promoter contracting with the band had to dress up in costume, wig, and full face makeup the night of the show. That night was David's turn. He said it was fun, except when you get an itch.

At 8:00 P.M. the opening act took the stage. The main event took place shortly after 9:00 P.M. Many in the crowd had waited over sixteen years to see the original band back together in costume playing the music of their teen-age years. The band brought the house down with the pyrotechnics and special effects on stage that were only reserved for a Kiss concert.

Kiss Dressing Room Requirements:

- 10 baked chicken breast fillets
- 1 fresh pasta with three sauces including marinara, alfredo, and oil and garlic
- fresh imported Parmesan cheese with grater
- steamed vegetables (no butter)
- 1 fresh fruit basket
- 1 tuna salad
- 1 garden salad
- 1 bottle lowfat Italian dressing
- 12 sourdough rolls
- 1 loaf rye bread
- 1 jar Coleman's mustard
- 1 jar Dijon mustard
- chocolate rice cakes
- caramel rice cakes
- 1 jar black raspberry jam
- 2 boxes of snack crackers including Wheat Thins
- 2 cans Pringles including regular and barbecue
- 12 liters spring water
- 1 liter natural apple juice

- 1 liter fresh-squeezed orange juice
- 2 half gallon milk including skim
- 10 liters red Gatorade
- 6 Caffeine Free Pepsi
- 12 cans Coke
- 12 cans Diet Coke
- 12 cans Pepsi
- 12 cans Diet Sprite
- 6 cans Squirt
- 6 bottles Diet Peach Snapple
- 6 bottles Snapple iced tea
- coffee and tea service including decaffeinated coffee
- hot cocoa
- 1 squeeze bottle of natural honey
- 12 dethorned long stem red roses

The Menu

Apple Cream Cheese and Toasted Almond Bagels
Seasonal Vegetable Puff Pastry
Low Fat Purée of Carrot Soup with Pernod
Chicken, Grape, and Walnut Salad

APPLE CREAM CHEESE AND TOASTED ALMOND BAGELS
(A MORNING FAVORITE)

1½ cups cream cheese

1½ cups mayonnaise or nonfat plain yogurt

1 cup real sour cream or nonfat sour cream

½ teaspoon salt

1½ tablespoons chopped Italian parsley

½ teaspoon white pepper

1 cup sugar

1 teaspoon cinnamon

8 cups peeled, cored, and sliced green apples

1½ cups golden raisins

1 cup toasted almonds

8 plain bagels, sliced through middle

1½ cups light brown sugar

1. In a large mixing bowl or kitchen mixer combine the cream cheese, mayonnaise or yogurt, sour cream, salt, parsley, pepper, sugar and cinnamon. Mix until creamy smooth.

2. Add the apples, raisins, and toasted almonds. Mix well.

3. Place the mixture on open-faced bagels, sprinkle generously with brown sugar, and broil until the brown sugar melts. Be careful not to overbroil!

SERVES 8

SEASONAL VEGETABLE PUFF PASTRY

1	tablespoon olive oil
1	teaspoon finely chopped fresh garlic
1	cup diced white onions
2	cups sliced mushrooms
1	cup sun dried tomatoes, poached and julienned
4	cups julienned assorted vegetables, (i.e. broccoli, cauliflower, carrots, asparagus, green beans, etc.)
1	tablespoon herbs de Provence
1	pound cream cheese, chunked
	salt to taste
	black pepper to taste
8	8-inch squares puff pastry
2	cups grated mozzarella cheese or Gruyere
2	eggs, whipped

1. In a large sauté pan heat the olive oil and sauté the garlic and onions over medium heat for 2 to 3 minutes. Add the mushrooms and sauté an additional 2 to 3 minutes. Add the tomatoes and vegetables and sauté 5 to 6 minutes more. Add the herbs de Provence and cream cheese chunks. Stir and continue to sauté. As the cheese begins to melt and create a creamy sauce, add salt and pepper to taste. Remove from the heat and set aside.

2. Place the pastry squares on a lightly floured pastry marble or cutting board. Using half of the grated cheese, place equal amounts into the center of each square.

3. Place equal amounts of the vegetable cream cheese mixture over the cheese. Use the remaining grated cheese to top the vegetables. Preheat the oven to 350°.

4. Brush the edges of the pastry squares with the egg mixture. Fold over a corner to meet the opposite corner, forming a triangle. Press the outer edges together with the prongs of a fork and clean up the edges with a pastry/pizza cutter if necessary.

5. Place the vegetable pockets on a nonstick baking sheet. Brush with the remaining egg mixture and bake for 12 to 15 minutes or until golden brown.

Can be served as a side dish with a Florentine sauce or as a vegetarian entree.

SERVES 8

LOW FAT PURÉE OF CARROT SOUP WITH PERNOD
(CAN BE VEGETARIAN)

1   tablespoon olive oil

1½   cups chopped white onions

2   pounds carrots, peeled and chopped

10   cups chicken stock or vegetable stock (if you prefer a vegetarian soup)

1   teaspoon salt

½   teaspoon white pepper

¼   cup Pernod (optional)

1½   pounds potatoes, peeled and chopped

1. In a large stock pot heat the olive oil and sauté the onions and carrots over medium heat for 5 to 7 minutes, stirring constantly.

2. Add the stock, increase the heat to high, and bring to a boil. Add salt, pepper, and Pernod, and stir well. Add the potatoes, reduce the heat to low, and simmer for 45 to 50 minutes.

3. Remove from the heat and let cool. Ladle a blender pitcher three-fourths full and blend the mixture at medium high for 3 to 4 minutes per batch or until the soup is completely puréed. Pour the soup into a fresh stock pot and continue the process until all ingredients have been blended.

4. Heat the puréed soup over medium heat until hot. Garnish with fresh chopped parsley.

SERVES 8+

CHICKEN, GRAPE, AND WALNUT SALAD

1½   cups real mayonnaise

½   cup diced red/Bermuda onion

2   tablespoons chopped fresh tarragon

1   teaspoon salt

½   teaspoon white pepper

1½   cups walnut pieces

3   pounds boneless, skinless chicken breasts, roasted or boiled, cubed

2   cups halved seedless grapes, red or white

1. In a large mixing bowl combine the mayonnaise, onion, tarragon, salt, and pepper. Mix until well blended. Add the walnut pieces and stir well.

2. Add the chicken and grapes, and toss thoroughly. Cover and chill for 1 hour.

3. Remove from the refrigerator and toss lightly. Serve on a French baguette with leaf lettuce and sprouts or atop a bed of mixed baby greens tossed with a Citrus Vinaigrette (see index).

SERVES 8

CHAPTER 33

FAITH HILL/TIM McGRAW

She didn't kiss the cook but she gave him the next best thing. . . .

Herb Crusted Tri-Tip

Zinfandel Sauce

Garlic and Rosemary Roasted Potatoes

Broccoli with a Parmesan Aioli

Tim McGraw and Faith Hill shared the marquee during their 1996 summer concert tour. Both country musicians and their crews hit the road on the "Spontaneous Combustion" tour. Country acts often tour in pairs or threesomes. It isn't that any one musician couldn't sellout their own show, but rather that, together they can pack the house and share tour expenses. Tim McGraw and Faith Hill were a perfect match on tour. Her music is a little softer, his a bit more rough.

Tim McGraw is a native of Louisiana. The singer moved to Nashville around 1989 and began to perform on the club circuit. His first self-titled album yielded three singles that landed on the country charts, "Two Steppin' Mind," "Memory Lane," and "Welcome to the Club." His second release, *Not a Moment Too Soon,* solidified Tim's country music career, containing dance hits such as "Indian Outlaw" and "Don't Take the Girl." The album has sold over five million copies, and it was *Billboard* magazine's sixth best-selling album of 1994. Tim's third album, *All I Want,* contained such chart-topping hits as "I Like It, I Love It," and the title track. Tim and his band, "The Dancehall Doctors," have toured the country over the years to promote his albums.

In 1996, Tim was joined on tour by country diva Faith Hill. The songstress is a favorite with country fans, especially young men. While Tim's washboard abs, which he chooses to accentuate with tight, sheer shirts, excite the women at his concerts, Faith Hill accentuates her 5' 8" figure with her brilliant smile and her country charm. Her honey-blonde hair and hazel eyes practically melt her male fans. Faith was born in Jackson, Mississippi, in 1967, and she performed at a mere seven years old at a 4-H club luncheon.

We had also catered for Faith in 1995, the year before her tour with Tim. She seemed younger and more casual on that tour. She was just coming into her own at that point, and she wasn't surrounded with management and the accompanying entourage. After enjoying dinner in the hospitality area, she approached our chef, Sean Fisher, and gave him a big hug and a "thank you" for the meal. She was very gracious, very sweet, and downright beautiful.

By 1996 and the "Spontaneous Combustion" tour, Faith had a new hairstyle and several people added to her entourage. She opted for short, cropped hair that year, as did country legend Reba McEntire. As she took to the stage, the crowd whistled and cheered for the stunning country charmer. She even pulled an audience member up onto the stage for a quick dance routine during the show. Even though her look had changed and she was a little more "protected" off-stage, Faith Hill was a sweetheart to everyone she came into contact with, from venue personnel, to fans— and yes, even to the caterer.

Tim was much more shy offstage. In his dressing room, marked with the sign

"Road Dog"—his nickname on the road—he would keep very much to himself. In fact, on one stop in Southern California, Tim chose to use his private tour bus as his dressing room, not entering the arena until he was cued to the stage. We even delivered his dinner to him on the bus, which was positioned at the top of a loading ramp in the parking lot. Although he didn't want to talk to or have contact with anyone that day, he emerged on stage that night to perform for 10,000 fans—who were anything but disappointed. That day happened to be during the time when there were rumors flying about his romance with Faith. The crew chalked up the extra need for privacy backstage to the media hype surrounding the romantic rumors. Of course, these days, Faith and Tim are married and well on their way to building a family.

Tim McGraw/Faith Hill Dressing Room Requirements:

FAITH HILL DRESSING ROOM REQUIREMENTS:
- hot tea with an assortment of decaffeinated tea
- 1 Lay's regular potato chips
- 24 bottles small Evian
- 1 bottle red wine (i.e. Columbia Crest Merlot)
- 1 fresh fruit basket
- 1 small tray of carrots

ROAD DOG (AKA TIM MCGRAW) DRESSING ROOM REQUIREMENTS:
- 48 bottles small Evian
- 12 cans Coke or Pepsi
- 24 bottles Bud, Coors or Miller Lite Beer

The Menu

Herb Crusted Tri-Tip

Zinfandel Sauce

Garlic and Rosemary Roasted
Potatoes

Broccoli with Parmesan Aioli

HERB CRUSTED TRI-TIP

2	tablespoons fresh rosemary
1	tablespoon coarse black pepper
1	tablespoon kosher salt
1	tablespoon dried diced onion
1	tablespoon dried whole thyme
1	tablespoon garlic powder
2	tablespoons firmly packed light brown sugar
½	teaspoon fennel seed
2	4-pound tri-tip roasts

1. In a mixing bowl combine all of the dry ingredients. Mix until well blended.

2. Preheat the oven to 450°.

3. Completely coat the outside surface of the roasts with the dry herb rub prepared in step 1.

4. Place the coated roast in a nonstick roasting pan (or spray a roasting pan with nonstick spray).

5. Roast the tri-tip for 15 minutes. Reduce the oven temperature to 350° and continue to roast for 40 to 50 minutes for rare to medium rare beef, or longer if you prefer your beef entrée more well done.

SERVES 8

ZINFANDEL SAUCE

1	tablespoon olive oil
3	tablespoons finely chopped white onion or shallots
½	cup brandy
1	cup zinfandel (a robust red wine)
2	tablespoons sugar
2	cups Demi-Glace (see index)
1	teaspoon coarse black pepper

1. In a 3-quart saucepan heat the olive oil and sauté the shallots or onions over a medium heat until translucent.

2. Add the brandy and flambé.

3. Add the zinfandel wine and sugar, and simmer over medium heat until the sauce thickens.

4. Add the Demi-Glace and pepper, and continue to stir until the sauce again thickens, approximately 5 minutes. If a thicker sauce is desired, thicken by beating in a roux mixture with a whisk.

GARLIC AND ROSEMARY ROASTED POTATOES

5   pounds red potatoes, quartered (small to medium size pieces)

½   cup olive oil

2   tablespoons chopped fresh rosemary

1   teaspoon salt

1   teaspoon coarse black pepper

3   tablespoons finely chopped fresh garlic

2   teaspoons paprika

    chopped Italian parsley for garnish

1. Preheat the oven to 400°. In a large roasting pan toss the potatoes with olive oil. Sprinkle the potatoes with rosemary, salt, pepper, garlic, and paprika. Toss again.

2. Roast in the oven for approximately 40 minutes or until golden and the skin appears slightly crisp. Toss the potatoes halfway through cooking time to assure even roasting.

   Serve as a side to beef or grilled chicken. Garnish with chopped Italian parsley, if desired.

SERVES 8

BROCCOLI WITH PARMESAN AIOLI

4   egg yolks

1   tablespoon chopped roasted garlic

1½ tablespoons cracked black pepper

¼   teaspoon salt

2   cups olive oil

½   teaspoon whole dry thyme

1   cup shredded Parmesan cheese

2   tablespoons lemon juice

3   pounds broccoli florets, steamed

1. In a blender, combine the egg yolks, garlic, pepper, and salt. Blend at medium speed for 1 minute. Gradually add the olive oil a little at a time until the mixture reaches a mayonnaise consistency.

2. Remove from the blender and place into a small mixing bowl. Stir in the thyme, Parmesan, and lemon juice with a whisk until the mixture appears creamy.

   Serve as a condiment dip for broccoli or any other vegetable of your choosing. This aioli also makes a wonderful sandwich spread or dressing.

SERVES 8

rush tour 1994

7-SAD

All Areas

World Tour 1992-1993 | BRUCE SPRINGSTEEN

U.S.A SO

Catherine

CHAPTER 34

~~~

AMY GRANT

This friendly pop diva is always careful to thank those who get her to the stage. She is an artist who realizes her success is not a one-person show, although her energy on stage might lead you to rethink that. "Load up the tomato stuff, I love it!" she exclaimed on her second trip through the buffet line prior to her performance.

Seared Ahi Salad with Mango Vinaigrette

Sicilian Chicken

Outstanding Caponata

Roasted Eggplant

Amy Grant began her recording career in high school in 1978. She began working on her first self-titled album during the spring of her junior year, and it was released the following spring, during her senior year. Amy continued her recording and performing career as she entered college in South Carolina. Her second album, *Father's Eyes,* was extremely popular with Contemporary Christian music fans. The artist continued to produce albums such as *Age to Age, Unguarded,* and *The Collection* (1986) at a rate of one per year throughout the 1980s. After *The Collection,* Amy only released one more album in the 1980s, entitled *Lead Me On.*

Her career then began to move in a new direction, as did her music. While her message and style didn't necessarily change, the 1990s brought a more mainstream Amy Grant to the listening audience. Her albums during this period, *Heart in Motion* (1991) and *House of Love* (1994), attracted a more diverse and widespread audience. The contemporary sounds of the albums transcended the realms of contemporary and Christian music. While Amy doesn't feel that her songs are any different or that any of her music has been compromised, something changed that led her to attract a broader base of fans. The "House of Love" tour of 1995 had the artist playing large venues, such as the Hollywood Bowl in Los Angeles, and packing in the fans as well.

The Hollywood Bowl concert was typical of most concerts played at the venue.

We loaded-in in the wee hours of the morning and the day seemed to progress quite smoothly. There were quite a few dressing rooms, however, which took a while to setup. This extra setup took away from the dinner preparation schedule. It was 5:20 P.M., and dinner was to be served in ten minutes. John was the chef that day. The kitchen food was prepared in a portable on-site kitchen, which was housed in a tent adjacent to the hospitality dining area. The menu for the evening included Sicilian Chicken with grilled vegetables in a puff pastry for the vegetarians. As they were putting the finishing touches to the meal, a server asked which type of sauce we were serving with the chicken. A look of sheer panic came over John's face. "Sauce?" he asked, "Oh, damn, I forgot to make the sauce." John quickly surveyed the ingredients available, looked at his watch, and said, "Okay, what can I make for 100 people in the next five minutes?" Quickly, he opted for a tomato curry sauce. Into the pot he dumped stewed Italian plum tomatoes, garlic, onion, curry powder, Tabasco sauce, lemon pepper, a bit of sugar, and the "miracle spice," also known as Salt Free-17. As the sauce began to boil, he frantically added a bit of tomato paste to give it some body, along with a few miscellaneous ingredients. Looking outside the tent doorway, John could see Amy and her band making their way to the dining tent.

Then came the moment of truth. Should he put the spicy curry sauce out for the guests or allow the band to eat the chicken naked? "What the hell," John resolved as he ladled the sauce over the chicken on the buffet and put the rest out as a side. He instructed the servers to guide the guests to the numerous other options available. Amy was first in line and asked what kind of sauce was on the chicken. The server explained that it was a very spicy tomato curry. The singer replied, "Great, I love spicy foods and tomatoes." Sweat beaded down John's forehead as Amy asked the server to pile on extra sauce. She sat down at a table in the tent with her band and began to enjoy her dinner. About halfway through the meal, she picked up her plate and came back to the line. John thought, "This is it. She hated the sauce." As she approached the table, she asked John if he was the chef. He explained that he was and nervously asked how her meal was. She responded enthusiastically that everything was great, but that she absolutely loved the sauce on the chicken. She helped herself to a second piece of chicken and to two ladles of sauce.

Unbelievably, the sauce was the talk of the meal. After 45 minutes, the tomato curry sauce was running out and John actually had to concoct a second batch! Amy left the dining area and commented that she was looking forward to dinner in San Diego the following night, which Sean Fisher was set to prepare. The performer was very gracious again in San Diego. Although there was no impromptu sauce, she asked for a "doggie bag" of the Eggplant Caponata to take with her on the bus. The artist signed a poster in San Diego for the catering crew. On it, she wrote: "To all my friends at Behind the Scenes. Fabulous food!! Love, Amy P.S. Thanks for my doggie bag."

―――

Amy Grant Dressing Room Requirements:

- tea service including Celestial Seasonings Peppermint
- 4 liters Evian or Mountain Valley water
- 1 bouquet fresh flowers

The Menu

Seared Ahi Salad with
Mango Vinaigrette

Sicilian Chicken

Outstanding Caponata

Roasted Eggplant

SEARED AHI SALAD WITH MANGO VINAIGRETTE

2½ pounds mixed baby greens
   Mango Vinaigrette (recipe follows)
1½ cups peeled and julienned carrots
1 cup cleaned and julienned red bell pepper
1 cup chopped green onion
1 cup radish sprouts
1 cup shredded radicchio
¼ cup thinly sliced red/Bermuda onion
8 6-ounce Seared Ahi Steaks (see p. 52)

1. In a large mixing bowl toss the baby greens with ¼ cup of Mango Vinaigrette.

2. Place equal portions of greens on serving plates. Sprinkle salads with equal amounts of prepared vegetables (carrots, peppers, green onions, sprouts). Drizzle with additional dressing. Finish with shredded radicchio and red onion.

3. Slice the ahi steaks at an angle, and fan one steak out atop each salad. Drizzle a bit more dressing atop the ahi and serve.

SERVES 8

MANGO VINAIGRETTE

1¼ cups chopped fresh mangos (or mango spears from a jar)
¼ cup seasoned rice wine vinegar
½ teaspoon ground ginger
   pinch salt
   pinch white pepper
1 tablespoon firmly packed brown sugar
4 tablespoons olive oil
2 tablespoons pistachio oil or olive oil or walnut oil

1. In a blender combine the mangos, vinegar, ginger, salt, pepper, and brown sugar. Blend on medium high for about 1 minute.

2. Continue blending, slowly adding the oils until the dressing emulsifies. Chill and serve.

SICILIAN CHICKEN

2	tablespoons chopped fresh garlic
2	tablespoons chopped red/Bermuda onion
2	tablespoons dry whole oregano
2	tablespoons cleaned fresh rosemary
1	cup lemon juice
1	teaspoon coarse black pepper
2	tablespoons chicken base
½	cup olive oil
8	6-ounce boneless, skinless chicken breasts
4	bay leaves

1. In a blender combine the garlic, onion, oregano, rosemary, lemon juice, pepper, and chicken base. Blend at medium speed for approximately 1½ minutes until smooth. Slowly add the olive oil while continuing to blend.

2. Place the chicken into a 6-quart bowl. Pour the blended marinade over the chicken. Stir the breasts around to assure they are well coated. Add the bay leaves to the marinated chicken. Refrigerate for 3 to 4 hours.

3. Preheat the grill to medium-high. Grill the marinated chicken for approximately 4 to 5 minutes on each side, simply to mark the chicken and seal in the flavor. Be sure not to overcook on the grill! The chicken will not be fully cooked. Place the grill-marked breasts on a baking sheet and finish for approximately 8 to 10 minutes in a 350° oven.

We often top with crumbled feta cheese, and Marinated Tomatoes and Cucumbers (see index), and serve with a side of Pesto Mayonnaise (see index), if served sandwich style.

SERVES 8

OUTSTANDING CAPONATA

2	tablespoons olive oil
1	cup diced white onion
1	tablespoon finely chopped fresh garlic
4	cups Roasted Eggplant (recipe follows)
⅓	cup capers
4	cups Red and Sassy Pomodoro Sauce (see index)
2	tablespoons whole dry oregano
2	tablespoons chopped fresh Italian parsley
1½	tablespoons shredded fresh basil
⅓	cup white wine vinegar
½	cup sugar
½	teaspoon cayenne pepper

1. In a large skillet heat the olive oil and sauté the garlic and onion over medium heat for approximately 5 minutes. Reduce the heat to low.

2. Add the remaining ingredients and stir well over low heat. Simmer for approximately 5 minutes. Remove from the heat.

3. Serve at room temperature or slightly warm. Great on sandwiches, as a side dish, atop crostini or with slightly warm and crusty sourdough bread.

SERVES 8+

ROASTED EGGPLANT

1   large eggplant, cubed (½")
¾   cup olive oil
2   tablespoons finely chopped fresh garlic
1   tablespoon finely chopped fresh Italian
parsley
1   tablespoon whole dry oregano
     salt to taste
     pepper to taste

1. Preheat the oven to 375°. In a large mixing bowl combine all of the ingredients and toss until the eggplant is well coated.

2. Place the seasoned eggplant on a baking sheet. Bake for 15 to 20 minutes or until golden brown.

CHAPTER 35

BROOKS & DUNN

A nervous server asked Ronnie Dunn to finish what was on his plate first when he requested a second pork chop. This casual country duo luckily found humor in the motherly request.

Stuffed Country Chops

Wild Mushroom Risotto

Steakhouse Chili

Brooks & Dunn is country music's hottest duo. Their energetic music and dance tunes have topped the charts consistently over their career. The duo's debut album, *Brand New Man,* was released in 1991 and has since gone quintuple platinum. Their 1993 follow-up album, *Hard Workin' Man,* has also been extremely popular, selling over 4 million copies. With songs such as "Boot Scootin' Boogie," and "Hard Workin' Man," the duo has burned up the charts and filled arenas for their live shows.

The duo is made up of Kix Brooks and Ronnie Dunn. The two teamed up in the early 1990s. Brooks is the one with the mustache who exemplifies nonstop excitement on stage. He used to perform in the dance halls and honky-tonks of the South. Ronnie Dunn was much more conservative on stage. The pair tried to influence each other a bit, but they finally realized that they could each do what they do and still entertain the crowd. Ronnie's gentler nature is now something they play with onstage. Kix's background is founded in what he calls a ". . . real wild Louisiana thing, where people basically raise hell on stage." Whatever the duo is doing, it seems to be working. They have racked up numerous awards, from Grammys to Academy of Country Music Awards. They are still as popular as ever on tour.

At their show in San Diego in February 1995, the pair arrived for sound check in the late afternoon. Ronnie donned his signature black cowboy hat and a rather patriotic flag shirt. Kix wore a sharp pair of boots and a black blazer. They joined our staff in the hospitality area for dinner after sound check. We had a new server working that evening. Ronnie picked up a plate and made his way to the buffet table. We were serving New York Steak and Stuffed Pork Chops that evening. He asked for one of each entrée. The server was conscious of the large portions and asked that he choose one or the other, not knowing who the musician was. Judging by the casual nature of the band, she thought they might be local radio personalities who weren't really supposed to be eating. The server came into the back and asked John if guests could have both entrées. He explained that that was all right, depending upon who the guest was. John peeked his head out to survey the group that was eating. He recognized Brooks & Dunn and asked if they were the people who were asking for both entrees. The server nodded yes. A little embarrassment ran down John's spine. With his head down, John approached the musician's table. "Is there anything else I can get you?" he asked. "More steak or pork chops, perhaps?" Ronnie looked over with a smile, "No, but thank you for watching my waistline." John smirked and apologized for the mistake. "No problem, no problem at all. I just hope your check cashes." Everyone got a good laugh and we went on with our evening.

Soon after this incident, a camera crew arrived in the hospitality area. It was a crew from CNN doing a three-part story entitled "Life on the Road." They were traveling with Brooks & Dunn on two of their concert stops to show what life backstage is like. They filmed our dining area and then followed the performers to the dressing rooms in an effort to catch them joking and bantering back and forth. The story aired on CNN the following month.

Brooks & Dunn Dressing Room Requirements:

- 6 cans Diet Coke
- 6 cans Sprite
- 4 liters Evian or Napa water
- assorted juices
- 1 bag tortilla chips and salsa

- 1 potato chips and dip
- coffee service

STUFFED COUNTRY CHOPS

1	1-pound box or bag stuffing croutons
⅓	cup golden raisins
1	cup fresh pears, peeled and chopped or canned pears, drained and chopped
½	cup diced white onion
½	cup diced celery
½	teaspoon dry sage
½	teaspoon whole dry thyme
½	teaspoon salt
½	teaspoon ground black pepper
1	cup chicken broth, hot
8	8-ounce pork chops (rib loin chops), 1½-inch thick
½	teaspoon salt
½	teaspoon ground black pepper
1	tablespoon finely chopped fresh rosemary
	Tuscan Chicken Balsamic Sauce (see index)

1. In a medium mixing bowl combine the stuffing croutons, raisins, pears, onion, celery, sage, thyme, salt, and pepper. Mix well.

2. Slowly add the hot chicken broth to the stuffing mixture, stirring constantly.

Depending upon the brand of stuffing croutons, you may need a little less broth or possibly a bit more. Continue to stir mixture until it clumps up and attains a moist consistency. Set aside.

3. Trim the excess fat from the chops, if any. Slice each chop horizontally through the center, three-fourths of the way to the bone, creating a cozy pocket.

4. Fill the pork pockets with stuffing mixture. Place the stuffed chops in a nonstick roasting pan and sprinkle with chopped rosemary, salt, and pepper.

5. Roast for approximately 40 minutes. Remove from the oven.

6. In a saucepan combine the Tuscan Chicken Balsamic Sauce and pork drippings or chicken stock. Heat through. Serve over the pork chops.

SERVES 8

WILD MUSHROOM RISOTTO

2	tablespoons olive oil
2	tablespoons finely chopped shallots
2	tablespoons finely chopped fresh garlic
4	cups assorted wild mushrooms (i.e. portabella, oyster, morel, chanterelle, porcini)
¼	cup brandy
2	cups risotto (short grain rice)
8	cups vegetable or chicken stock
½	cup heavy whipping cream
3	tablespoons chopped Italian parsley
1	teaspoon salt

½   teaspoon coarse black pepper

1½ cups shredded Parmesan cheese

1. In a large saucepan heat the olive oil and sauté the shallots and garlic over medium heat for about 2 to 3 minutes. Add the mushrooms and sauté for an additional 5 to 6 minutes. Add the brandy and flambé. Add the risotto and continue to sauté for an additional 2 to 3 minutes.

2. Add 4 cups of stock and bring to a boil. Reduce heat to medium-low and simmer for 20 to 25 minutes. Stir in 1 cup of stock every 5 minutes as the liquid dissipates.

4. Stir in the heavy cream, 2 tablespoons of parsley, salt, pepper, and ¾ cup of Parmesan cheese. Simmer for an additional 5 minutes or until the risotto appears saucy and slightly thickened. Serve promptly with Parmesan and Italian parsley garnish.

SERVES 8

STEAKHOUSE CHILI

2   tablespoons olive oil

3   pounds lean stewing beef (chuck)

2   cups diced white onions

1   tablespoon finely chopped fresh garlic

3   cups red beans, pre-soaked overnight

3   tablespoons chili powder

1½ tablespoons salt

1   tablespoon coarse black pepper

1   teaspoon cayenne pepper

2   medium green bell peppers, cleaned and diced

¼   cup cleaned and chopped fresh cilantro, (no stems)

1   tablespoon ground cumin

12   cups spring water

1   10-ounce can tomato paste

1   28-ounce can stewed tomatoes, chopped

2   sprigs epazote (fresh herb found in mexican specialty stores)

      New York Sharp Cheddar cheese for garnish

1. In a large stock pot, heat the olive oil. Add the beef, onions, and garlic, and sauté over medium-high heat until the meat is browned, approximately 10 minutes.

2. Add the presoaked beans, chili powder, salt, black pepper, cayenne pepper, green peppers, cilantro, and cumin. Stir well.

3. Add the spring water and increase the heat to high. Bring to boil. Add the tomato paste, stewed tomatoes, and epazote. Reduce the heat to medium and simmer for about 30 minutes, stirring occasionally.

4. Reduce the heat to low and continue to simmer, stirring occasionally, for approximately 55 to 60 minutes.

5. Remove the epazote sprigs from the chili, and thicken if necessary with flour and water mixture. This chili is often served to bands and road crews in hollowed out sourdough bowls that are slightly toasted. We garnish the hot dish with shredded New York Sharp Cheddar cheese and chopped scallions.

SERVES 8+

CHAPTER 36

GREEN DAY

The alternative music icons were like kids in a candy store during their first-ever arena concert—on Halloween of all nights. "You mean we get dinner, too?"

Grilled Vegetable Lasagna

Béchamel Sauce

Ratatouille

Green Day has become one of the hottest punk-rock bands in the 90's. The group consists of Billie Joe Armstrong (guitar and vocals), Mike Dirnt (bass), and Tre Cool (drums). They are a very young yet very popular band. Green Day's music has mainstreamed the "punk rock" of Generation X. Their success can be gauged by the popularity of their first major album, *Dookie,* which was released in January of 1994. That debut album sold over eleven million copies. The band went on to headline the "Lollapalooza" tour and was among the most talked-about groups at the Woodstock Reunion Festival. Green Day released its second album in October 1995, titled *Insomniac.* The album was a huge hit, containing such chart toppers as "Welcome to Paradise," "When I Come Around," and "Basket Case."

All three members of Green Day were born in 1972. Billie Joe wrote and recorded his first song at age twelve, just two years after he and Mike met at school. In 1987, the duo played their first gig as the group "Sweet Children." Two years later, the two renamed the band "Green Day." They started their first U.S. tour in 1990, the day after Mike's high school graduation. Their original drummer, John Kiftmeyer, decided at the same time to leave the band and go to college. It wasn't until 1993 that they signed with a major label, Reprise Records. Shortly after they chose Reprise, they released their smash-hit *Dookie* and made history as the first punk band to sell over eleven million albums. The band continued to tour the nation, selling out arenas coast to coast. They were labeled another "Gen-X" band by the alternative-rock community. But however their critics choose to label them, their music remains popular and they continue to sell millions of albums.

Green Day's San Diego concert performance kicked off their 1994 U.S. arena tour. The concert was on Halloween and brought fans to the Sports Arena wearing costumes, masks, and some, their usual punk garb. The sold-out concert brought in youth of all types. The crowd was mixed from clean-cut surfer dudes to pink- and green-haired sixteen-year-olds with pierced noses and eyebrows. The excited crowd quickly filled the arena.

This excitement was carried backstage, as well. The band was thrilled to be playing in a large arena. All of their previous gigs had been in local clubs or music halls. The young band members walked around in a near stupor as they surveyed the stage and participated in the sound check. They were very gracious and thankful to everyone throughout the evening. They were like kids in a candy store. It was endearing, and we couldn't help but be excited with them. It was a wonderful experience being a part of this major event for the group.

Prior to the band's performance, they ran out of beer in the dressing room after inviting several guests to join them backstage. Billie Joe Armstrong, the lead singer, entered the production office looking for some additional beer for the guests. Within ten minutes we had additional ice cold beers delivered to the dressing room. The band and their guests were thrilled. In fact, one of the dressing room visitors remarked, "Damn, all you do is ask and they bring whatever you want?" "Yeah, pretty much," responded one of the band members with a look of contentment.

—*mm*—

Green Day Dressing Room Requirements:

- 24 Pete's Wicked Ale
- 1 bottle red wine
- 1 bunch bananas
- 1 bunch seedless grapes
- 6 cans Diet Mountain Dew
- 6 cans Diet Coke
- 2 cases Pepsi
- 6 cans Sprite
- 6 cans A&W Root Beer
- 1 quart orange juice
- 1 quart apple juice

- 1 quart cranberry juice
- coffee and tea service
- 12 liters spring water
- 2 bags natural tortilla chips
- 1 jar hot salsa

The Menu

Grilled Vegetable Lasagna
Béchamel Sauce
Ratatouille

GRILLED VEGETABLE LASAGNA

2   cups ricotta cheese

2½   cups shredded parmesan cheese

1   tablespoon finely chopped fresh garlic

1   tablespoon chopped fresh basil

1   tablespoon chopped fresh oregano

1   teaspoon chopped Italian parsley

1   teaspoon salt

½   teaspoon black pepper

4½   cups Béchamel Sauce (recipe follows)

2   pounds lasagna noodles, cooked al dente

3   pounds Grilled Assorted Vegetables (see
index): yellow squash, zucchini, eggplant, car-
rots, onions, asparagus, mushrooms, etc.

3½   cups grated mozzarella cheese

1. Preheat the oven to 350°. In a medium bowl combine the ricotta, 2 cups of Parmesan cheese, the garlic, basil, oregano, parsley, salt, and pepper. Mix thoroughly and set aside.

2. In a lasagna pan (approximately 13" x 9" x 3") sprayed with nonstick spray, spread ½ cup of Béchamel on the bottom of the pan. Add a single layer of one-third of the lasagna noodles. Spread half of the ricotta mixture evenly over the noodles.

3. Next, layer half of the grilled vegetables over the ricotta mixture. Spread 1½ cups of Béchamel over the vegetables. Spread 1 cup of mozzarella over the sauce. Layer another third of the lasagna noodles, the remaining ricotta, the remaining grilled vegetables, half of the remaining Béchamel, and 1 cup of mozzarella cheese.

4. Place the final layer of noodles over the mozzarella cheese, spread with the remaining Béchamel sauce, the remaining Parmesan, and the remaining mozzarella cheese.

5. Tent the baking pan with a layer of foil. Bake for approximately 45 to 50 minutes.

6. Remove the foil, increase the heat to 375°, and bake for an additional 10 minutes or until the cheese is lightly browned and the lasagna is bubbling. Remove and let stand 10 to 12 minutes before cutting and serving.

SERVES 8+

BÉCHAMEL SAUCE
(YOUR BASIC WHITE SAUCE)

4½ cups whole milk

½ teaspoon salt

½ teaspoon black pepper

½ teaspoon ground nutmeg

¼ cup French Roux, approximately

(see index)

1. In a saucepan combine the milk, salt, pepper, and nutmeg and bring to almost a boil over medium-high heat. Do not boil—the milk will scorch!

2. Reduce the heat to medium and gradually add the roux mixture until the sauce thickens. Depending upon the temperature and type of milk, you may use a bit more or a bit less (¼ cup is an estimate). Add gradually to prevent overthickening.

RATATOUILLE

¼ cup olive oil

2 large eggplants, cubed (¾")

2 tablespoons finely chopped fresh garlic

2 cups coarsely chopped white onions

½ cup red wine

2 28-ounce cans ground Roma tomatoes in purée

1 tablespoon chopped fresh oregano

2 tablespoons sugar

1½ teaspoons salt

1 teaspoon black pepper

¼ teaspoon cayenne pepper

1 large green bell pepper, coarsely chopped

1 large red bell pepper, coarsely chopped

1 large yellow bell pepper, coarsely chopped

2 tablespoons chopped fresh basil

2 tablespoons chopped Italian parsley,

½ cup capers

1. In a large stock pot heat the olive oil over medium-high heat for 3 to 4 minutes. Add the eggplant and sauté for 3 to 5 minutes. Add the garlic and onions and sauté for an additional 5 minutes.

2. Add the red wine and tomatoes and reduce the heat to medium low. Simmer for 5 minutes. Add the oregano, sugar, salt, pepper, and cayenne pepper. Reduce the heat to low, cover, and simmer for 25 minutes, stirring occasionally.

3. Remove the lid, and stir in the peppers, basil, parsley, and capers. Cover and simmer an additional 20 to 25 minutes. Remove the cover and serve!

SERVES 8

CHAPTER 37

~~~

SHERYL CROW

Man's best friend was kind enough to clean up the dinner buffet shortly after the band filled their plates.

Linguini Carbonara
Mediterranean Tuna Salad
Roasted Eggplant Sandwich
Salsa Siciliana

*S*heryl Crow was born in a small town in southeastern Missouri. Her parents were amateur jazz musicians who taught her how to understand and appreciate music as an art form. Already an accomplished pianist, Sheryl began composing as early as age thirteen. Her big break into the music industry came in 1986, when she moved to Los Angeles after receiving her college degree in music composition. Not knowing a soul in Los Angeles, she figured she didn't have anything to lose. She took a job as a waitress and did some singing for commercials. While she was singing, she overheard a conversation about auditions for a Michael Jackson tour. Sheryl simply showed-up at the audition, even though it was by invitation only. She ended up with a job as a backup singer on Michael Jackson's "Bad" world tour. This break kept her busy for two years. After the tour ended, she moved into the studio to do backup vocals for such artists as Rod Stewart, Sting, and Don Henley. She continued to sell her songs to other artists such as Eric Clapton, Lisa Lisa, and Wynonna Judd.

Finally, prompted by advice from Henley, she quit doing backup vocals and tried a solo career with her own music. Sheryl didn't work for two years as she pursued this dream. Eventually, she was asked to join the Tuesday Night Music Club. This invitation was the beginning of her music career. Soon, the composer and performer released her first album, entitled *Tuesday Night Music Club.*

We have had the opportunity to cater for this beautiful young star on numerous occasions. The first of these was at the San Diego Street Scene, a food and music festival held in the Gaslamp District downtown. The annual festival brings together over a hundred bands on fifteen stages for three days. Crowds walk the barricaded streets drinking, eating, shopping the crafts booths, and enjoying music at each of the theme stages. The acts are booked a year in advance, and Sheryl Crow was booked to appear before her album was released and started to blaze up the charts. She honored her appearance and attracted one of the largest crowds ever to the Street Scene stage.

Six months later, we had a more intimate opportunity to serve Sheryl and her band. This was on her first major tour, the "Tuesday Night Music Club" tour. She was basking in the first wave of her popularity on this tour. Her album was selling well and she was receiving a great deal of radio air time.

After sound check, Sheryl and some of the band members made their way backstage for dinner. In tow was the artist's beautiful retriever, who accompanied her on tour. We never did get the dog's name, as Sheryl would refer to him (or her) as "Puppy" or "Baby." Sheryl picked up a plate and made her way through the buffet line. Her lifelong companion followed her through the line. Unfortunately, the adorable dog's nose was at table level, and he conveniently cleaned the excess food from the front end of the table. We quickly followed the dog's trail to remove any licked or sniffed items. The crew sat and chuckled, very used to the dog's behavior. Sheryl sold out the 4,000+ seat arena that night.

The artist was very friendly to her band and crew, and to our staff, as well. She even brought her dirty plate to the kitchen when she was finished eating, before we had a chance to pick it up from the table. The singer, full of life, practiced her music on her acoustic guitar after dinner. The music could be heard throughout the halls of the venue. At around 8:00 P.M., the opening act, Freedy Johnston, took the stage. Sheryl took the stage at about 9:00 P.M. She played her heart out to the captivated crowd. She had finally made it in the music industry.

CHAPTER 37

Sheryl Crow Dressing Room Requirements:

- 12 bottles Evian
- 1 gallon Ocean Spray cranberry juice
- 12 cans Coke
- 12 cans Diet Coke
- 1 two liter Diet Mountain Dew
- 48 bottles Rolling Rock or Beck's
- 12 bottles Amstel Light
- 4 bottles of red wine (Beaujolais, Merlot or Bordeaux)
- 1 bottle Makers Mark bourbon

- deli tray
- fresh fruit basket
- assorted chips
- 1 bag pretzels
- M&M almond and peanut candies
- Reese's peanut butter cups

3. Add the cooked pancetta to the Parmesan mixture and continue to whisk. Add the warm cream and whisk thoroughly. Add the piping hot linguine and butter. Toss vigorously, coating the pasta. Serve with Parmesan and Italian parsley sprigs as a garnish.

SERVES 8

The Menu

Linguini Carbonara
Roasted Eggplant Sandwich with Salsa Siciliana
Mediterranean Tuna Salad

LINGUINI CARBONARA

8   egg yolks

1   teaspoon salt

1½ tablespoons cracked black pepper

1   cup shredded fresh Parmesan

2   tablespoons chopped Italian parsley

4   cups heavy whipping cream

1½ cup chopped pancetta, sautéed crisp (approximately 2 pounds uncooked) or prosciutto

2   pounds linguini, cooked al dente

4   tablespoons butter

8   sprigs Italian parsley for garnish

1. In a large mixing bowl whisk the egg yolks with the salt, pepper, Parmesan, and chopped parsley.

2. In a small saucepan, warm the whipping cream over low heat. Do not boil!

297

ROASTED EGGPLANT SANDWICH WITH SALSA SICILIANA

2   medium eggplants, sliced into ¼-inch rings

½   cup olive oil

1   tablespoon fresh garlic

1   teaspoon salt

½   teaspoon black pepper

1   tablespoon oregano or Italian seasoning

8   fresh sandwich rolls (oval)

2   cups Salsa Siciliana (recipe follows)

16 slices Provolone or mozzarella cheese (thin sliced)

1. Preheat oven to 375°. On nonstick baking sheet(s), place the sliced eggplant in a single layer. Brush with olive oil.

2. In a small mixing bowl combine the remaining olive oil, garlic, salt, pepper, and oregano. Spread the mixture evenly over the eggplant. Bake for 10 to 12 minutes or until lightly browned. Remove from the oven and set aside.

3. Slice the sandwich rolls through. Toast or griddle the tops of the bread. Place 3 rings of eggplant on each roll bottom, spoon on 2 to 3 tablespoons of salsa and top with 2 slices of Provolone or mozzarella cheese. Bake for 3 to 4 minutes or until the cheese is melted. Remove from the oven, cap, and serve.

SERVES 8

SALSA SICILIANA

1½ cups Red and Sassy Pomodoro Sauce (see index)

¼   cup capers

¼   cup chopped kalamata olives

1   teaspoon finely chopped fresh garlic

1   tablespoon chopped fresh oregano

1   tablespoon chopped fresh basil

3   tablespoons sugar

2   tablespoons olive oil

1   tablespoon chopped Italian parsley

2   tablespoons rice wine vinegar

¼   teaspoon cayenne pepper

2   tablespoons finely diced red/Bermuda onion

1   teaspoon salt

½   teaspoon coarse black pepper

1. In a small mixing bowl combine all ingredients and stir well.

2. Transfer to a serving bowl and serve immediately or place in a container with a lid and refrigerate until needed.

MEDITERRANEAN TUNA SALAD

3   pounds white albacore tuna, in spring
water (3 16-ounce cans)

1   cup diced celery

¾   cup diced red/Bermuda onion

1   cup olive oil

½   cup lemon juice

1/4 cup caper

2   tablespoons pitted and diced greek olives

1½   tablespoons whole dry oregano

1½   tablespoons chopped fresh Italian parsley

1   teaspoon salt

1   teaspoon black pepper

1. In a medium mixing bowl chunk the tuna.
    Do not crumble and create "cat food."

2. Add the remaining ingredients and toss
    thoroughly. Cover and refrigerate for at
    least 1 hour.

3. Remove from the refrigerator, lightly toss,
    and serve.

    *This salad may also be served atop
    mixed greens or on a crusty sandwich
    roll with Roma tomatoes and butter leaf
    lettuce.*

SERVES 8

CHAPTER 38

CLINT BLACK

A good ol' country boy, Clint Black has loads of talent and a healthy appetite. Like many country musicians, Black makes time for his fans before and after his concert appearances.

Baby Back Ribs
Homestyle Barbecue Sauce
Achiote Barbecue Corn
Pancetta Potato Salad
Fat Free Black Bean Chili

Clint Black is one of many country music artists whose career was launched in the late 1980s. Country music's popularity soared at the time, and with that popularity came a group of attractive young musicians trying to make a name for themselves. Clint was one of those musicians, and he soon stood tall above the pack with his debut album *Killin' Time* in 1989. The album produced five consecutive number one singles. In fact, his first three albums combined sold over six million copies.

Clint was born in New Jersey in 1962, however, he grew up in Houston, Texas. His break came when the aspiring singer hooked up with manager Bill Ham (of ZZ-Top fame) and guitarist Hayden Nicholas. Ham put Clint in touch with the right people who put together his record deal. Nicholas joined Clint's band and has been an integral part of writing some of his most popular hits.

Clint's second album, *Put Yourself in My Shoes* did modestly well. In 1992, he made up for the lackluster second album with his next release, *The Hard Way*. This third album solidified his place at the head of the country music pack. Clint quickly developed a reputation for his professionalism, friendliness, and sheer energy on stage. Crowds flocked to see him perform in stadiums and arenas across the country. The artist has earned numerous awards including the Country Music Association's Male Vocalist of The Year. In interviews, Clint is modest about his successes. He once commented that

the notoriety is great but he felt that individuals should be judged by their relationships with those they work with. Using that standard, Clint would rate very high.

During his 1995 tour, sponsored by Keebler, Clint was most hospitable to all the guests and staff backstage. His wife, television actress Lisa Hartman-Black, would join him on occasion to greet the numerous guests that the tour sponsor invited to the show. We had set up a sumptuous buffet for the guests and Clint took the time to greet each person individually, signing autographs and posing for pictures. There were several children present at the Meet & Greet, and Clint would get down on one knee and introduce himself to each one with his genuine southern charm.

After the Meet & Greet, Clint moved into the hospitality area for dinner. We cooked up a good old-fashioned barbecue dinner—with a slight California flair. The band and crew loved the meal. It was a warm September evening and the concert was held at an outdoor venue on the waterfront. Crowds packed the grassy peninsula and sailboats lined the rocky coastline, all to view the country entertainer.

At 8:00 P.M., the sun drifted down over the rippling water and the lights on the stage came up. Clint hit the stage, working the crowd with hits from *Killin' Time* such as, "A Better Man" and "Nothing's News." Clint finished his set to a standing ovation. He exited the stage and quickly retreated to his dressing room to change. As he emerged from his room, preparing to leave the venue, the artist made a point to thank each member of our staff for the wonderful hospitality throughout the day. Flashing his boyish grin, he said that he looked forward to their next stop in San Diego. With his thank yous said, he turned and boarded his tour bus for the ride to his next stop.

Clint Black Dressing Room Requirements:

- coffee and tea service including Earl Grey and Lipton
- 2 bags Guiltless Gourmet tortilla chips
- 1 Guiltless Gourmet spicy black bean dip
- 2 jars Pace hot picante sauce
- 2 packages of fat free cookies—prefer Snackwells devils food
- 4 assorted non-fat yogurts
- 15 roasted skinless, boneless chicken breasts—prepared with no butter or oil
- 1 loaf of 40 calorie wheat bread
- fresh fruit basket
- lettuce and tomato tray

- celery sticks and carrots in cold water
- 1 half pound turkey breast
- 2 quarts non-fat milk
- 1 quart orange juice
- 1 quart apple juice
- 1 cranberry juice
- 6 cans Diet Orange Slice
- 12 cans assorted soda
- 6 cans unsweetened iced tea
- 12 Caffeine Free Diet Coke

The Menu

Baby Back Ribs

Homestyle Barbecue Sauce

Achiote Barbecue Corn

Pancetta Potato Salad

Fat Free Black Bean Chili

BABY BACK RIBS

4 racks baby back pork ribs

1½ tablespoons seasoning salt

3 medium green bell peppers, cleaned and julienned

2 medium red/Bermuda onions, julienned

4 cups spring water

Homestyle Barbecue Sauce (recipe follows)

1. Preheat the oven to 300°.

2. Season the ribs on both sides with seasoning salt. Place the seasoned ribs in a large roasting pan (spread out evenly). Cover with even amounts of onions and peppers, and add the water. Cover the pan tightly with foil. Roast in the oven for approximately 3 hours.

3. Remove from the oven and discard the onions, peppers, and excess liquid. Let the ribs stand for approximately 35 minutes. Preheat the grill to medium/medium-high heat.

4. Place the ribs on the grill for about 10 minutes, continually rotating at 90 second intervals. Also continually baste the ribs with your favorite or our famous Homestyle Barbecue Sauce. Remove from the grill, slice apart, and serve.

We often serve this finger lickin' recipe with Bonnie Raitt's Red Beans and Rice (see index) and Black Jack Peas (see index).

SERVES 8

HOMESTYLE BARBECUE SAUCE

4	cups tomato ketchup
½	cup strong brewed coffee
1	cup tomato paste
½	teaspoon salt
¼	cup lemon juice
½	teaspoon black pepper
3	tablespoons apple cider vinegar
¼	cup honey
2	tablespoons sugar
2	tablespoons Worcestershire sauce
1	tablespoon chili powder
1	teaspoon ground cumin
1	teaspoon onion powder
1½	teaspoons granulated garlic
2	tablespoons firmly packed dark brown sugar
2	tablespoons molasses
1½	teaspoons ground oregano
½	teaspoon cayenne pepper

1. In a medium saucepan, combine all of the ingredients over medium low heat and stir well. Simmer over low heat for 10 minutes.

2. Increase the heat to medium for an additional 10 minutes or until the sauce is hot. Remove from the heat and let cool. Store any excess sauce in an airtight container in the refrigerator.

ACHIOTE BARBECUE CORN

6	quarts water
1½	teaspoons salt
8	ears fresh corn, husked and cleaned
½	teaspoon olive oil
2	tablespoons diced red/Bermuda onion
1	tablespoon finely chopped fresh garlic
¼	cup tequila
½	cup achiote condimentido (spiced annato seed paste)
2	cups chicken or vegetable stock
1	teaspoon chili powder (mild)
¼	teaspoon black pepper
¼	cup honey
	pinch cayenne pepper
1	tablespoon lemon juice
1	tablespoon red wine vinegar
1	tablespoon chopped fresh cilantro

1. In a large stock pot bring 6 quarts of water to a boil with 1 teaspoon of salt. Add the corn to the boiling water and poach for 5 to 7 minutes. Remove the corn from the water and cool.

2. In a large saucepan, heat the olive oil over medium-high heat and sauté the onions and garlic for approximately 5 minutes. Add the tequila and flambé.

3. Add the achiote, stock, chili powder, ½ teaspoon of salt, pepper, honey, cayenne pepper, lemon juice, and vinegar. Reduce the heat to medium and simmer for 10 to 12 minutes, stirring occasionally, until the glaze thickens.

4. Remove from the heat and add the cilantro. Set aside.

5. Preheat the grill to medium. Spray the wire rack with nonstick cooking spray. (Be careful not to spray the can too close or for too long near the grill as the spray is flammable and under pressure.) Place the ears of corn on the grill and thoroughly baste with glaze. Grill, rotating and basting constantly, for approximately 3 to 5 minutes, just long enough to lightly char the kernels. Be careful not to overcook.

Remaining glaze can be heated and served as a side sauce to the meal. The corn is great with southern style or southwest style barbecues.

SERVES 8

PANCETTA POTATO SALAD

¼ cup chicken base

4 pounds small red potatoes, quartered

1 pound pancetta or bacon, chopped, cooked crisp and drained

1½ cups diced red/Bermuda onion

1½ cups mayonnaise

¼ cup whole grain mustard

1½ teaspoons cracked black pepper

1 teaspoon salt

2 tablespoons fresh italian parsley, chopped
julienned red and yellow bell peppers for garnish

1. In a large stock pot combine the chicken base, cut potatoes, and water (enough water to fill the pot 1 inch above the potatoes). Bring to a boil over high heat and cook approximately 15 to 20 minutes until the potatoes are fully cooked but still firm.

2. Remove the potatoes from the heat, drain, and rinse with cool ice water. This will stop the potatoes from continuing to cook.

3. In a separate large mixing bowl combine the remaining ingredients. Stir well.

4. Fold the potatoes into the dressing, delicately, taking care not to break up the potatoes. Cover and refrigerate for at least 2 hours or until well chilled.

5. Remove from the refrigerator, toss and serve. Garnish with julienned red and yellow bell peppers.

SERVES 8+

FAT FREE BLACK BEAN CHILI
(VEGETARIAN)

1	tablespoon ground cumin
2	tablespoons chili powder (mild)
10	cups spring water
1	cup finely chopped white onions
1	cup finely chopped red/Bermuda onions
1	cup peeled and chopped carrots
1	16-ounce can chunky tomato sauce
4	cups black beans, uncooked, presoaked
overnight	
2	cups chopped green bell pepper
1	teaspoon salt
1	teaspoon black pepper
½	teaspoon cayenne pepper
¼	cup chopped fresh cilantro, (no stems)
1	cup fat free sour cream
	cilantro sprigs for garnish

1. In a large stock pot combine the cumin and chili powder. Lightly toast the spices over medium heat, stirring constantly. This will bring out the full flavor of the seasonings.

2. Add 10 cups of water, the onions, carrots, tomato sauce, and presoaked black beans. Increase the heat to high and bring to a rockin' boil. Stir occasionally and boil for 10 minutes.

3. Reduce the heat to low and simmer for approximately 1 hour, stirring occasionally.

4. Add the bell peppers, salt, and peppers. Simmer for an additional 20 to 25 minutes. The beans should be tender, if needed additional water may be added to thin the chili. Stir in the cilantro, top with a dollop of fat free sour cream, and garnish with a sprig of cilantro.

SERVES 8+

CONCLUSION

Over the past thirteen years of catering to the music industry, we have pretty much seen and heard it all. From Clint Black to Hootie & the Blowfish; from Frank Sinatra to Poison some groups continue to entertain, while others have faded into the background. We have seen bands go from selling out 14,000 seats in an arena to playing small, regional clubs. Fame can be—and is—fleeting, that we have learned. Yet in our many years catering to these famous musicians we have seen many trends develop.

In the mid-1980s, when alcohol and drug use went unnoticed in some cases, health conscious menus were not a concern. Life on the road was long and hard and as a result the road crew and musicians would often reward themselves with lavish dressing room displays, indulgent dinners, and backstage parties with full bars for the guests. This trend faded with the end of the decade. The music industry was generating billions of dollars in CD sales and backstage became much more of a business environment. Artists continued to receive their special requests; however, there were now budgets to adhere to. Alcohol was usually only consumed by band members and the crew after their performances and

respective jobs were complete. It was a much more responsible atmosphere.

With the 1990s also came a focus on health-conscious menus. The call for wheatgrass shakes was heard more often, from groups such as Aerosmith. Rock musicians began to request expensive wines for their dressing rooms rather than five cases of domestic beer. The pasta sauce was to be made with less cream, and more steamed vegetables were requested. The wave of fad diets also hit the backstage. Artists requested dishes made with no oils or animal fats. No butter was to be used or served backstage in some cases. Breakfast tables contained more fresh fruits and blenders to concoct smoothies. Grilled menu items became popular, replacing fried foods. Baked chips and fat-free snacks were the rave.

In the 1990s some artists travel with home gym systems to get in a quick workout on the road. These health-conscious attitudes, however, still left room for life's little pleasures. Green Day had the backstage area wired for televisions and video games to pass the time at their first sold-out arena concert. Pearl Jam had the backstage converted to recreation area as well with a half-court basketball court. The idea is to make the artist happy so that they perform at peak levels and earn money to keep the tour accountant happy.

Sponsorship of concert tours became popular in the 1990s as well. Corporate America began to buy out entire tours and use them as savvy marketing tools. Keebler bought Clint Black's tour and would host backstage autograph parties for local VIPs and sales staff in various cities. Companies would use Meet & Greet parties as community outreach events, inviting local children or community groups backstage. Many just wanted to place their logo on the sides of the stage to associate their company with a popular musician.

Some artists rejected this money concept and really just wanted to perform for their fans. That feeling is obvious when you find big name musicians that could sell out an arena playing venues that barely hold 1,000 fans. Many artists even have turned the tables on the cor-

porate sponsors by sponsoring their own tour and donating the proceeds to charity. If a corporation wanted to be a part of the tour, it would take a hefty donation to the charity of the artist's choosing. Touring musicians realized how much influence they can have, and with the 1990s they began to harness that power.

All of these observations brings us back to the purpose of *Backstage Pass*. For years, the image fans had of what it is like backstage at a concert has been limited to local television news stories and magazine articles—often a distorted view. We hope *Backstage Pass* gives you a new perspective on life behind the stage. In doing so, we offer our insight, our famous recipes, and our interesting stories providing a fresh look into this private world. Bon Appetit!

Alphabetical Listing of Recipes

INFORMATION AND MEASUREMENTS

All the recipes in this book have been tested with standard American measuring cups and measuring spoons (8 ounces = 16 tablespoons; 1 tablespoon = 3 teaspoons). All measurements are level, unless otherwise indicated. Liquids are measured in standard 8-ounce glass measuring cups, at eye level.

- All sugar is granulated white sugar unless otherwise specified.
- All brown sugar is firmly packed when measured.
- All pepper is ground pepper unless otherwise specified.
- Unsalted butter is used unless otherwise specified.
- ⅓ to ½ teaspoon dried herbs can be substituted for each tablespoon of fresh herbs. Crumble herbs before using to release flavor.

COOKING TEMPERATURES AND TIMES

Cooking temperatures and times are approximate for meat. They depend not only on the weight and kind of meat, but also on its shape, temperature, and bone and fat content. Use a meat thermometer to test.

Temperatures

250 to 275	Very Slow
300 to 325	Slow
350 to 375	Moderate
400 to 425	Hot
450 to 475	Very Hot
500 to 525	Extremely Hot

TIPS FROM THE CHEFS

───〜〜〜───

- If you have over-salted soup or vegetables, add cut raw potatoes and discard once they have cooked or try a teaspoon each of cider vinegar and sugar.
- To thicken a sauce, mix flour and cornstarch and water, which has been mixed to a smooth paste, add gradually, stirring constantly, while bringing to a boil.
- Cooking for a larger group: It is hard to mix highly seasoned foods in big batches evenly. Plan on mixing the recipe in smaller batches.
- Plan on taking meats out of the oven 30 to 40 minutes before serving time. They will hold their heat until cut and will carve better if allowed to stand a few minutes at room temperature.
- If fresh vegetables are wilted or blemished, take off brown edges, sprinkle with cool water, wrap in a paper towel and refrigerate for an hour or so.
- You'll shed fewer tears if you cut off the root end of the onion last.
- Meat loaf will not stick to the pan if you place a slice of bacon on the bottom of the pan.
- A few teaspoons of cooking oil added to water when boiling rice or pasta will prevent it from boiling over.
- Grating a stick of butter softens it faster.
- A dampened paper towel or terry cloth brushed downward on a cob of corn will remove every strand of corn silk.

- Thaw frozen fish in milk. The milk draws out the frozen taste and provides a fresh caught flavor.
- Be cautious with strong herbs and spices. Remember, you can always add more. Start with pinches and build up to taste.
- To separate excess fat from meat stock quickly, pour into a tall cup and place immediately in cold water. The fat will rise to the top and can be skimmed off easily leaving stock. Or wrap ice cubes in a paper towel or cheesecloth and skim over the top of soup.
- Add leftover coffee to barbecue sauce, beef and pork gravies for a richer flavor (about 1½ cups of coffee to 3 or 4 cups sauce or gravy).
- Use sugar as a seasoning. A pinch or two in vegetables gives them fresher taste without making them sweet.
- Fruit purées, such as pear or applesauce, add sweetness to baked goods. Purées also help baked goods stay moist, and can lower the fat content of your favorite baked goods. Use one quarter of the oil called for and substitute purée for the rest.

───〜〜〜───

Spice Glossary

Basil (Sweet Basil)
  sweet with clovelike spicy tang
Bay Leaves (Laurel)
  aromatic
Cayenne Pepper
  hot, peppery
Cinnamon
  pungent and sweet
Cloves
  strong, pungent and sweet
Cumin
  strong, dry taste
Epazote
  aromatic, Spanish seasoning
  (anti-gas herb)
Ginger
  pungent and spicy, aromatic
Mint
  sweet with a cool aftertaste
Nutmeg
  sweet with warm and spicy
  undertone
Oregano
  strong, aromatic with pleasantly bitter
  undertones

Paprika
  dry taste with slightly bitter
  undertones
Parsley
  mild and pleasant
Pepper
  penetrating odor, hot, biting and very
  pungent
Rosemary
  sweet aroma and fresh sweet flavor
Sage
  aromatic, slightly bitter
Sesame Seed
  rich nutlike flavor
Tarragon
  reminiscent of Anise
Thyme
  aromatic, pungent flavor

GLOSSARY OF BACKSTAGE TERMS

Backstage pass
Credential issued to staff, crew, band members, and guests allowing them to access specified areas of the backstage.

Call time
The scheduled time the crew is to be ready to start work.

Crew call
Start time for working, usually referring to the local crew.

Dressing room
The area or room set aside for the artist(s) to prepare for the show or concert.

Flies
Term sometimes used by the road crew and local crew in reference to backstage guests (often radio contest winners).

Lighting truss
Metal rails used to secure and suspend lights and sound equipment above the stage.

Load-in
The process of unloading the trucks, unpacking the equipment, and setting up the equipment, lighting, sound and stage props.

Load-out
The process of breaking down and packing up the lighting and sound equipment and stage props and loading the trucks.

Local crew
The crew hired in each city to help off load, set up, and reload the equipment.

Local promoter
The company or individual who books the performer and sells the tickets to the particular concert/show.

Meet & Greet
Scheduled reception for fans and guests to meet and talk with the musician, often backstage.

Production manager
The person in charge of logistics and details surrounding the setup, functioning and breakdown of a concert/show.

Pyro-room/yard
Room set aside for the pyrotechnic technicians to prep and store stage fireworks to be used during concert.

Quick change
A tent/enclosure on or near the stage, used for quick wardrobe changes during performances.

Rider
The contract between the promoter and/or venue and the artist or group that specifies the artist's compensation and detailed requirements for the

performance (i.e. catering needs, power source requirements, hotel rooms, etc.).

Riggers

Individuals who climb to the venue rafters to secure lighting and sound equipment that is to be suspended above the stage.

Road cases

Rolling suitcases of a sort, that sound, lighting, and other equipment are packed and transported in.

Road crew

The crew hired to tour with the band to set up and run the equipment at each concert or show.

Set list

The list of songs in the order played at a concert.

Settling

The process of negotiating the final amount of moneys due the band or artist from the local promoter or venue, includes fee for performance as well as a percentage of merchandise sales and sometimes concessions.

Sound check

Time set aside, usually in the late afternoon, to check instruments, sound, and lighting, prior to the actual performance.

Tour accountant

The person responsible for collecting all moneys due the artist or group, settling with the local promoter or the venue, and distribution of all moneys to local vendors and road crew members.

Tour bus

Custom coach used to transport road crew and band members from city to city.

Tour manager

The person responsible for the functioning and running of the entire tour.

Venue

Location, building, or site where the concert is performed.

GLOSSARY OF RECIPE TERMS

Al dente
A term used in Italian cooking to describe the degree (barely tender) to which pasta, rice and vegetables should be cooked

Au gratin
Food topped with bread crumbs and/or grated cheese and broiled or baked until brown

Au jus
French term referring to natural, unthickened juices of meat obtained in the cooking and served with meat

Béchamel
French term for basic white sauce

Caper
Flower bud from a Mediterranean shrub; the bud is pickled

Chopped
Cut into small even pieces

Chunked
Cut into medium to large even pieces

Chutney
Spicy, somewhat sweet relish of East Indian origin, made from several fruits and/or vegetables

Cleaned
Washed with water thoroughly and de-seeded or stems removed if applicable

Diced
Cut into very small even pieces

En brochette
French term for cooked on a skewer

Frittata
Italian omelet

Garnish
The finishing touch on a recipe, choice of garnish should complement the creation. People taste 20% with their tastebuds, 10% with their nose, and 70% with their eyes.

Julienne
Cut into matchlike strips

Peeled
Outer skin removed

Poached
Lightly cooked in a boiling or hot water bath; brings out the color and flavor of fresh vegetables

Polenta
Italian cornmeal side dish

Reconstituted
Rehydrated, brought back to its natural level, normally done with dried vegetables; soak in warm water

Roux
Cooked mixture of flour and butter used to thicken sauces; can lighten roux and use water in place of butter for certain recipes

U21/30

Size measurement of shrimp, refers to approximate number of shrimp per pound. (For example U21/30 has 21 to 30 shrimp per pound.)

Zest

The yellow/orange outer peel of lemons and oranges, which contains a strong flavor. The white part underneath is somewhat bitter and should not be used when grating peel for zest.

CONVERSION TABLE

1 pinch = less than ⅛ teaspoon (dry)
1 dash = 3 drops to ¼ teaspoon (liquid)
3 teaspoons = 1 tablespoon = ½ ounce (liquid)
2 tablespoons = 2 ounces (liquid and dry)
4 tablespoons = 2 ounces (liquid and dry) = ¼ cup
5⅓ tablespoons = ⅓ cup
16 tablespoons = 8 ounces = 1 cup = ½ pound
16 tablespoons = 48 teaspoons
32 tablespoons = 16 ounces = 2 cups = 1 pound
64 tablespoons = 32 ounces = 1 quart = 2 pounds
1 cup = 8 ounces (liquid) = ½ pint
2 cups = 16 ounces (liquid) = 1 pint
4 cups = 32 ounces (liquid) = 2 pints = 1 quart
16 cups = 128 ounces (liquid) = 4 quarts = 1 gallon
1 quart = 2 pints (dry)
8 quarts = 1 peck (dry)
4 pecks = 1 bushel (dry)

Approximate Equivalents
1 quart (liquid) = about 1 liter
8 tablespoons = 4 ounces = ½ cup = 1 stick butter
1 cup all-purpose presifted flour = 5 ounces
1 cup stoneground yellow cornmeal = 4½ ounces
1 cup granulated sugar = 8 ounces
1 cup brown sugar = 6 ounces
1 cup confectioners sugar = 4½ ounces
1 large egg = 2 ounces = ¼ cup = 4 tablespoons
1 egg yolk = 1 tablespoon + 1 teaspoon
1 egg white = 2 tablespoons + 2 teaspoons

INDEX

O

P

Printed in the USA
CPSIA information can be obtained
at www.ICGtesting.com
JSHW052014140824
68134JS00027B/2475